SERIES ENDORSEMENTS

"There are so many fine commentaries available today, but it's great to have a reliable author you can turn to for solid Reformed reflections on Scripture. In this case, there are sixteen of them—friends and fellow shepherds who have given me great insight into God's Word over the years. I'm looking forward eagerly to each one of these sermonic commentaries!"

Michael S. Horton
J. Gresham Machen Professor of Apologetics and
    Systematic Theology at Westminster Seminary California
Host of the *White Horse Inn* Radio Show
Editor-in-Chief of *Modern Reformation* magazine

"Those of us who have promoted and practiced *lectio continua* expository preaching through the years eagerly await the volumes announced in The Lectio Continua Expository Commentary on the New Testament. We are equally eager to read such a series written by pastors who have practiced the method in their churches. The international and interdenominational character of the series will only add to the richness of its insights."

T. David Gordon
Professor of Religion and Greek at Grove City College
Author of *Why Johnny Can't Preach*

"As the history of preaching is unfolded, it becomes clear how important the orderly, systematic preaching through the Scriptures has been, and why it has been a favorite homiletic approach over the centuries. One is surprised to discover how many of history's great preachers made a regular practice of preaching through one book of the Bible after another. Origen, the first Christian preacher from whom we have any sizable collection of sermons, preached most of his sermons on the *lectio continua*. We find the same with John Chrysostom, who is usually referred to as the greatest Christian preacher. We find the same true of Augustine as well. At the time of the Protestant Reformation, Zwingli, Calvin, Bucer, and Knox followed this system regularly, and they passed it on to the Puritans. Today, we see a real revival of *lectio continua* preaching. The Lectio Continua Expository Commentary on the New Testament represents a wonderful opportunity for the church to recover a truly expository pulpit."

Hughes Oliphant Old
Formerly John H. Leith Professor of Reformed Theology
   and Worship at Erskine Theological Seminary
Author of *The Reading and Preaching of the Scriptures in the
   Worship of the Christian Church*

"The concept behind this series is a fascinating one and, given the list of authors, I am confident that the final product will not disappoint. This promises to be a great resource for churches seeking to know the Word of God more fully."

Carl R. Trueman
Paul Wooley Chair of Church History and
   Professor of Church History at
   Westminster Theological Seminary in Philadelphia

Ephesians

THE LECTIO CONTINUA
EXPOSITORY COMMENTARY ON THE NEW TESTAMENT

Series Editors

Joel R. Beeke | Jon D. Payne

Other available books in this series:
First Corinthians — Kim Riddlebarger
Galatians — J. V. Fesko
Hebrews — David B. McWilliams
Revelation — Joel R. Beeke

Ephesians

Ian Hamilton

REFORMATION HERITAGE BOOKS
Grand Rapids, Michigan

Reformation Heritage Books
2965 Leonard St. NE
Grand Rapids, MI 49525
616-977-0889 / Fax 616-285-3246
orders@heritagebooks.org
www.heritagebooks.org

Printed in the United States of America
17 18 19 20 21 22/10 9 8 7 6 5 4 3 2 1

Library of Congress Cataloging-in-Publication Data

Names: Hamilton, Ian, 1950- author.
Title: Ephesians / Ian Hamilton.
Description: Grand Rapids, Michigan : Reformation Heritage Books, 2017. | Series: The Lectio Continua expository commentary on the New Testament
Identifiers: LCCN 2017039485 | ISBN 9781601785411 (hardcover : alk. paper)
Subjects: LCSH: Bible. Ephesians—Commentaries.
Classification: LCC BS2695.53 .H36 2017 | DDC 227/.5077—dc23
LC record
available at https://lccn.loc.gov/2017039485

For additional Reformed literature, request a free book list from Reformation Heritage Books at the above regular or e-mail address.

For
Mark, Fiona, and Lindsay
Steadfast friends and ever faithful encouragers

Contents

St. Giles Cathedral in Edinburgh, Scotland, where John Knox preached from 1560–1572.

Series Introduction

The greatest need of the church today is the recovery of sound biblical preaching. We need preaching that faithfully explains and applies the text, courageously confronts sin, and boldly trumpets forth the sovereign majesty, law, and gospel promises of God. This type of powerful proclamation has vanished in many quarters of the evangelical church only to be replaced by that which is anemic and man-centered. Instead of doctrinally rich exposition which strengthens faith and fosters Christian maturity, the standard fare has become informal, chatty, anecdote-laden messages, devoid of instruction in the truths of the Christian faith. This approach leaves unbelievers confused and keeps believers in a state of chronic spiritual adolescence.[1]

There is indeed a dire need for the recovery of solid biblical preaching. Not only does reformation of this sort lead Christ's sheep back to the verdant pastures of His soul-nourishing Word, it also provides a good example for present and future generations of

---

1. A stinging, yet constructive, critique of modern-day preaching is found in T. David Gordon's *Why Johnny Can't Preach: The Media Have Shaped the Messengers* (Phillipsburg, N.J.: P&R, 2009). "I have come to recognize that many, many individuals today have never been under a steady diet of competent preaching.... As starving children in Manila sift through the landfill for food, Christians in many churches today have never experienced genuine soul-nourishing preaching, and so they just pick away at what is available to them, trying to find a morsel of spiritual sustenance or helpful counsel here or there" (Gordon, *Why Johnny Can't Preach*, 17). Elements of this introduction are adapted from Jon D. Payne, "The Roaring of Christ through *Lectio Continua* Preaching," *Modern Reformation* 19, no. 6 (Nov.–Dec. 2010): 23–24, and are used by permission of the publisher.

ministers. For this reason, we are pleased to introduce The Lectio Continua Expository Commentary on the New Testament, a new series of expository commentaries authored by an array of seasoned pastor-scholars from various Reformed denominations on both sides of the Atlantic.

What is the *lectio continua* method of preaching?[2] It is simply the uninterrupted, systematic, expository proclamation of God's Word—verse by verse, chapter by chapter, book by book—that endeavors to deliver the whole counsel of God (Acts 20:26–27). Christian discipleship is impoverished when large portions of Scripture are ignored. Carried out faithfully, the *lectio continua* method ensures that every passage is mined for its riches (even those verses which are obscure, controversial, or hard to swallow). Paul states that "all scripture is given by inspiration of God, and is profitable for doctrine, for reproof, for correction, for instruction in righteousness: that the man of God may be perfect, thoroughly furnished unto all good works" (2 Tim. 3:16–17 KJV).

Lectio continua preaching has a splendid heritage. It finds its roots in the early church and patristic eras. Its use, however, was revived and greatly expanded during the sixteenth-century Protestant Reformation. When Huldrych Zwingli (d. 1531) arrived at the Zurich Grossmunster in 1519, it was his desire to dispense with the standard lectionary[3] and introduce *lectio continua* preaching to his congregation by moving systematically through the Gospel of Matthew. At first, some members of his church council were suspicious. They were uncomfortable replacing the lectionary with this

---

2. In Christianity, *lectio continua* (Latin for continuous reading) originally referred to the practice of reading Scripture sequentially in public worship, as was the practice of the ancient church. This practice is recommended by the Westminster divines in the Directory for Public Worship, which, in turn, served as an impetus for *lectio continua* preaching. Sadly, Scripture reading in this manner has been neglected in Reformed and Presbyterian churches for many generations, perhaps as far back as the eighteenth century, when public worship was reduced to sermon-hearing sessions.

3. A lectionary is a plan or table of Scripture passages to be read in the services of church for each day or week of the year.

seemingly new approach. But Zwingli explained that the *lectio continua* method of preaching was not new at all. On the contrary, important figures such as Augustine (d. 430), Chrysostom (d. 407), and Bernard of Clairvaux (d. 1153) all employed this homiletical approach. Zwingli is quoted by his successor, Heinrich Bullinger (d. 1575), as saying that "no friend of evangelical truth could have any reason to complain" about such a method.[4]

Zwingli rightly believed that the quickest way to restore biblical Christianity to the church was to preach the whole counsel of God verse by verse, chapter by chapter, book by book, Lord's Day after Lord's Day, year after year. Other Reformers agreed and followed his pattern. In the city of Strasbourg, just ninety miles north of Zurich, preachers such as Martin Bucer (d. 1551), Wolfgang Capito (d. 1570), and Kaspar Hedio (d. 1552) practiced *lectio continua* preaching. Johannes Oecolampadius (d. 1531) boldly preached the *lectio continua* in Basel. And let us not forget John Calvin (d. 1564); between 1549 and 1564, the Genevan Reformer preached sequentially through no fewer than twenty-five books of the Bible (over two thousand sermons), which he was able to do because he also preached regularly for weekday services.[5]

The example of these Reformers has been emulated by preachers throughout the centuries, from the post-Reformation age down to the present. In the last half of the twentieth century, Donald Grey Barnhouse (1895–1960), Martyn Lloyd-Jones (d. 1981), William Still (d. 1997), James Montgomery Boice (d. 2000), and John MacArthur all boldly preached straight through books of the Bible from their pulpits. But why? Surely we have acquired better, more

---

4. It is interesting to note that the year before Zwingli began preaching sequentially through books of the Bible, he had received a new edition of Chrysostom's *lectio continua* sermons on Matthew's gospel. See Hughes Oliphant Old, *The Patristic Roots of Reformed Worship* (Black Mountain, N.C.: Worship Press, 2004), 195. Cf. Hughes Oliphant Old, *The Reading and Preaching of the Scriptures in the Worship of the Christian Church*, vol. 4: *The Age of the Reformation* (Grand Rapids: Eerdmans, 2002), and Timothy George, *Reading Scripture with the Reformers* (Downers Grove, Ill.: IVP Academic, 2011), 228–53.

5. T. H. L. Parker, *Calvin's Preaching* (Edinburgh: T&T Clark, 1992), 159.

contemporary methods of preaching? Is the *lectio continua* relevant in our twenty-first-century context? In a day when biblical preaching is being increasingly undermined and marginalized by media/story/therapy/personality-driven sermons, even among the avowedly Reformed, these are important questions to consider.

Shortly before the apostle Paul was martyred in Rome by Emperor Nero, he penned 2 Timothy. In what proved to be some of his final words to his young disciple, he wrote, "I charge thee therefore before God and the Lord Jesus Christ...*preach the word;* be instant in season, out of season; reprove, rebuke, exhort with all longsuffering and doctrine" (2 Tim. 4:1–2 KJV). This directive was not meant only for Timothy. It is the duty of every Christian minister (and church) to heed these timeless words; according to God's divine blueprint for ministry, it is chiefly through the faithful proclamation of the Word that Christ saves, sanctifies, and comforts the beloved church for which He died.[6] In other words, the preaching of the gospel and the right administration of the sacraments are the divinely sanctioned and efficacious means by which Christ and all His benefits of redemption are communicated to the elect. For this reason alone the *lectio continua* method of preaching is a helpful practice in our churches, providing a steady diet of law and gospel from the entirety of God's Word.

Some may ask, "Why another expository commentary series?" First, because in every generation it is highly valuable to provide fresh and reliable expositions of God's Word. Every age possesses its own set of theological, ecclesiastical, and cultural challenges. Thus, it is beneficial for both current and rising ministers in every generation to have trustworthy contemporary models of biblical preaching. Second, these volumes uniquely feature the expositions of an array of pastors from a variety of Reformed and confessional traditions. Consequently, this series brings a wealth of exegetical, confessional,

---

6. See Matthew 28:18–20; Romans 10:14–17; 1 Corinthians 1:18–21; 1 Peter 1:22–25; Westminster Shorter Catechism, Q. 89.

experiential, and practical insight, and furnishes the reader with an instructive and stimulating selection of *lectio continua* sermons.

This series is not meant to be an academic or highly technical commentary. There are many helpful exegetical commentaries written for that purpose. Rather, the aim is to provide *lectio continua* sermons, originally delivered to Reformed congregations, which clearly and faithfully communicate the context, meaning, gravity, and application of God's inerrant Word. Each volume of expositions aspires to be redemptive-historical, covenantal, Reformed and confessional, Trinitarian, Christ-centered, and teeming with spiritual and practical application. Therefore, we pray that the series will be a profound blessing to every Christian believer who longs to "grow in the grace and knowledge of our Lord and Savior Jesus Christ" (2 Peter 3:18).

We are pleased to announce that this series of commentaries is now being published by Reformation Heritage Books, which graciously agreed to take over this large task from Tolle Lege Press. We thank Tolle Lege for printing the first three volumes (*First Corinthians* by Kim Riddlebarger, *Galatians* by J. V. Fesko, and *Hebrews* by David B. McWilliams). We, Joel Beeke and Jon Payne, look forward to coediting the remainder of the series for Reformation Heritage Books. The goal is to publish two volumes per year in the King James or New King James Version, according to the choice of each author.

In addition to thanking Reformation Heritage Books and its faithful team for producing this series, we wish to thank our churches, Christ Church Presbyterian, Charleston, South Carolina, and the Heritage Reformed Congregation, Grand Rapids, Michigan, for warmly encouraging us as ministers to work on projects such as this one that impact the wider church. Furthermore, we thank our dear wives, Mary Beeke and Marla Payne, and our precious children for their heartwarming support, which makes editing a series like this one possible. We both feel that God has greatly blessed us with God-fearing wives and children who mean more to us than words can express.

Finally, and most importantly, thanks and praise must be given to our blessed triune God, the eternal Fountain of all grace and truth. By His sovereign love and mercy, and through faith in the crucified, resurrected, and ascended Christ, we have been "born again, not of corruptible seed, but of incorruptible, by the word of God, which liveth and abideth for ever. For all flesh is as grass, and all the glory of man as the flower of grass. The grass withereth, and the flower thereof falleth away: but the word of the Lord endureth for ever. And this is the word which by the gospel is preached unto you" (1 Peter 1:23–25 KJV).

— Joel R. Beeke and Jon D. Payne, Series Editors

Introduction

John Owen, the great English Puritan, wrote, "Our greatest hindrance in the Christian life is not our lack of effort but our lack of acquaintedness with our privileges." In his letter to the Ephesians, Paul elaborates and expands in a most wonderful way on the God-given, Christ-secured, Holy Spirit–applied privileges of the Christian life. Here, perhaps more than anywhere else in the New Testament, we are brought face-to-face with the "unsearchable riches of Christ" (3:8). Step by adoring step, Paul introduces us to the spiritual blessings that are the predestined (1:4–5), blood-bought (1:7) privileges of everyone who has put their self-abandoning trust in Jesus Christ.

Paul's letter to the Ephesians is a spiritual Mount Everest. It turns us away from ourselves and places the spotlight of God's great salvation on Christ and His perfect work of redemption.

A Pastoral Letter

It is vital to remember that Ephesians is a pastoral letter written to encourage, instruct, challenge, rebuke, and inspire Christians. It is not a handbook of Christian doctrine. In his final greetings (6:21), Paul gives what may be a simple, though pastorally rich reason why he wrote this letter: "That you also may know my affairs and how I am doing, Tychicus, a beloved brother and faithful minister in the Lord, will make all things known to you." The gloriously rich theology embedded in Ephesians may have developed out of this initial, caring, pastoral impulse. At the very least, Paul is showing us that the gospel of God's great grace in Christ is embodied in the day-to-day life and fellowship of God's people. Theology that is not pastoral is remote from the theology we find in God's Word.

Paul's intention throughout Ephesians is to deliver us from "our morbid pre-occupation with ourselves," which Martyn Lloyd-Jones called "the peculiar error of this present [twentieth] century." Paul wants to give us a panoramic and exhaustive understanding of the greatness of our Savior, the salvation He has won for us, and the exalted calling we have in Christ. "What we need primarily," wrote Lloyd-Jones, "is not an experience, but to realise what we are, and who we are, what God has done in Christ and the way He has blessed us." As Christians, we so often live like spiritual paupers when we are spiritual billionaires, blessed in Christ "with every spiritual blessing in the heavenly places" (1:3).

Ordinary Christians
We should never forget that the New Testament letters were written to ordinary Christian men and women to establish them in their faith, to warn them against the encroaching deceitfulness of false teaching and teachers, and to enrich their experience of Christ. They shared the same struggles and battles that we face. They had to battle each day against indwelling sin, against the seduction of a dying world, and against the wiles of the devil. Perhaps unlike most of us, these Christians in Ephesus probably suffered social ostracism, material hardship, and physical pain because of their faith in the Lord Jesus Christ. They were a colony of heaven in the midst of a pagan, Christ-opposing, polytheistic world. So Paul wrote to them. He had spent three years in Ephesus (Acts 20:31). During those three years, he did not shrink from teaching them anything that was profitable and especially from declaring to them the "whole counsel of God" (Acts 20:20, 27). What an immense privilege these Ephesian believers had, listening day after day to Paul teaching them "the gospel of the grace of God" (Acts 20:24).

Ephesus

Ephesus was one of the great cities of the Roman Empire. It was the capital of the Roman province of Asia and a renowned religious center, famous for its worship of the emperor and of the goddess Diana (Artemis). The temple of Diana was four times the size of the Parthenon in Athens and was considered one of the Seven Wonders of the Ancient World. To such a city Paul came with the good news of Jesus Christ and for three years labored to see a church of converted men and women established in that center of pagan idolatry. Acts 19:20 recounts the great opposition Paul experienced and the wonderful blessing that God gave to his preaching: "So the word of the Lord grew mightily and prevailed."

Written from Prison

Paul wrote this letter from prison, probably in Rome (4:1; 6:20). Characteristically, even though he was in prison, Paul's great concern was for Christ's church. So he wrote this letter to encourage, strengthen, and challenge God's people to "walk worthy of the calling" to which they had been called (4:1). Paul longed to see these forgiven, heaven-bound sinners live the kind of lives that honored the Savior who loved them and gave Himself for them.

As we have noted, Paul also wanted the church at Ephesus to know how he was and what he was doing (6:21). To that end he was sending them Tychicus, "a beloved brother and faithful minister in the Lord" (6:21). It is easy to see the familial intimacy that marked all Paul's dealings with the various churches he wrote to. He was "an apostle of Jesus Christ by the will of God" (1:1), but these Christians were "members of the household of God" (2:19)—that is, family— his "brethren" in Christ (6:23). There is nothing remotely clinical in anything Paul writes in this letter. He stands alongside his fellow believers, never lording it over them (see especially the striking use of the plural pronouns in 2:3–7).

A Second Letter

There is, however, another letter to the church in Ephesus in the New Testament. In Revelation 2:1–7, the risen Lord, who held "the seven stars in His right hand" and who walked "in the midst of the seven golden lampstands" wrote to the church in Ephesus a stinging, searching letter. After initially commending the church for its works, toil, patient endurance, and doctrinal faithfulness (vv. 1–3), Jesus said, "Nevertheless I have this against you, that you have left your first love" (v. 4). So seriously did the Lord take this declension in love that He threatened to come and decimate the church unless it repented and returned to its first love (v. 5).

This letter is a solemn warning to us that the best of churches, even churches founded by apostles, can quickly depart from the "faith which was once for all delivered to the saints" (Jude 3). It is little wonder Jesus commanded His disciples, and indeed all disciples, to "watch and pray" (Matt. 26:41; Mark 13:33; Luke 21:36). We can never take gospel orthodoxy for granted. Sadly, we can easily forget that there is such a thing as heart heresy as well as head heresy (John 13:34–35). This was a conviction embedded within the "Princeton tradition." B. B. Warfield, perhaps the greatest of the Old Princeton biblical theologians, told his students that "any proper preparation for the ministry must include these three chief parts—a training of the heart, a training of the hand, a training of the head—a devotional, a practical, and an intellectual training."[1] Warfield reflects the consistent Reformed tradition that the head and the heart are indissolubly united. Where one is emphasized at the expense of the other, the result is either doctrinal aridity or doctrineless piety.[2] Paul's letter

---

1. As quoted in David B. Calhoun, *Princeton Seminary: The Majestic Testimony 1869–1929* (Edinburgh: Banner of Truth Trust, 1996), 425.

2. The English Puritan John Owen understood this better than most: "Where light leaves the affections behind it ends in formality or atheism; and where affections outrun light, they sink in the bog of superstition, doting on images and pictures, or the like. But where things go not into these excesses, it is better that our affections exceed our light from the defect of our understandings, than that our light exceed our affections from the corruption of our wills." *The Works of John Owen*, ed. William H. Goold (Edinburgh: Banner of Truth Trust, 1966), 1:401.

to the Ephesians beautifully conjoins heart and head. For War-field this conjunction was of the utmost importance. He wrote in the *Presbyterian and Reformed Review*, "The systematic theologian is preeminently a preacher of the gospel; and the end of his work is obviously not merely the logical arrangement of the truths which come under his hand, but the moving of men, through their power, to love God with all their hearts and their neighbors as themselves; to choose their portion with the Savior of their souls; to find and hold him precious; and to recognize and yield to the sweet influences of the Holy Spirit whom He has sent."[3]

The Immeasurable Riches of God's Grace (1:1–3:21)

Ephesians can be divided into two main sections. In the first section, Paul expounds the great doctrines of the gospel of Christ. Before he calls the Ephesians to live lives of holy obedience to Christ, he sets before them "the unsearchable riches of Christ" (3:8). This is always how the Bible approaches the Christian life. Before there are any appeals or exhortations to obedience and godliness, God sets before us the riches of His grace. Appeals to faithfulness and obedience always flow out of gospel exposition. The gospel has a particular grammar: the indicatives of grace always precede the imperatives of duty. This is not a New Testament phenomenon. God's Ten Words are prefaced by the significant statement, "I am the LORD your God, who brought you out of the land of Egypt, out of the house of bondage" (Ex. 20:2). For the Christian, the cross is the great incentive and encouragement to obedience. If Christians are reluctant or halfhearted in their obedience to Christ, the answer is not to press them with a flood of exhortations but to speak of Christ, His cross, His salvation! The root reason our faithfulness and obedience are so often less than they should be is because we become disconnected from our Savior. The glory of His cross becomes lost to us. The longing to serve and obey Christ is most evident in lives that glory in His cross.

---

3. As quoted in Calhoun, *Princeton Seminary*, 424–25.

Living Worthy of the Gospel of God's Grace (4:1–6:23)

In this section Paul spells out what it means to live a life worthy of such a great Savior as Jesus Christ. How can men and women for whom the Son of God died—whose precious blood has saved them from God's holy wrath—who are now, through Christ's sin-bearing sacrifice, God's own "dear children" (5:1), walk any longer "as the rest of the Gentiles walk" (4:17)? The gospel obliges, even compels, Christians to live godly lives. Union with Christ (1:3) reveals itself in Christlike living in those who seek to be "imitators of God as dear children" (5:1).

This leads to the longest coherent section in the letter, in which Paul highlights the various relationships, familial and social, that are transformed by the gospel of Christ. Perhaps more than anything else, Ephesian society needed to see the transformative power and grace of the gospel in family life as much as to hear its unique message. The gospel of God's grace in Christ comes to change who and what we are. It re-centers our lives in God, it transforms our minds, it fills us with hope, it rescues us from the guilt and power of sin and from the "spiritual hosts of wickedness in the heavenly places" (6:12), and it makes us new creations (2 Cor. 5:17). In a deeply morally fractured society, the new life inherent in the gospel was to be manifested in how wives related to husbands and husbands to wives, children to parents and parents to children, servants to masters and masters to servants.

In his excellent commentary on Ephesians, John Stott identified four main concerns that dominate the landscape of Paul's letter:[4]

1. *The new life* that God gives to everyone who believes in His Son (1:3–2:10). Paul wants Christians to understand and rejoice in "every spiritual blessing" (1:3) that is theirs through faith in Jesus Christ. "This is your gospel inheritance," Paul is telling us. "Grasp its immensity."

---

4. John R. W. Stott, *God's New Society: The Message of Ephesians* (Leicester, U.K.: IVP, 1979), 25.

2. *The new society* that God has created through the saving
   work of Christ (2:11–3:21). Becoming a Christian brings
   you into a family, "the household of God" (2:19). The
   Lord Jesus did not come simply to save sinners; He came
   to transform forgiven, saved sinners into a new society, a
   family for God. It is striking that all the pictures of the
   church in the New Testament are corporate: the church
   is "the household of God"; the "temple" of the Holy
   Spirit (1 Cor. 3:17); the "bride" of Christ (Rev. 21:2); and
   the "body" of Christ (1 Cor. 12:12–31).

3. *The new standards* that God expects of this new society
   (4:1–5:20). Chief among those new standards are unity
   and purity. Christians are not only forgiven and saved
   people but they are a changed people, people who live
   to please and serve their Savior and heavenly Father,
   people whose lives are shaped and styled by God's commands, not the ever-changing fads and fashions of a
   passing world.

4. *The new relationships* into which God brings believing
   men and women (5:21–6:24). We can summarize these
   new relationships like this: God looks to see His people
   live harmoniously and happily in their homes and in
   resolute hostility to the devil and his wicked ways. The
   gospel comes to change everything—your relationship
   with God, the world around you, your family, your work,
   your leisure, and your hopes and ambitions. The gospel
   of Christ comes to make everything new. Paul made this
   point dramatically in 2 Corinthians 5:17: "If anyone is
   in Christ, he is a new creation; old things have passed
   away; behold, all things have become new." Paul is not
   particularly thinking here of the character transformation the gospel of God's grace accomplishes in our lives.
   He is telling us that "in Christ," we are a "new creation"!
   A Christian is someone who has come to experience

the beginnings of the cosmic transformation that Jesus
Christ inaugurated by His incarnation, death, and resurrection. That cosmic transformation is not yet complete,
but it has begun in Christ, and all Christians share in
that "now" but "not yet" transformation.

The "now" but "not yet" motif is built into the fabric of God's
new covenant revelation (e.g., 1 John 3:2). It highlights the unfolding eschatological reality of the Christian life, a life that will only
be finally complete when Christ returns and inaugurates the new
heaven and the new earth (Rom. 8:23; 2 Peter 3:13).

1

Paul's Greeting

EPHESIANS 1:1–2

Paul, an apostle of Jesus Christ by the will of God, to the saints who are in Ephesus, and faithful in Christ Jesus: Grace to you and peace from God our Father and the Lord Jesus Christ.

Paul begins his letter by placarding his ministerial credentials. He is "an apostle of Jesus Christ" (v. 1). An "apostle" was a uniquely commissioned ambassador of Christ.[1] Paul was once, by his own admission, "a blasphemer, a persecutor, and an insolent man" (1 Tim. 1:13). "But," he said, "I obtained mercy" (1 Tim. 1:13). Paul was a trophy of sovereign, saving grace. God had dramatically invaded his life as he journeyed to Damascus in search of Christians to persecute (Acts 9:1–2). He was filled with hate, "exceedingly enraged" (Acts 26:11) against Christ and His people. "But God" (Eph. 2:4)! If anyone knew what it was to be converted, it was Paul. One moment he "made havoc of the church…breathing threats and murder against the disciples of the Lord" (Acts 8:3; 9:1), and the next he was lying in the dust saying, "Who are You, Lord?" (Acts 9:5). Blinded by the light of the risen Christ, Paul was led meekly by the hand into Damascus, where Ananias laid his hands on him, and he was "filled with the Holy Spirit" and was baptized (Acts 9:17–18). Paul recognized that he was "the least of the apostles, who [was] not worthy

---

1. "Apostles" in the New Testament not only refers to the Twelve and to Paul, but to a wider group of gospel ambassadors. Barnabas is called an apostle (Acts 14:14), as well as Silas and Timothy (1 Thess. 1:1; 2:6), and possibly Apollos (1 Cor. 3:22; 4:6, 9).

to be called an apostle, because I persecuted the church of God"
(1 Cor. 15:9). He never forgot that he was what he was "by the grace
of God" (1 Cor. 15:10).

What was true of Paul is true for every Christian, but not in
the sense that Paul's conversion was a pattern or paradigm of Christian conversion. There were unique reasons why his conversion was
so dramatic. To be an apostle, he needed be a witness to Jesus's
resurrection (Acts 1:22). For his conversion to be credible to the
church in which he had "made havoc" (Acts 8:3), it needed to be
undeniable. Paul's conversion to Christ, however, is a pattern for all
conversions to Christ in this respect: he owed his conversion to God
alone. He "obtained mercy" (1 Tim. 1:13). Apostles are unique. They
belong to the church's foundation (Eph. 2:20). There are no apostles
today, only Christians with an apostolic testimony: "By the grace of
God I am what I am" (1 Cor. 15:10).

Sovereignty in Salvation

The sovereignty of God in salvation is not just a Calvinistic distinctive; it is a biblical distinctive. Except for God's sovereign,
interposing mercy in Christ, we would all be without hope and
without God (Eph. 2:12). Here is the fountainhead of the gospel of
our Lord Jesus Christ. Here is where we cast our anchor and rejoice
that our salvation does not rest in our frail hold of Him, but in His
mighty, merciful grasp of us. Here is where thanksgiving to God
is nurtured. Here is where we begin to learn the Christlike grace
of humility and say with the psalmist, "Not unto us, O LORD, not
unto us, but to Your name give glory" (Ps. 115:1).

By God's Will

Paul also wanted the Ephesians to know that he was an apostle "by
the will of God" (1:1). This was deeply significant for Paul. He did
not choose or initiate this calling. God set him apart and chose him
to be an apostle of His Son (Gal. 1:1). Paul lived under the lordship of Christ, and his life was not his own. He had been redeemed
through Christ's blood (1 Cor. 6:19–20; Eph. 1:7). God's will, not

his own desires, shaped his life. In this, Paul is a pattern for all Christians. We are not our own because we have been bought with a price, and the only right and reasonable response is to glorify God in our bodies (Rom. 12:1–2; 1 Cor. 6:20) and to "walk worthy of the calling with which [we] were called" (Eph. 4:1).

The Recipients

Significantly, in verse 1, Paul addresses the believers in Ephesus as "saints" who live in "Ephesus," and who are "faithful in Christ Jesus." Believers are saints, which means they have been set apart by God and for God. Paul is not describing their inward condition as much as their outward belonging. A saint is a holy one, someone who has been decisively and irreversibly set apart by God to be one of "His own special people" (1 Peter 2:9). All believers in Ephesus were saints, not just the especially saintly. Remarkably, Paul told the Christians in Corinth that they were "those who are sanctified in Christ Jesus" (1 Cor. 1:2).

In using this language, Paul is highlighting the believer's union with Christ. United to Christ through faith, all believers have "died to sin" (Rom. 6:2) and have been raised with Him to live a new life (Rom. 6:4–5). Yes, we are to grow up into Christ. Yes, we are to "grow in the grace and knowledge of our Lord and Savior Jesus Christ" (2 Peter 3:18). But this growth in grace is built upon and predicated upon our foundational union with Christ in His death to sin (Rom. 6:10) and in His resurrection to a new life (Rom. 6:5, 9–10). Union with Christ is the Spirit-wrought dynamic that ensures our growth in likeness to Christ.

This is a truth that we must take to heart. Because, as Christians, we no longer belong to sin or Satan but to God, sin and Satan's dominion have been forever broken in our lives. Sin is still there to trouble us, but it no longer has any claim on us. We are, in Christ, God's saints, His holy ones.

Do you know who you are? If you are in Christ, you are God's special possession. This glorious truth is calculated to breathe godly dignity and much-needed encouragement into our lives.

A Double Identity

Verse 1 tells us that these saints live in Ephesus. Some manuscripts omit "in Ephesus" and thereby suggest that Ephesians is a circular letter, intended by Paul to be read in a number of churches in the western part of the Roman province of Asia. The absence of personal greetings and the general character of Paul's writing may give some support to this suggestion. It is impossible, however, to make a decisive judgment on the letter's destination. What is undeniable is that the recipients of the letter are living out their set-apart lives in the midst of a godless world. They live "in Christ" but also "in Ephesus."

What was true of the believers in Ephesus is true for believers in every age. We have, by the grace of God, a heavenly zip code, "in Christ," but we also have an earthly zip code—Ephesus, New York, London, Singapore, Beijing. This reality lay behind the Lord Jesus's prayer for His disciples in John 17:15: "I do not pray that You should take them out of the world, but that You should keep them from the evil one." That prevailing prayer continues to be prayed by our now risen and ascended Savior (Rom. 8:34; Heb. 7:25). He knows well the trials, struggles, challenges, and temptations that assail His people in Ephesus—or wherever. And He prays for us unceasingly. As our Great High Priest and King, Jesus intercedes for us before His Father. Not only do we have the indwelling Holy Spirit helping us (Rom. 8:26) and the rich promises of God sustaining us, we have a Great High Priest who is interceding for us—and He is always heard by His Father. His continuing ministry guarantees the perfect efficacy of His finished work on our behalf.

The "Faithful in Christ Jesus"

Paul's reference to the "faithful in Christ Jesus" in the first verse could mean one of two things: it could mean that the people to whom Paul is writing are believers, men and women who have come to a personal trust in Jesus Christ as Savior and Lord. The church is a fellowship of believers. It is more than that, but not less than that. But more likely Paul means that these saints have been tried and found to be trustworthy, loyal, dependable believers. The

Christians in Ephesus were not fair-weather believers. Their faith was marked by faithfulness, and they stuck with their Savior in bad times as well as good times. "Faithful" is what God is to us. He is a faithful God, unchanging and unfailing in His love and commitment to His people. Is this what you are to Him? Are you faithful to His cause and kingdom? We are not justified by our faithfulness, but the reality of our justification is seen in our faithfulness. Our Lord Jesus was the prototypical faithful man. He was "obedient to the point of death, even the death of the cross" (Phil. 2:8). It is the present ministry of the Holy Spirit to reproduce in us what He first produced in our Savior. This faithfulness is "in Christ Jesus." We live out the life of faith vitally united to our Lord Jesus (Gal. 2:20).

In Christ

"In Christ" is Paul's most frequent description of a Christian (nine times in the first fourteen verses). Faith in Christ—self-renouncing, self-abandoning faith—takes you into Christ. Faith is your passport into Christ and into all the blessings that are found in Him (1:3). These Christians were "in Ephesus," but by God's amazing grace they were also "in Christ Jesus." Christians live in a fallen world but do so in vital union with the Savior, Jesus Christ. He is our life (Gal. 2:20; Col. 3:4). He is the true vine to whom we have been united by the grace of our heavenly Father, through faith (John 15). Outside of Christ we are lost, "children of [God's] wrath" (Eph. 2:3), heading for a ruined eternity. But in Christ we are everlastingly secure. Nothing and no one is able to snatch us out of Christ's hand—a hand held in the everlasting grasp of His Father (John 10:28–30).

The Central Truth

John Murray calls union with Christ "the central truth of the whole doctrine of salvation."[2] This union has a number of facets. It is a *federal, or covenantal, union.* Jesus Christ is the appointed head and representative of His church, which is His body. It is a *personal*

---

2. John Murray, *Redemption, Accomplished and Applied* (Edinburgh: Banner of Truth Trust, 2009), 153.

union. We are united personally and vitally in the gospel to Jesus Christ Himself. It is a *spiritual union.* This union is forged by the Holy Spirit, whereby Christ indwells His people and they indwell Him. It is a *faith union.* Faith in Christ brings us experientially into union with Him (Eph. 1:13). This glorious union is not the privilege and preserve of elite Christians; it is the God-given birthright of every believer in the Lord Jesus Christ.

Do you begin to see how radical and wonderful the gospel is? It, or better He, takes us out of the kingdom of sin and Satan and brings "us into the kingdom of the Son of His love" (Col. 1:13). In Christ we have a new identity, a new master, and a new destiny.

Grace and Peace

To such people God gives His "grace…and peace" (v. 2). Thomas Goodwin offered this definition of grace: "Grace is more than mercy and love, it superadds to them. It denotes not simply love, but the love of a sovereign, transcendent superior, one that may do what he will, that may wholly choose whether he will love or no.… Now God, who is an infinite Sovereign, who might have chosen whether ever He would love us or no, for Him to love us, this is grace."[3]

When Paul adds "peace," he is not blessing these believers with the prospect of a trouble-free life. "Peace from God our Father" (v. 2) is the joy and assurance of the Father's love to us in Christ. The heavenly Father desires all His children to rejoice in the assurance of His love. Lack of assurance is not a mark of Christian humility; it is usually the sign of a distempered Christian life. Assurance of our Father's love is deepened and strengthened the more we look outward to Christ, who He is and what He has done.[4]

---

3. *The Works of Thomas Goodwin* (Edinburgh: James Nichol, 1861), 2:222.

4. John Owen wrote, "How few of the saints are experimentally acquainted with this privilege of holding immediate communion with the Father in love! With what anxious, doubtful thoughts do they look upon him! What fears, what questionings are there of his good-will and kindness! At the best, many think there is no sweetness at all in him towards us, but what is purchased at the high price of the blood of Jesus." *Works,* 2:32.

2

So Great a Salvation

EPHESIANS 1:3–7

Blessed be the God and Father of our Lord Jesus Christ, who has blessed us with every spiritual blessing in the heavenly places in Christ, just as He chose us in Him before the foundation of the world, that we should be holy and without blame before Him in love, having predestined us to adoption as sons by Jesus Christ to Himself, according to the good pleasure of His will, to the praise of the glory of His grace, by which He made us accepted in the Beloved.

In Him we have redemption through His blood, the forgiveness of sins, according to the riches of His grace.

One year, my wife and I went to London for a vacation, and while we were there, we visited the Tower of London to see the crown jewels. They were magnificent. They were, however, out of reach, locked away in bulletproof glass cages. Not out of sight, but out of reach. In these verses Paul is displaying the crown jewels of the gospel—jewels that are not out of reach and which are, by God's grace in Christ, the permanent possession and present experience of every Christian, even if it is not always consciously done. More particularly, Paul is describing to us the glory of salvation, which is the crown jewel in the Christian's inheritance. Here, as perhaps nowhere else, we see what it means to be a saved sinner. Paul wants these believers in the church at and beyond Ephesus to see how fabulous the jewels of God's grace in Christ are. He understands that our greatest need is to grasp and to be grasped by the wonder of the gospel.

When we are gripped by the greatness and glory of our salvation in Christ, everything else, in a sense, takes care of itself. When Paul encouraged the church in Corinth to give generously to the needs of the poor saints in Jerusalem, he reminded them of "the grace of our Lord Jesus Christ" (2 Cor. 8:9). This, as we have already noted, is the theological grammar of the Bible. The imperatives of duty are rooted in and flow out of the indicatives of grace. It is this foundational pattern that keeps the Christian life from becoming cold, clinical, and metallic. The great preservative against legalism and the great encouragement to true holiness in the Christian life is the exposition and consideration of who God is and His amazing grace to us in Christ.

Paul has a deeply pastoral reason for writing as he does in Ephesians 1:3–14. Ephesus was a noted center of idolatry. Luke recounts this in Acts 19. As Paul begins his letter to God's little flock in the great city of Ephesus, he clearly wants to encourage them to grasp something of the "width and length and depth and height" of God's love to them in Christ (Eph. 3:18–19). Paul understands that this, more than anything else, will help them to stand faithfully for Christ, no matter how sore the opposition and persecution. The application to us should be obvious. If we are to live courageously for our Savior in an increasingly anti-Christian world, we must sink our hearts and minds into the "unsearchable riches of Christ" (Eph. 3:8).

Blessed Be God

In verse 3, Paul begins the substance of his letter by blessing "the God and Father of our Lord Jesus Christ," because He has "blessed us with every spiritual blessing in the heavenly places…in Christ." It is imperative for the apostle that we understand God the Father is the originator and giver of our spiritual blessings. Within the Holy Trinity, the Father is the initiator in salvation. Each person of the Trinity is intimately and actively involved in the work of salvation. But within the Trinity, the Father takes the lead in originating salvation, the Son in accomplishing salvation, and the Holy Spirit in applying salvation. The Holy Trinity together is actively involved

in every phase of creation, providence, redemption, and consummation. As John Owen explained in his magisterial work *Communion
with God*, however, while the three persons do all they do together,
the Father "by way of eminency" plans, the Son "by way of eminency" procures, and the Spirit "by way of eminency" applies.[1]

What does it mean to bless God? We cannot add anything to
God. He is perfect in all He is and in all He does. He is "the blessed
and only Potentate, the King of kings and Lord of lords" (1 Tim.
6:15). To "bless" means, literally, to "speak well of." When we bless
God, we speak well of Him; we declare that He is all that He says
He is and that He is worthy of our unceasing praise. King David
exhorted himself to "bless the LORD" for the multitude of the Lord's
blessings to him (Ps. 103:1–5) and promised that he would do so
"at all times" (Ps. 34:1). Blessing the Lord is the response of our
redeemed hearts to His overflowing blessing of us in Christ, "who
has blessed us with every spiritual blessing in the heavenly places."

There probably is not a more profound statement in the Bible.
In Christ, which is Paul's most characteristic description of a
Christian, God the Father has truly blessed us. In verses 3–7, Paul
explores the riches of the "so great a salvation" (Heb. 2:3) that God
has provided for us in His Son.

The Extravagance and Extensiveness of Salvation

In giving us His Son, our heavenly Father has wrapped up in Him
"every spiritual blessing in the heavenly places" (v. 3). Nothing has
been withheld from us that could bring us blessing. This is just
another way of telling us that Jesus Himself is the great salvation
that is ours through faith alone in Him. Salvation is not so much a
state as a person, the blessed person of God's own Son. Jesus is the
one who has won for all believers the spiritual blessings God had
destined for them. This is the reality behind Paul's assurance to the

---

1. Owen, *Works*, 2:18–19. Salvation, Owen wrote, comes from the Father "by the
way of original authority"; from the Son "by the way of communicating from a purchased treasury"; and from the Holy Spirit "by the way of immediate efficacy" (16).

Christians in Rome that God the Father, having given "His own Son" for us, will certainly "with Him also freely give us all things" (Rom. 8:32). There is always the danger that we seek God's blessings apart from seeking Christ, in whom all the blessings of God are found. Jesus Christ is our "wisdom from God—and righteousness and sanctification and redemption" (1 Cor. 1:30). This is why the prevailing pulsebeat of the Christian life animated the apostle Paul: "I also count all things loss for the excellence of the knowledge of Christ Jesus my Lord" (Phil. 3:8). The greatest practical good for the Christian derives from an ever-deepening knowledge of and communion with Jesus Christ.

The Present Reality of Salvation

The apostle tells us that this "so great a salvation" (Heb. 2:3) is not a potential blessing to anticipate but a present blessing to enjoy. In Christ, the Father "has blessed us with every spiritual blessing in the heavenly places" in Christ (1:3). The blessings of the gospel come to us not in discreet parcels but in all their perfection and fullness when we believe on the Lord Jesus Christ and are brought into saving union with Him. This wonderful truth absolutely rules out every form of "second blessing" theology or experience. The fundamental flaw in every second blessing theology is the failure to understand that Jesus Christ Himself is the gospel and is inseparable from His benefits. He is the good news, the gift that has come from the loving heart of the heavenly Father. He is indivisible.

This does not mean that the life of faith is static and humdrum. The Christian life is to be an unceasing exploration and ever-deepening experience of the spiritual blessings the Father has blessed us with in Christ. Jesus is the "living water" who continually satisfies our thirst for life (John 4:10–14); He is the "true bread from heaven" who satisfies our hunger for life (John 6:32–35)—and He is inexhaustible.

This is why we are to bless our heavenly Father. What He has done for us in His Son surely prompts us to bless Him, to glory in Him, admire Him, and rejoice in Him. If our individual and corporate Christian lives should be marked by anything, they should be marked by joyful, thankful glorying in the God of our salvation. Our public worship services should pulse with the wonder of sinners forgiven by grace and blessed in Christ with every spiritual blessing by a loving heavenly Father. The reason our worship services do not always throb with life is not because our liturgies are antiquated, our praise lacks modernity, and our surroundings are formal. The reason is more basic and serious: we are not captivated and overwhelmed by the gospel! This is not a plea to abandon modernity and embrace antiquity. It is a plea to cry out to the Lord that we might be freshly acquainted with our privileges in Christ. This is the church's great need—yours and mine also.

Because every blessing we possess has been given to us in Christ by our heavenly Father, we have nothing to boast about (1 Cor. 4:7–8). We are and ever will be debtors to the God of undeserved kindness. The mark of a life that has been gripped by grace is not pride but humility. A proud Christian is the ultimate oxymoron. God's mighty, sovereign grace crushes the pride out of us and causes us to cry out,

> Not unto us, O LORD, not unto us,
> But to Your name give glory,
> Because of Your mercy,
> Because of Your truth. (Ps. 115:1)

It is a tragedy that Calvinism has such a bad reputation in the Christian church. Too often people (usually men) who claim to be Calvinists have been harsh in their espousing of the doctrines of grace. But the God of grace is kind to sinners, rich in mercy, longsuffering, and abounding in goodness and truth (see Ex. 34:6–7). And the Son of God, incarnate in our flesh, does not break bruised reeds or quench smoking flax (see Isa. 42:3). It should not surprise us that Paul urges "the elect of God" to "put on tender mercies, kindness, humility, meekness, longsuffering," and much else (Col. 3:12–14).

God's Electing Love

Paul tells us that the "so great a salvation" (Heb. 2:3) these saints in Ephesus have come to possess originated in God's sovereign, electing love (see vv. 3, 4, 11). Salvation does not begin with my choice of Christ, but with God's choice of me. "Before the foundation of the world," before you or I or anyone was thought of, far less born, the Father chose us in Christ (v. 4).

God's choosing love, His electing mercy, is underlined throughout these verses by the word "grace." Grace is God's undeserved mercy and love to judgment-deserving sinners. If salvation depended on one iota of anything in you or in me, we could never be saved. But salvation originates in "the good pleasure [purpose] of His will" (v. 5). It comes to us from the planned purpose of God's loving heart (see v. 4). God's love is the fountainhead of the gospel (John 3:16; 1 John 4:10). God's Son did not come into the world to persuade the Father to love us or to win His love for us; He came as the gift of the Father's love to us. Sinners are saved because God is pleased to save them. God is under no obligation to save anyone. We are all fallen in Adam (Rom. 5:12–20). All of us "have sinned and fall short of the glory of God" (Rom. 3:23). The wonder is not that God saves some but that God saves any.

The Transforming Purpose of Salvation

Paul highlights the revealed purpose of God's "so great a salvation" (Heb. 2:3) in Christ. The Holy Spirit is far more concerned that we understand the purpose of God's gracious election of sinners than its mystery. God's purpose in election is that "we should be holy and without blame before Him" (v. 4). Salvation is not just a completed act; it is a continuing process. Think of a master sculptor who seeks to create a marble masterpiece. He first chooses an unshaped block of marble and then slowly but surely begins the long process of transforming it into the form his mind has conceived. God's ultimate purpose, as the divine Sculptor, is to conform us to the likeness of His Son (Rom. 8:29). This requires that we become "holy and without blame before Him" (v. 4), just as His Son is perfectly holy and blameless. It is the particular ministry of the Holy Spirit to replicate in us the likeness He first etched in the life of the Lord Jesus Christ. As we will later see (Eph. 4:17–23), this ministry of replication involves us in an unending battle with indwelling sin, a godless world, and an unholy adversary.

Set Apart

The heart of biblical holiness is being set apart by God, for God. We would never choose to be holy because we have no will, desire, or strength to be holy. Sin has captured the citadel of our hearts. It is not an occasional, troublesome intruder; it is an enslaving master (John 8:34; Rom. 6:16–17). "But God" (Eph. 2:4)! In times eternal God decreed to set apart a people for His praise, to separate us from our sin and make us "His own special people" (1 Peter 2:9).

Without Blame

More than that, God chose us to be "without blame" (v. 4) before Him. "Without blame" does not mean without sin. It means to be undeviatingly consistent, not open to public charges of inconsistency and hypocrisy. To be without blame is to live a life that can be examined in the light and found faithful. But what do holiness and blamelessness actually look like? They look like Jesus. What, then, were the distinguishing features of our Lord Jesus's earthly life? He loved his Father and lived to please and obey Him (John 14:31). He loved His disciples (John 13:1, 34–35). He was gentle and patient with His disciples and with sinners in general (Matt. 12:17–21, quoting Isa. 42:1–4). He was full of kindness and compassion for the lost (Matt. 9:36). This is the life all God's saved people have been called to in Christ. Paul urges God's holy, elect people to "put on tender mercies, kindness, humility, meekness, longsuffering; bearing with one another, and forgiving one another, if anyone has a complaint against another; even as Christ forgave you, so you also must do" (Col. 3:12–13). Do you recognize yourself? This is the holy and blameless life. Is it the desire of your heart to be "holy and without blame before Him"?

Before Him

The words "before Him" (v. 4) remind us that the Christian life is to be lived first before God. We live in the world and are to live before this unbelieving world the life of faith in our Lord Jesus. But first and foremost, we are to live "before Him." Our primary gaze is not to be looking around, wondering what the world thinks of us, but looking up into the face of our great and gracious God, living first to please Him.

The manifest lack of holiness in the modern evangelical church robs our gospel testimony of credibility and power. We have too often been seduced by the mantra of modernity telling us that credibility lies in relevance, slickness, presentation, and coolness. We spend more time trying to be relevant and accepted than seeking after heart holiness and moral integrity. The church in Corinth had been in part seduced by charismatic teachers. Paul's response to his detractors highlights his absolute conviction that the church's lasting impact on this fallen world rests in "not walking in craftiness nor handling the word of God deceitfully" (2 Cor. 4:2). On the contrary, Paul declared that "by manifestation of the truth" he would commend himself "to every man's conscience in the sight of God" (2 Cor. 4:2). Here is a man living before the face of God (*coram Deo*). This is the life that God invariably blesses with His presence and power.

Lovingly Predestined

If God's election highlights His sovereignty in salvation, His predestination highlights His purpose in salvation. Probably more than any other biblical truth, predestination, along with its sister truth election, arouses the ire of unbelievers as well as the perplexity of many believers. It will help us, however, if we recognize that God's predestination of sinners for adoption is neither cold nor arbitrary. His predestination is rooted in his love: "In love, having predestined us to adoption" (vv. 4–5).

It is grammatically possible, however, that "in love" qualifies what precedes it rather than what follows it. This would mean that, following the New King James Version (NKJV), the holiness and blamelessness that God purposes for our lives is to be animated and defined by love. Love to God for His grace to us in Christ is the mother of all other graces. Without love, all our other graces are empty shells. We might "speak with the tongues of men and of angels," possess prophetic powers, understand all mysteries, and have all faith, but if we "have not love," we are sounding brass and clanging cymbals (1 Cor. 13:1–2). When a lawyer asked Jesus what was the greatest commandment, He replied, "You shall love the LORD your God with all your heart, with all your soul, and with all your mind" (Matt. 22:36–37; see also Deut. 6:5). Love to God, heart and soul affection to God in Christ, gives holiness a humility and gentleness that prevents it from becoming insufferably proud.

It is more likely, however, that the English Standard Version (ESV) rightly punctuates the apostle's thought. In Romans 8:29, Paul tells us that it was those God "foreknew" whom He "predestined to be conformed to the image of His Son." In this context, to "foreknow" is to love. "It means," wrote John Murray, "whom he set regard upon" or "whom he knew from eternity with distinguishing affection and delight," and is virtually equivalent to "whom he foreloved."[2] God's predestination is rooted in His love for His people and reflects His holy passion to give them His best.

Predestination, Not Fatalism

Too often Christians have allowed the unbiblical idea of fatalism to influence their understanding of divine predestination. Fatalism is nothing more than blind chance, the idea that what will happen, will happen; that we are helpless pawns in a cosmic game. God's predestination, however, is thousands of miles away from fatalism. Divine predestination is rooted in the heavenly Father's love, which is beyond our fathoming. But it is the same love that sent the Son of God into the world to be the Savior of the world. It is a love we can trust, even when we cannot, through our present

---

2. John Murray, *The Epistle to the Romans* (London: Marshall, Morgan and Scott, 1960), 317.

creaturely sinfulness, fully comprehend. The cross of the Savior is where we bring all our perplexities, not to have them solved but to be reminded that "He who did not spare His own Son, but delivered Him up for us all, how shall He not with Him also freely give us all things?" (Rom. 8:32).

It is to be expected that God's revelation of Himself and His purposes will far transcend our understanding. Paul's stunning conclusion to his exposition of the gospel of God in Romans 11:33 captures the adoring humility of the believing heart and mind in the face of God's unabridged sovereignty: "Oh, the depth of the riches both of the wisdom and knowledge of God! How unsearchable are His judgments and His ways past finding out!"

There is no escaping the fact that the God of the Bible predestines (see Eph. 1:11). Predestination is not a Calvinistic peculiarity; it is the plain teaching of Holy Scripture.

A Cause of Controversy

Sadly, God's election and predestination in salvation has been a cause of controversy among Christians. It is undoubtedly true that good men and women—faithful, Bible-believing Christians—have differed, sometimes with great acrimony, in their understanding of God's election of sinners to salvation and His predestination of them for adoption. Some Christians have insisted that God's election follows His foreknowledge; that is, God foresees who will believe in His Son and elects or chooses them for salvation. God's choice of us, then, follows our choice of Him. Others have felt that if God's election precedes our choice of Him and is itself the cause of our choice of Him, then pride and presumption necessarily follow.

History is littered with the moral tragedies of men and women who have used the doctrine of election to excuse their sins. Nonetheless, it has to be said that God's Word unambiguously teaches divine, gratuitous election and subsequent predestination. The Christian's concern should not be how to puzzle through the mysteries of God's sovereignty, but to bow in worship before the sovereign God who loves us and gave His own Son for us. Divine sovereignty is never

presented to us in the Bible as a puzzle to solve but as a comfort
to cherish.

By Their Fruit You Will Know Them

As Paul has made plain in Ephesians 1:4, God's sovereign and gracious election of sinners to salvation is productive of holiness, not
an excuse for sin. Where there is no holiness of life, there has been
no election unto salvation. Jesus said, "Therefore by their fruits you
will know them" (Matt. 7:20; John 15:1–8). We cannot say this or
hear this too often. God's election is "in Christ," the Christ who is
"holy, harmless, undefiled, [and] separate from sinners" (Heb. 7:26).
It is often claimed that belief in divine sovereignty enervates true
spirituality and the pursuit of godliness. The reverse is true. When
it dawns on forgiven sinners that salvation has come to them as the
gift of God's grace, that though they were deserving of God's wrath
and judgment God set His electing love upon them when they were
"dead in trespasses" (Eph. 2:5), they will have but one desire, to live
"to the praise of the glory of His grace" (Eph. 1:6).

A Stimulus to Humility

God's sovereign and gracious election of sinners to salvation is presented in the Bible as a stimulus to humility rather than a cause
for boasting (Eph. 2:8–9). What do we have that we did not first
receive? And if we have received all that we have as a gift from God,
how can we ever boast (1 Cor. 4:7–8)? John Calvin made the point
eloquently: "God's election is free and beats down and annihilates
all the unworthiness, works and virtues of men."[3] One of the hallmarks of men and women whose lives have been mastered by God's
sovereign, gracious, electing love is humility of heart. The realization
that we are debtors to mercy alone humbles us to the dust and fills
us with the desire to present our bodies as a living sacrifice to God
(Rom. 11:33–12:2).

---

3. John Calvin, *Sermons on the Epistle to the Ephesians* (Edinburgh: Banner of
Truth Trust, 1974), 33.

The Family Character of Salvation

Paul highlights the staggering truth that God has not only chosen us in Christ to be "holy and without blame" (v. 4), but He has
"predestined us to adoption as sons by Jesus Christ" (v. 5). God's
salvation in Christ has a familial shape. Adoption has been called
the apex, or omega point, of God's blessings to us in Christ. In
our union with Adam, our first head, we fell into sin and became
"children of wrath" (Eph. 2:3). In union with Christ, our second and
ultimate Head, we are brought into the consummate heights of sonship to God. Jesus is the eternal Son of God in our flesh. Because
of God's predestined purpose "by Jesus Christ," we have received
adoption as sons (v. 5). Jesus has "brothered" us in His gospel. He
has done this, first, by becoming one with us in His incarnation
(Heb. 2:11), then as our representative covenant Head who died in
our place, bearing God's just condemnation on our sin and rising
for our justification (Rom. 4:25).

God's gracious adoption of sinners is a much-neglected truth.
He chose us, saved us, and sanctified us in order to make us His
adopted children. God is our Father in Christ. We are His sons
and daughters, with all the privileges of sons and daughters. The
Westminster Confession of Faith, chapter 12, has a magnificent
explanation of adoption:

> All those that are justified, God vouchsafeth, in and for his only
> Son Jesus Christ, to make partakers of the grace of adoption:
> by which they are taken into the number, and enjoy the liber-
> ties and privileges of the children of God; have his name put
> upon them; receive the Spirit of adoption; have access to the
> throne of grace with boldness; are enabled to cry, Abba, Father;
> are pitied, protected, provided for, and chastened by him as by
> a father; yet never cast off, but sealed to the day of redemption,
> and inherit the promises, as heirs of everlasting salvation.

The Pleasure of His Will

Paul tells us that this glorious privilege, like other blessings we possess in Christ, comes to us "according to the good pleasure of His

will" (v. 5). Paul never wearies of reminding us that every blessing we possess is in Christ and is the result of God's sovereign good pleasure and purpose. That is why praise belongs to God alone and especially "to the praise of the glory of His grace" (v. 6). Grace is glorious not just because it has lavished upon us every spiritual blessing in the heavenly places, but because it is itself truly glorious. It originates in the good pleasure of His will and is wholly and immeasurably undeserved. Grace is not first a theological or denominational distinctive; it is a cause for doxology. Unceasing praise, not self-preening pride, is the mark of a sovereignly saved sinner.

It is not surprising that Paul once again reminds us that this grace of adoption has come to us "in the Beloved" (v. 6). Faith brings us, by the grace of the Holy Spirit, into actual, vital union with Christ, the Son of God, the God-man in our flesh. He is the "firstborn among many brethren" (Rom. 8:29) and is not ashamed to call us His brothers because we are "of one" (Heb. 2:11). During the Son's life on earth, the Father split the heavens to speak of and to Him: "This is My beloved Son" (Matt. 3:17; 17:5). Because Christ is the beloved Son, everyone in Him is no less God's beloved son. He is the beloved Son from eternity; we are the beloved sons from time, made sons not by any merit in us but solely by "the glory of His grace" (1:6). What a gospel! What a God!

Blood Redemption

In verse 7, Paul proceeds to highlight what it cost God to secure this "so great a salvation" (Heb. 2:3) for sinners. "Redemption" is one of the great words in the Bible. To understand its significance, we need to appreciate its Old Testament roots. In the Old Testament, the great act of redemption was God's deliverance of Israel from bondage and slavery in Egypt. Redemption, however, means more than deliverance; it means deliverance through costly effort. Redemption is costly. This point is made in Exodus 13:14: "By strength of hand the LORD brought us out of Egypt, out of the house of bondage." Rescuing His people from their bondage was not an effortless act on God's part. It was "by strength of hand"—that is, by the exertion of His almighty power—that God rescued His people from their captivity in Egypt.

Why We Need Redemption

But the great captivity that enslaves God's people is not to any mere earthly power. Jesus said, "Most assuredly, I say to you, whoever commits sin is a slave of sin" (John 8:34). Paul tells the Christians in Rome that they "were slaves of sin" (Rom. 6:17). The sad and tragic state of every human being is that we follow "the prince of the power of the air" and are "by nature children of [God's] wrath" (Eph. 2:2–3). Sin is not an occasional, troublesome intruder; it is an enslaving power. And we are powerless in and of ourselves to do anything about this bondage to sin and its master, Satan. This is why we need redemption. We need to be rescued from this sorry servitude and set free to become "slaves of righteousness" (Rom. 6:18). This is what the Lord Jesus Christ has done for us: "In Him we have redemption through His blood, the forgiveness of sins" (v. 7). Redemption from the guilt and domineering power of sin and Satan is one of the glorious blessings of our union with Christ.

The Price Paid

The question arises, but how does the blood of Christ effect our redemption from sin and Satan? Again, we need to go back to the Old Testament to fully appreciate the connection between the blood and redemption. In the rich symbolism and typology of the Old Testament sacrificial system, God's holy wrath and just judgment were turned aside by the offering up of a spotless sacrifice in the place of the sinner. The letter to the Hebrews wonderfully captures the heart of the Old Testament sacrificial system and explains its significance: "But Christ came as High Priest of the good things to come.... Not with the blood of goats and calves, but with His own blood He entered the Most Holy Place once for all, having obtained eternal redemption" (Heb. 9:11–12). Jesus paid in full the price of our redemption. He offered Himself as our substitute to pay the ransom that we could never pay—the price of removing the sin that enslaved us to Satan. Our sin had made a separation between us and God (Isa. 59:2).

If we were ever to be rescued from our enslaved and hell-bound state, we needed God to step in and do for us what we were power-less to do for ourselves: remove the sin that separated Him from us and made us Satan's captives. This He has done, unimaginably and unfathomably, in His Son, Jesus Christ. God is holy and could never simply wave a wand and make our sin disappear. But in His glorious grace and in His beloved Son, God has found a righteous and holy way to punish our sin and rescue us from our abysmal captivity to sin and Satan.

It is imperative that we rightly understand what Paul is telling us. He is not saying that a gracious, love-filled Son persuaded His Father to redeem us through His sin-bearing death on the cross. The Son of God is always the Sent One of His Father. It was the love of the heavenly Father that sent forth Jesus "as a propitiation by His blood, through faith" (Rom. 3:25).

A Representative Substitute

There is nothing unbecoming or inappropriate in the Lord Jesus Christ taking our place on Calvary's cross. From the moment of His conception in the womb of the Virgin Mary, through the overshad-owing power of the Holy Spirit, God's Son in our flesh was living and breathing and acting not for Himself, but for us. All that Jesus did He did for all those He represented before God. Just as we fell in Adam, our first head, so we are raised in Christ, our second and last Head (see Rom. 5:12–21; 1 Cor. 15:21–23, 47–49). His death on Calvary's cross was of infinite significance and infinite effective-ness. He was the spotless Lamb of God on whom the Father laid all our iniquity (Isa. 53:6, 10). He paid in His own blood the price of our sin.

By His representative, substitutionary shedding of His blood on Calvary, God's Son, in our flesh, won for us the forgiveness of our sins. The righteous judgment and condemnation our sin against

God deserved was executed on God's own Son, the representative God-man.

It is little wonder that, once again, Paul tells us that God did this for us "according to the riches of His grace" (v. 7). He never tires of reminding us that everything we now possess in Christ is the result and fruit of the riches of God's grace. Salvation is of the Lord.

Jesus Christ is our covenant Head, the one appointed in eternity by God to be the Redeemer of His elect. In His own Son, God executed the unimaginable judgment that our sin deserved: "For He made Him who knew no sin to be sin for us, that we might become the righteousness of God in Him" (2 Cor. 5:21). This was Jesus's self-conscious understanding of His mission: "For even the Son of Man did not come to be served, but to serve, and to give His life a ransom for many" (Mark 10:45).

The Forgiveness of Sins

The first benefit flowing to us from Christ's redemption is "the forgiveness of sins" (v. 7). To be a forgiven sinner, to know that God is no longer against you but for you in Christ, is truly liberating. If Christ has atoned for us in our sin and rebellion and paid in the shedding of His blood the price for our sin, then we are free to live unto God as His now forgiven, adopted sons. Do we sufficiently marvel at the forgiveness of sins? In Christ, God has blotted out all our sins (Acts 3:19) and removed them from us "as far as the east is from the west" (Ps. 103:12). "In Him we have redemption" (v. 7). Redemption in Christ is a settled fact—an unchangeable, never-to-be-altered fact.

Christ's redemption of sinners by the shedding of His blood has an immediate implication for and application to sinners. His redemption means that we are not our own, for we have been bought with a price. "Therefore," Paul tells the Corinthians, "glorify God in your body" (1 Cor. 6:20). It is one thing to confess the truth of the blood redemption of Christ and another thing to live as a blood-redeemed, forgiven sinner, glorifying God concretely in our bodies. We bring every thought in submission to Christ and yield up our bodies to God as living sacrifices, which is our "reasonable service" (Rom. 12:1).

And, not surprisingly, Paul once again tells us that this redemption in Christ is "according to the riches of His grace" (v. 7). Paul never wearies of magnifying the God of grace. He wants us never to forget for a moment that we are and ever will be debtors to mercy alone. The grace of God is more than a theological or denominational distinctive. The mark of a man or woman captured and captivated by grace is a humble heart and a worship-filled life. Doxology is the first resting place of biblical, authentic Calvinism. If it is not, then gospel grace is absent.

3

God's Ultimate Plan

…which He made to abound toward us in all wisdom and pru-dence, having made known to us the mystery of His will, according to His good pleasure which He purposed in Himself, that in the dispensation of the fullness of the times He might gather together in one all things in Christ, both which are in heaven and which are on earth—in Him. In Him also we have obtained an inheritance, being predestined according to the purpose of Him who works all things according to the counsel of His will, that we who first trusted in Christ should be to the praise of His glory.

In Him you also trusted, after you heard the word of truth, the gospel of your salvation; in whom also, having believed, you were sealed with the Holy Spirit of promise, who is the guarantee of our inheritance until the redemption of the purchased possession, to the praise of His glory.

The Bible has a breathtaking panoramic understanding of redemp-tion. God's redeeming work in Christ transcends rescuing sinners from their bondage to sin and to Satan. There is, therefore, in Ephe-sians 1 a developing or unfolding connection between verse 7 and verses 8–10. God's redeeming work in Christ embraces the totality of the cosmos. The redeeming grace that God has "made to abound toward us in all wisdom and prudence" (v. 8) has an ultimate end in view that goes beyond the redemption of individual sinners. What God in the gospel of redeeming grace makes known to us is noth-ing less than "the mystery of His will" (v. 9).

A Gospel Mystery

A gospel mystery is not a truth that remains an insolvable puzzle. Rather, it is a truth that we could never know, except God in His grace reveals it to us. The word "mystery" appears sixteen times in Paul's letters, including six times in Ephesians (1:9; 3:3, 4, 9; 5:32; 6:19). The gospel is the revealed plan and purpose of God for His glory and for bringing justified and sanctified sinners to share in His glory (Rom. 5:2; 8:17). In Ephesians 3:4–6 Paul speaks of "the mystery of Christ…as it has now been revealed by the Spirit to His holy apostles and prophets: that the Gentiles should be fellow heirs, of the same body, and partakers of His promise in Christ through the gospel." The unity of Gentiles and Jews in the same body is a prelude to and a foretaste of the cosmic unity that Paul highlights in verse 10.

The mystery that God has revealed (v. 9) is His "dispensation of the fullness of the times, [that] He might gather together in one all things in Christ, both which are in heaven and which are on earth—in Him" (v. 10). When Adam sinned, God's good creation was defaced. Sin came into the world (Rom. 5:12), and Satan, the enemy of our souls, became the god of this whole world as it came under his diabolical rule (2 Cor. 4:4; 1 John 5:19). The whole creation is presently in "bondage of corruption" and waits to obtain "the glorious liberty of the children of God" (Rom. 8:21). Adam's sin was cosmic tragedy, but God already had a purpose to "gather together in one all things in Christ, both which are in heaven and which are on earth" (v. 10). Paul makes a similar statement in his letter to the Colossians, where he speaks of God reconciling all things to Himself in Christ, things in heaven and things on earth, "having made peace through the blood of His cross" (Col. 1:20). The whole creation that was lost to God through the fall will be restored to God through Christ.

Paul uses a vivid verb in verse 10 to capture the glorious cosmic unity that God is in the process of accomplishing in Christ.[1] The

---

1. The verb is ἀνακεφαλαιόω (I sum up or recapitulate). The early church father Irenaeus (c. 115–c. 202) understood that the atonement of Christ reversed

ESV translates it "to unite all things in him"; the New International Version (NIV), "to bring unity to all things…under Christ"; the King James Version (KJV) and the NKJV, to "gather together in one all things in Christ"; and the New American Standard Bible (NASB), "the summing up of all things in Christ." The verb appears in only one other place in the New Testament, Romans 13:9, where Paul says that God's commandments are "summed up (ἀνακεφαλαιοῦται) in this saying, namely, 'You shall love your neighbor as yourself.'" It is clear that ἀνακεφαλαιόω contains the idea of "gathering together and bringing into a unity."

The context, however, suggests another way to translate this Greek compound. In Ephesians 1:22, Paul tells us that the Father has given Christ as "head over all things." Creation has a head, who is Jesus Christ. The term ἀνακεφαλαιόω is literally "to head up again." It may be better to understand that Paul is telling the Ephesians that God's purpose, which He set forth in Christ, was to head up again all things in Him. Before Adam's rebellion, God's Son was the head of creation. The triune God's lordship of creation was mediated through the Son. God's ultimate purpose, then, is to reestablish the Son as the Head of creation.

It is imperative for us to understand that God's purpose in salvation does not ultimately focus on us, but on His Son. Paul makes this explicit in Romans 8:29: "For whom He foreknew, He also predestined to be conformed to the image of His Son, that He might be the firstborn among many brethren." The ultimate cosmic glory of the Son is the Father's preeminent purpose in redeeming sinners. If nothing else, this should teach us that our blessedness is tied to Christ's exaltation as head over all things. Modern evangelicalism

---

the tragedy of Adam's cosmically significant sin of disobedience. Irenaeus maintained that Christ's life recapitulated all the stages of human life and, in doing so, reversed the course of disobedience initiated by Adam. He saw Christ as the new Adam, who reversed everything Adam did. Where Adam was disobedient to God's command concerning the fruit of the tree of the knowledge of good and evil, Christ was obedient even to death on the wood of a tree. Irenaeus saw Christ as "recapitulating" or "summing up" the life of humanity.

has often been infiltrated—even scarred—by the self-centeredness of modernity. It is as if God exists to make our lives complete. God's purpose for us indeed is to make our lives complete, but that completeness is bound up with the cosmic triumph of our Head, Jesus Christ.

Our Spirit-Sealed Inheritance

Paul continues to unpack the riches of God's grace that have come to us in Christ. Uppermost in the apostle's mind is the "inheritance" that we have come to possess in Christ (vv. 11, 14). An inheritance comes into effect when a testator dies (Heb. 9:15–16). Before a testator dies, an inheritance is only a prospect. It may be a tantalizing prospect full of fabulous riches, but until the testator dies, it remains out of reach. But "in Him also we have obtained an inheritance" (v. 11). There has been a death. On Calvary's cross, our Lord and Savior died and left us an unimaginable and ultimately indescribable inheritance. In Hebrews 9:15 we read that this inheritance is eternal. In his first letter, Peter tells us that this inheritance is "incorruptible and undefiled and…does not fade away, [and is] reserved in heaven for you, who are kept by the power of God through faith for salvation ready to be revealed in the last time" (1:4–5). Paul has been exploring something of the vastness and glory of this inheritance in Ephesians 1:3–10, and now he has even more to tell us about this inheritance.

Predestinating Grace

Paul tells us that we have obtained this inheritance, "being predestined according to the purpose of Him who works all things according to the counsel of His will" (v. 11). The inheritance of the riches of God's grace in Christ has come to us not because we deserve it in any way. We are "by nature children of wrath, just as the others" (Eph. 2:3). What we deserve from God is His righteous wrath, not a glorious inheritance. And yet we have obtained this inheritance. How could this be? Because God predestined that we should obtain this inheritance.

If God's election highlights the sovereignty of His salvation, His predestination highlights the purpose of His salvation. Of His good pleasure and purpose, God predestined—that is, destined in times eternal—that believing sinners should obtain a glorious inheritance. There is inexplicableness to God's saving purposes. All He does, verse 11 says, He does "according to the counsel of His will." He works in accordance with a preconceived plan. He is not influenced by anything or anyone outside Himself. He does all He pleases. This is why there can never be a trace of self-congratulation in a Christian's thinking or behavior. God's predestination is far from being a doctrine to shun; it is the most comforting and reassuring of truths. It tells us that our God reigns, that He is never playing "catch-up," and that behind the mayhem of a fallen world are the directing wisdom and power of a good, gracious, and just God.

The Necessity of Faith

God's sovereign, predestinating grace in no sense denies the need for faith. On the contrary, faith is required. This inheritance is the possession of everyone who believes "in Him" (v. 13). In verses 12 and 13, Paul distinguishes two groups of people: "we who first trusted in Christ" and "you also." "We who first trusted in Christ" seems to refer to the Jews who had come to believe in Jesus as the promised Messiah. The purpose of God in predestinating a people to obtain an inheritance was that they "should be to the praise of His glory" (v. 12). The Westminster Shorter Catechism puts this memorably: "Man's chief end is to glorify God and enjoy Him forever." God Himself is our highest good. It is not that God is supremely absorbed in Himself and wants His creation simply to admire and praise Him. The gospel of Christ flows out of God's astonishing love for His rebellious, sinful world (John 3:16; 1 John 4:10). Redeemed sinners, transformed by the grace of God, are indeed to the praise of His glory, which is not only ineffable but also rich in goodness and mercy (Ex. 33:18–19; 34:6–7). God's revealed glory is "full of grace and truth" (John 1:14). This inheritance and this calling to be to the praise of His glory is not, however, the privileged possession of God's ancient covenant people alone. In Ephesians 3:4–6, Paul informs his readers of "the mystery of Christ" that God has revealed to His apostles and prophets, "that the Gentiles should be fellow heirs, of the same body, and partakers of His promise in Christ through the gospel."

Sharing in the Inheritance

Through the gospel, men and women who were "aliens from the commonwealth of Israel and strangers from the covenants of promise, having no hope and without God in the world" (Eph. 2:12), have come to share in the glorious inheritance that is the possession of everyone who believes in Christ, according to verse 13. In Christ, "the middle wall of separation" has been broken down (Eph. 2:14). No longer does the inheritance have a particular national identity. The church is God's international people, "of all nations, tribes, peoples, and tongues" (Rev. 7:9). The one qualification for obtaining this inheritance is hearing the "word of truth" (v. 13) and believing in the Savior therein proclaimed and held forth. Believing in Christ takes us experientially into Christ. God has chosen us in Christ before the foundation of the world. But that wholly gracious election in Christ in eternity becomes our possession only when we believe on the Lord Jesus Christ. Paul unambiguously highlights the exclusiveness of faith as the means by which we come into possession of our inheritance. In the Bible as a whole, faith is never conceived in purely theoretical terms. Faith is more than assent to certain truths. It is acknowledging with the mind and embracing with the heart the truth and person of Christ. It is self-renouncing trust in the Son of God who loved us and gave Himself for us (Gal. 2:20). Gospel faith sees nothing good in itself. This faith takes us into Christ, in whom God the Father has blessed us with every spiritual blessing (Eph. 1:3).

Guaranteed Inheritance

In Christ and by faith in Christ, believers have obtained an inheritance. It is a present possession. But in verse 14 Paul writes of an inheritance yet to be possessed, "until the redemption of the purchased possession." Here we encounter a truth that runs through the New Testament, the "already, but not yet." In Christ the kingdom of God has come in power, but not yet in its fullest revelation. In Christ, the salvation of God has been achieved, but not yet in its fullest sense. Paul highlights this truth in Ephesians 4:30: "And do not grieve the Holy Spirit of God, by whom you were sealed for the day of redemption."

Verse 7 tells us that in Christ we are already redeemed, but that redemption will be fully realized only in the day of redemption, when Christ returns and consummates history and unites our redeemed souls with our resurrection bodies. Paul makes this point dramatically in Romans 8:23–24: "We also who have the firstfruits of the Spirit, even we ourselves groan within ourselves, eagerly waiting for the adoption, the redemption of our body. For we were saved in this hope."

In Romans 8:15, Paul told the Roman Christians that they had "received the Spirit of adoption by whom we cry out, 'Abba, Father.'" They were the sons of the living God, and yet they awaited the fullness of their sonship. Christians possess their heavenly inheritance already, but not yet in its eschatological fullness. But that fullness is guaranteed because God has "sealed [us] with the Holy Spirit of promise" (v. 13). God Himself is the guarantee that our inheritance will never perish, spoil, or fade.

The Holy Spirit Himself is the seal who guarantees our inheritance. Some people have thought that the sealing of the Spirit is a second work of grace in believers' hearts, confirming their salvation or assuring them of it. There should be no doubt that ordinarily the Holy Spirit graciously and often confirms to God's children the truth of their adoption. What Paul writes about here, however, is not a second work of grace but a perspective on the epochal work of grace that brought these Ephesian believers out of their darkness and into the light and life of God's Son. This understanding is confirmed by what Paul writes in Ephesians 4:30. The Holy Spirit is our seal, the guarantee that we will not fail to obtain the inheritance won for us by our Savior. When these Ephesians heard the word of truth, the gospel of their salvation, and "believed," that moment they "were sealed with the Holy Spirit of promise" (v. 13).

Whatever hindrance comes our way, the Holy Spirit of promise will see to it that we will not fail to enter our eternal inheritance. The mention of the Holy Spirit *of promise* emphasizes the new covenant dimension of the gospel. The Holy Spirit has always indwelled believers. Without His indwelling, sanctifying presence, there would be no believers! But with the coming of the Messiah and the inauguration of the new covenant in His blood (Luke 22:20), the Holy Spirit has come in His new covenant ministry as the Spirit of the now-exalted and glorified Christ (John 7:37–39; Gal. 3:14).

Christ Is the Inheritance

We have not yet unpacked precisely what the inheritance is that we have obtained in Christ. Paul has described much of its richness in verses 3–10. We need to understand, however, that our blood-bought inheritance is not at heart a collection of blessings, even the glorious blessings so wonderfully described in verses 3–10. Our inheritance is "in Christ," because He is our inheritance. We must never attempt to separate Christ from His blessings and benefits. He is our salvation, just as He is our peace (Eph. 2:14) and our "wisdom from God—and righteousness and sanctification and redemption" (1 Cor. 1:30). God in Christ is the believer's inheritance. This is the incalculable and unfathomable inheritance that God gifts to us when we believe in the Lord Jesus Christ. It is little wonder Paul concludes this section with the words "to the praise of His glory" (v. 14).

The Holy Trinity

In these opening verses of Ephesians, Paul has shown us the active involvement of each person of the Holy Trinity in our salvation. John Calvin wrote about a passage in an oration by fourth-century theologian Gregory Nazianzen, which, he said, "vastly delights me": "No sooner do I conceive of the One than I am illumined by the splendor of the Three; no sooner do I distinguish them than I am carried back to the One. When I think of any one of the Three I think of him as the whole, and my eyes are filled, and the greater part of what I am thinking escapes me."[2]

Can you relate to Calvin's vast delights and to Gregory's overwhelming sense of the wonder of God's triunity? What time do we give, as Christian believers, to pondering the revealed glory of our triune Savior God? What honor do we ascribe, in our personal and corporate worship, to the persons, being, and acts of our triune God? The Christian faith rests upon and centers in the triune God: "For of Him and through Him and to Him are all things, to whom be glory forever. Amen" (Rom. 11:36).

This is what Paul has shown us in these opening verses of Ephesians. Salvation in all its parts is founded in and flows from the three persons of the Godhead—Father, Son, and Holy Spirit. The Father has chosen us, blessed us in Christ with every spiritual blessing, adopted us as His sons, and predestined us according to His own eternal purpose. The Son has redeemed us by His own blood, and in union with Him we come to possess and experience the riches of God's grace. The Holy Spirit has sealed us and is the guarantee of our inheritance. In all of this the Trinity has worked as one.[3]

It should be the default of our spiritual lives and of our theological confession that before all else, we give glory to our triune God. In recent times, evangelicalism has often oscillated between Christomonism and Spirit-monism. But we do a huge disservice to Christ and the Spirit if we ever think of them apart from the Father and from one another. Jesus is always the Sent One of the

---

2. John Calvin, *The Institutes of the Christian Religion*, Library of Christian Classics, vol. 20 (Philadelphia: Westminster, 1960), 1.13.17. Calvin is quoting Gregory's "On Holy Baptism," oration 40.41.

3. The church has always confessed the *opera ad extra trinitatis indivisa sunt* (the external works of the Trinity are indivisible). The persons of the Trinity never act independently. What one does, they all do. It was not the Father or the Spirit who died on Calvary's cross, but it was "through the eternal Spirit" that Jesus "offered Himself without spot to God" (Heb. 9:14).

Father, His Servant Son. The Spirit is always the One sent from the Father and the Son to indwell us as the Spirit of Christ, ministering to us out of the riches of Christ (John 14:23). And the Father is always to be thought of as the Father who "so loved the world that He gave His only begotten Son" (John 3:16; 1 John 4:10). The Christian faith is pervasively Trinitarian: Christian worship is Trinitarian (Eph. 2:18); Christian salvation is Trinitarian (Rom. 11:36); and Christian baptism and missions are Trinitarian (Matt. 28:18–20).[4]

Thinking God's thoughts after Him—that is, having our minds and hearts shaped by His Trinitarian self-revelation—will enrich our lives and give expansiveness to our communion with God, both personal and corporate. Many churches experience poverty in worship because they practically ignore the revealed richness of God as Trinity. Perhaps for many Christians the doctrine of the Trinity is considered recondite, a biblical truth that should be believed and confessed but that belongs to the niceties of the study, not the daily life of the believer. Nothing could be further from the truth. Jesus said that eternal life was knowing the only true God (John 17:3), and the only true God is triune. Our present relationship with God and our eternal relationship with God are shaped by His triune being. We come to the Father through the Son, and by the Spirit (Eph. 2:18).

---

4. A careful study of John Owen, *On Communion with God*, will reveal how foundational and glorious the Christian life is as it is lived in fellowship with the Father, the Son, and the Holy Spirit.

4

Prayer for the Church

EPHESIANS 1:15–19

Therefore I also, after I heard of your faith in the Lord Jesus and your love for all the saints, do not cease to give thanks for you, making mention of you in my prayers: that the God of our Lord Jesus Christ, the Father of glory, may give to you the spirit of wisdom and revelation in the knowledge of Him, the eyes of your understanding being enlightened; that you may know what is the hope of His calling, what are the riches of the glory of His inheritance in the saints, and what is the exceeding greatness of His power toward us who believe, according to the working of His mighty power.

These verses focus on Paul's prayer for the church in Ephesus. Do you pray for your church? What do you pray for your church? Are you persuaded that "Jesus loves to answer prayer"?[1] Martin Luther, the German Reformer, believed that God ordinarily does nothing but in answer to prayer. He taught that the Christian life is composed of three spiritual realities: prayer (*oratio*), testing (*tentatio*), and meditation (*meditatio*). The modern evangelical church is often at its weakest where our forebearers were at their strongest. For many modern churches, prayer—especially congregational prayer— is supplemental and not fundamental, peripheral and not central to the church's life and mission. The church today is strong on activities, plans, and programs; it is often weak on seeking God in prayer. We need to be reacquainted with the New Testament's teaching on

---

1. John Newton, "*Come My Soul, Thy Suit Prepare*," in the public domain.

the priority of prayer. It is surely significant that the first description of the church after Peter's Pentecost sermon highlights its devotion to prayer: "They continued steadfastly in the apostles' doctrine and fellowship, in the breaking of bread, and in prayers" (Acts 2:42).

In Paul's prayer in Ephesians 1 we are shown God's great priorities for the life of His church. Paul could have prayed many things as a matter of priority for this church. It was in one of the great centers of the Roman Empire, a city noted for its devotion to the goddess Diana (see Acts 19:23–41). The early Christians in Ephesus had experienced opposition and persecution. What does Paul say he is praying for them? When you struggle to know what to pray for yourself, your loved ones, and your church (Rom. 8:26), Paul's prayer (and other prayers in the Bible) is a model to emulate. There are three things we should note before we examine Paul's particular petitions for the church in Ephesus.

Prayer and Praise

Paul's prayer for the Ephesian church follows his praise to God for His great grace to them in Christ: "Therefore," he begins (v. 15). Praise leads inevitably to prayer. As Paul recounts the astonishing blessings of God's grace in Christ to the Ephesians and to himself, he is brought to his knees in prayer (see Eph. 3:14). Prayer for others is fueled by praise to God. When you find yourself struggling to pray, thoughtful meditation and reflection on "the riches of His grace" (Eph. 1:7) will frame your heart and mind to pray for others and for yourself. So Paul prays that these Christians might know the truth and power and glory of these blessings of God's amazing grace—not merely know what they are, but know in their hearts, in their inmost beings, the sweet, praise-fueling truth of them! There is a huge difference between knowing about someone and actually knowing that person, being personally and intimately related to him or her. You can be acquainted with the doctrines of grace and yet be a stranger to the power and grace of God's love and mercy in Christ. The Christian life is natively experiential and affectional. Paul's final words in this letter, "Grace be with all those who love our Lord

Jesus Christ in sincerity" (6:24), underscore the deeply personal nature of the believing life.

The Fruit of Faith

Notice how Paul describes the Christians he is praying for. In verse 15, he commends them for their "faith in the Lord Jesus and [their] love for all the saints." Where there is faith, self-abandoning trust in the Lord Jesus Christ, there will inevitably be love toward all His people. Faith in Christ brings us into the family of God, into the body of Christ, His church (1 Cor. 12:12–31). The apostle John has strong words for professing Christians who say they belong to Christ but do not love their fellow Christian brothers and sisters: "If someone says, 'I love God,' and hates his brother, he is a liar; for he who does not love his brother whom he has seen, how can he love God whom he has not seen?" (1 John 4:20). Jesus impressed on His disciples the centrality of brotherly love: "By this all will know that you are My disciples, if you have love for one another" (John 13:35). Where brotherly love is absent, the saving grace of God cannot be present (1 John 3:17; 4:20–21).

Jesus's teaching is deeply heart-searching. In Mark's gospel, Jesus's disciples try to stop a man from casting out demons in Jesus's name, "because he does not follow us" (Mark 9:38). Jesus strongly rebuked the narrow-heartedness of His disciples. The disciples had fallen into a sin that sadly has too often marked the Christian church—the sin of partiality. This partiality takes many forms, but it is seen most prevalently in denominational partiality. All denominations, even the most orthodox, are marked by sin and weakness.

It should be our absolute conviction that if the heavenly Father has elected sinners to eternal life, and if our Lord Jesus has died bearing the guilt and shame of their sin, and if they are indwelt by the Spirit of God, then they are family, brothers and sisters to be loved and cherished. This does not mean that we are ever to ignore sin, doctrinal or moral, in any fellow Christian or Christian denomination. It does mean that we are to bear with one another in love and forgive one another as the Lord Himself has forgiven us (Col. 3:13).

Clearly the Lord's disciples took to heart His teaching on brotherly love. In John's first letter, love to the brothers is one of the essential marks of authentic Christian profession. Neither Jesus nor John were suggesting that Christians should not speak or act boldly and, if necessary, confrontationally, to fellow believers. Paul confronted Peter to his face "because he was to be blamed" (Gal. 2:11). Rather, the mark of loving other Christians, whoever they are, is essentially twofold: we treat them as brothers and seek their present and eternal good, even when it costs us to do so:

> By this we know love, because He laid down His life for us. And we also ought to lay down our lives for the brethren. But whoever has this world's goods, and sees his brother in need, and shuts up his heart from him, how does the love of God abide in him?

> My little children, let us not love in word or in tongue, but in deed and in truth. (1 John 3:16–18)

The Puritan Thomas Watson wrote, "There is but one God, and they that serve him should be one. There is nothing that would render the true religion more lovely, or make more proselytes to it, than to see the possessors of it tied together with the heart-strings of love." Paul says the same thing in Romans 15:7: "Receive one another, just as Christ also received us, to the glory of God." How heart-searching God's Word is!

A Thankful Apostle

In verse 16, Paul tells the Ephesians that he thanked God for them unceasingly. He wanted them to *know* that he always gave thanks to God for them. The apostle was always quick to tell Christians how much he loved them, prayed for them, and thanked God for them. He especially told them that he unfailingly remembered them in his prayers. Clearly Paul believed that the greatest and best thing he could do for these believers was to pray for them.

Do you share Paul's conviction? Do you express your care for Christ's church, your brothers and sisters in Christ, by diligently, faithfully, and determinedly praying for them? The great ones in the church are those who give themselves to prayer.

It is easy to see the heart intimacy that Paul enjoyed with fellow believers. He wore his heart on his sleeve. His Christianity was never stoic, passive, or indulgently introspective. Certainly our church life would be transformed if we regularly told other believers in the church that we thanked God and prayed unceasingly for them.

The church in Ephesus had many needs. Paul could have prayed many legitimate and necessary things for these Christians. In his prayer here he tells the Ephesians what their great and pressing needs are. What we, as Christians, think our great needs are may not be what our great needs really are. It is like going to the doctor: you might think you need a particular medicine, but the doctor sees that you actually need something quite different. It is striking that nowhere in his prayer does Paul ask the Lord to protect the Ephesians from persecution, to give them good health, or to provide them with employment (not that it's wrong to ask for these things). No doubt the Ephesian church had many pressing needs, but in Paul's prayer for them we see what he believed their pressing needs really are.

Prayer to the Father

Paul prayed to "the God of our Lord Jesus Christ, the Father of glory" (v. 17). He prayed to the Father. There is a usual, if not invariable, Trinitarian character to prayer, and indeed to all Christian worship. We pray to the Father, through the Son, in the grace and power of the Holy Spirit. This Father to whom Paul prayed was the "Father of glory," but He was no less "the God of our Lord Jesus Christ." Paul is striking two significant notes in his description of the heavenly Father. He is the "Father of glory," the glorious Father, the Father of an infinite majesty. But He is also "the God of our Lord Jesus Christ"; the God who "so loved the world that He gave His only begotten Son" (John 3:16); the God "who did not spare His own Son, but delivered Him up for us all" (Rom. 8:32). There is a wonderful conjunction of majesty and mercy in the

Christian gospel. The God of glory is not to be trifled with, nor is He to be kept at a distance. He is rich in mercy and kind to sinners, and He has come near to us in His only Son. He is a God to whom we can come with humble confidence that He will hear us and answer us out of the overflow of His goodness and mercy.

The Ephesians' Great Need

Paul's first, foundational petition that God would give them "the spirit of wisdom and revelation in the knowledge of Him" (v. 17) is remarkable. Of all the important and pressing needs of the Ephesians, Paul recognized that their greatest need was the enlightening ministry of the Holy Spirit. They needed, wrote Calvin, "a larger measure of the Spirit."[2] Jesus had promised that the Holy Spirit would come and guide His disciples "into all truth" (John 16:13). Although Jesus was clearly speaking about the unique ministry of His apostles, we can hardly confine the illuminating ministry of the Spirit to those first apostles. Earlier in His ministry, Jesus had encouraged His disciples to ask the heavenly Father to give them the Holy Spirit. They were Spirit-indwelled men, but Jesus wanted them (and us) to know that our generous-hearted "heavenly Father [gives] the Holy Spirit to those who ask Him!" (Luke 11:13). Here Paul is praying that the generous-hearted Father of glory will give the Holy Spirit as the Spirit of "wisdom and revelation" to Jesus's disciples in Ephesus. This was their greatest need.

Paul is not asking that further, fresh revelations from God will come to these believers. He is using the word "revelation" in the sense of "illumination," as the following verses make clear. Calvin captures the central thrust of Paul's prayer: "Until we have been taught by the Spirit our master, all that we know is folly and ignorance."[3] It is the great new covenant ministry of the Holy Spirit

---

2. John Calvin, *The Epistles of Paul the Apostle to the Galatians, Ephesians, Philippians and Colossians* (Edinburgh: St. Andrew Press, 1965), 134.

3. Calvin, *Galatians, Ephesians, Philippians and Colossians*, 134.

to introduce us to the grace and glory of our salvation and, more significantly, of our great God and Savior, Jesus Christ.

Knowing Him

The ministry of the Holy Spirit is not to give us spiritual excitement, but to bring us to "the knowledge of Him, the eyes of our understanding being enlightened" (vv. 17b–18a). This was their greatest need: to know God better. Jesus defined eternal life as knowing "the only true God, and Jesus Christ whom You have sent" (John 17:3). The reason the Holy Spirit has come into our lives is to bring us into an ever-deeper knowledge and experience of the God of our salvation. Paul told the church in Corinth, "We have received…the Spirit who is from God, that we might know the things that have been freely given to us by God" (1 Cor. 2:12).

God made you and me to know Him. He sent His Son into the world that through His sinless life, His sin-bearing death, and His resurrection as our covenant Head, we might be restored to His fellowship. The Christian faith is essentially relational, personal, and intimate. We grow up into Christ as our lives sink down into the unfathomable and inexhaustible depths of knowing our God. It is the people "who know their God" who "shall be strong, and carry out great exploits" (Dan. 11:32). And it is the particular ministry of the Holy Spirit, the Spirit of the risen, ascended Christ, to illumine our hearts and minds to know God and the grace of His love. So Paul is not being abstractly doctrinal. He knows that if these Christians in idol-filled Ephesus are to stand and continue standing in the faith of Christ, they need, as a matter of first importance, to know God better.

It is a moment of seismic significance when it dawns on a young Christian—or any Christian—that doctrine matters and is morally transformative. God's truth is not a brute chunk of fact. Wielded by the Holy Spirit, God's truth is "living and powerful" (Heb. 4:12). What enables us to stand against the assaults of the unholy trinity of the world, the flesh, and the devil is an ever-deepening, personal, affectional knowledge of God. The Holy Spirit delights to give us this. Ask Him!

Paul's Burden

The Christian's Hope

The Spirit-illumined knowledge of God that Paul requested for these believers would be attained, in measure, by their grasping three things. First, he prayed that "the eyes of your understanding [would be] enlightened; that you may know what is the hope of His calling" (v. 18). God's calling takes us back to the beginning of our Christian lives (Rom. 8:30; 1 Cor. 1:9); it is His gracious, sovereign summons that wonderfully and effectually delivers us out of Satan's kingdom and plants us in Christ's kingdom (Col. 1:13).

God's calling is the irresistible summons of the eternal King. What then is this hope to which God has called us in the gospel? The Christian's hope is nothing less than the "hope of the glory of God" (Rom. 5:2). Paul is praying that we might *know* this hope, be assured of its certainty. The Christian hope is not something vague or uncertain. The writer to the Hebrews tells us that "this hope we have [is] an anchor of the soul, both sure and steadfast, and…enters the Presence behind the veil, where the forerunner has entered for us, even Jesus" (6:19–20). God wants all His believing children to know for sure who they are and where they are going. Lack of assurance of salvation is not a mark of spiritual humility; it can be tremendously debilitating and hugely distracting. One of Satan's prime tactics is to sow seeds of doubt into our minds, which prompts us to ask questions like, Am I really saved? Is heaven truly my ultimate destiny? Assurance of salvation frees us from self-absorption so that we can live without distraction for our Savior. So Paul prays that the Holy Spirit would indelibly assure these hard-pressed Christians of the great and glorious hope that is theirs in Christ.

But this hope is not reserved for the future; it is the present possession and experience of every Christian. Paul tells the Christians in Colossae that Christ in them is, presently, "the hope of glory" (Col. 1:27). So much of the Christian life is lived in the tension of the "already, but not yet." We presently possess all things (1 Cor. 3:21–22), but we do not presently possess all things in their eschatological fullness, although one day we will. As you wait for the appearing of our great God and Savior, if you lack assurance, if you are struggling with doubts, pray that the Holy Spirit, the gift of the risen Christ to His church, will enlighten the eyes of your heart to know the hope He has called you to in Christ.

God's Inheritance

Second, Paul prays that the eyes of the Ephesians' understanding will be enlightened so that they may know "what are the riches of the glory of His inheritance in the saints" (v. 18). It is a wonderful truth that God Himself is the inheritance of His people (see the earlier discussion of Ephesians 1:14). Even more wonderfully, if unfathomably, Paul tells us that believers are God's inheritance: "the riches of the glory of His inheritance in the saints."

The thought here is almost unimaginable. Peter says something similar to the exiles of the Dispersion: "But you are a chosen generation, a royal priesthood, a holy nation, His own special people" (1 Peter 2:9; see Ex. 19:5). This little community of faith in the midst of idol-obsessed Ephesus was the living God's inheritance. Through the blood redemption of Christ (Eph. 1:7), God had made them His special possession, a people to the praise of His glory. He is our inheritance, and we are His inheritance. The thought is staggering! The prophet Zephaniah exhorted God's people at a perilous time in their history not to

> fear....
> The LORD your God in your midst...
> will rejoice over you with gladness,
> He will quiet you with His love,
> He will rejoice over you with singing. (Zeph. 3:16–17)

Nothing is more calculated to lift up our weary hearts and calm our distempered minds than a reawakened sense of how precious we are to God. Paul writes of "the riches of the glory of His inheritance."

When we look at ourselves we see, rightly, sin and failure and inconstancy. We do not love the Lord with all our heart, soul, mind, and strength. We leave undone much that should be done, and we do much that we should never do. We are a mass of contradictions. But in Christ we are God's inheritance—"the glory of His inheritance." We are His dearly loved children in Christ. We are precious to Him because we are the blood brothers of His eternal Son.

Do you see how practical Paul is? He is a true pastor. He understands that the spiritual well-being of these believers and their gospel effectiveness do not lie principally in exhortation but in exposition. Paul is not slow to press exhortations on Christians, and he will do so in Ephesians 4–6. But the gospel effectiveness of exhortation depends on its being rooted and grounded in the glorious truth of the gospel of God's grace in Christ. When Christians are struggling in any way, their first great need is to hear, "Behold your God." When churches find themselves wracked by disputes, disagreements, and even divisions, their first great need is to hear, "Behold your God." Only in the light of the astonishing riches of God's revealed grace in Christ are we fit to hear and act upon the exhortations and challenges of the gospel. This is Paul's almost invariable pastoral method. The priority of indicatives over imperatives is the spiritual grammar of the Bible. Before it is anything else, the religion of the Bible is a world of grace. This is the keynote of all authentic pastoral ministries.

God's Power

Third, Paul prays that the eyes of the Ephesians' understanding will be enlightened so that they may know "what is the exceeding greatness of His power toward us who believe" (v. 19). Paul longs for these believers to grasp with their hearts as well as their heads the immeasurable greatness of the resources they have as men and women in Christ, God's own inheritance.

If there were one thing these Christians in Ephesus felt they lacked it was probably power. They were few in number and were probably marginalized; possibly even some of them had been disinherited. But nothing less than "the exceeding greatness of [God's] power" was "toward" them (or perhaps "in" them). Paul is struggling to convey in human language the greatness of this power that is "toward us who believe." He writes of the "exceeding greatness" of God's power, which cannot be measured because it is the power of the immeasurable God.

The ruling power in Ephesus was all-conquering Rome. Rome's power was intimidating, even frightening. Caesar has spoken! But who is Caesar compared to the God who works all things according to the counsel of His own will (Eph. 1:11)? Unlimited, exceeding power is "toward" or "in" these Ephesian believers: power enabling them to overcome temptation like Joseph (Genesis 39); power to resist the pressure to compromise like the apostles (Acts 4:18–31); power to cope with blasted hopes (Rom. 4:20–24; Phil. 4:13); power to overcome indwelling sin (Rom. 8:13); and power to persevere to the end (Phil. 1:6), bloodied maybe, but still standing. It is vital to grasp that this power is not the possession of the favored few, of some elite category of Christian. It is "toward us who believe." All Christians, however young or weak, have the same immeasurably great power acting for them and in them. Weak faith is not as comforting or as joyful as strong faith, but because it is united to Christ it is the recipient of God's immeasurable power. Christians need to believe in and live in the good of this power and not be overwhelmed by the power of the enemies of the gospel or by their own variableness. If God is for us, who can be against us (Rom. 8:31)?

5

The Power That Resides in the Church

EPHESIANS 1:20–23

…which He worked in Christ when He raised Him from the dead and seated Him at His right hand in the heavenly places, far above all principality and power and might and dominion, and every name that is named, not only in this age but also in that which is to come.

And He put all things under His feet, and gave Him to be head over all things to the church, which is His body, the fullness of Him who fills all in all.

Characteristically, Paul is carried away with the mention of God's power, and his mind soars at the thought of this power that is "toward us who believe" (Eph. 1:19). This power has been manifested in three spheres of God's activity.

Resurrection Power

The power of verse 19 is the power that raised Christ from the dead. The resurrection was absolutely central to the apostolic gospel and to apostolic preaching (1 Cor. 15:1–28). For Paul, Christ's resurrection was an indisputable fact, a gospel commonplace. On the third day, God the Father raised His Son from the dead, never to die again. He had conquered sin and death and hell. He was "declared to be the Son of God with power according to the Spirit of holiness, by the resurrection from the dead" (Rom. 1:4). The power that raised Christ from the dead, the power of almighty God, is the same power that is now "toward us who believe." It is sin-vanquishing,

Satan-defeating, death-conquering power. Nothing is more calculated to breathe hope and encouragement into our embattled lives than the doctrines of the gospel. What God has done in His Son is the foundation and wellspring of all our hopes.

Heaven-Exalting Power

In verse 20, Paul tells us that this power exalted Christ to the "right hand" (1:20) of the heavenly Father. Christ is presently "seated" at His Father's right hand "in the heavenly places," and, astonishingly, Christians are seated with him there (see Eph. 2:6). Christians think too little about the exaltation of Christ. How great must this power be that is "toward us who believe"! This power exalted Christ in His resurrected body through the heavens and seated Him in the place of honor in the heavenly places (Heb. 1:3). Paul is teaching us rich theology that is calculated to minister encouragement and comfort to our hard-pressed lives. This same power that exalts Christ to heaven is "toward us who believe." You can almost hear Paul saying, "Lift up your heads. Be undaunted. If God is for you, who can be against you?"

Cosmic Enthroned Power

This power enthroned Christ "far above all principality and power and might and dominion, and every name that is named, not only in this age but also in that which is to come" (v. 21). Jesus, not Caesar and even less the authorities in Ephesus, rules and reigns. Whatever powers and authorities may yet arise in this world, every one of them is under Christ's rule and dominion. This same power that gave Christ cosmic and endless rule and dominion is toward or in God's people in Ephesus and everywhere else. As a pastor, Paul understood that God's people's greatest need was to anchor their lives in the grace of the Lord Jesus Christ. Christian doctrine is foundational to Christian living, anchoring us deeply in the midst of life's storms (Paul will develop this analogy in Ephesians 4:11–14). This is the perspective of the life of faith, and it is breathtaking.

The language and thought of verses 20–22 echo Psalm 110:1 ("Sit at My right hand, till I make Your enemies Your footstool") and Psalm 8:6 ("You have made him to have dominion over the works of Your hands; You have put all things under his feet"). What the old covenant Scriptures looked forward to in hope has been realized in the resurrection and exaltation of Christ. The Father has given "all authority…in heaven and on earth" to His Son (Matt. 28:18). Abraham Kuyper (1837–1920), the great Dutch theologian and polymath, wrote, "There is not a square inch in the whole domain of our human existence over which Christ, who is Sovereign over all, does not cry: 'Mine!'"[1] The Father has put all things under the feet—the dominion and rule—of His Son, nothing excepted. And yet writing to the church in Corinth Paul says, "For 'He has put all things under His feet'" (quoting Ps. 8:6), and "When all things are made subject to Him, then the Son Himself will also be subject to Him who put all things under Him, that God may be all in all" (1 Cor. 15:27–28). All things are now under Christ's rule and dominion. But the full reality of that dominion will not be seen or experienced until Christ returns. There is an "already, but not yet" dimension to every facet of the gospel.

As we look out on this fallen, gospel-rejecting world, it does not seem that our Lord Jesus has the dominion and rule, but He does. The Father has given it to Him. One day every knee will bow and every tongue confess "that Jesus Christ is Lord, to the glory of God the Father" (Phil. 2:10–11). Then all will see what God has revealed to us in His Word—that Jesus is Lord!

For the Church

But the cosmic enthronement and rule of Christ is not for His enjoyment alone. He is "head over all things to the church, which is His body, the fullness of Him who fills all in all" (vv. 22–23). Christ

---

1. Abraham Kuyper, "Sphere Sovereignty" (public address, Free University of Amsterdam, October 20, 1880), trans. George Kamps, http://www.reformationalpublishingproject.com/pdf_books/Scanned_Books_PDF/Sphere Sovereignty_English.pdf.

exercises His cosmic sovereignty for the good of His church. As
the God-man, the Mediator of the new covenant, the Lord Jesus
Christ exercises His universal dominion. He is the Head of the
church, "which is His body." The picture of the church as the body
of Christ is unique to Paul. He develops the picture at some length
in Romans 12:4–8 and especially in 1 Corinthians 12:12–31. There
doesn't appear to be any Old Testament background to this way of
picturing the church. It is possible that as Paul reflected on Christ's
union with His believing people, the picture of the body with its
dominating, distinguishing, directing head readily and graphically
displayed to him the unity of the church with its Savior.

Remarkably, Paul speaks of the church as "the fullness of Him
who fills all in all" (v. 23). He could hardly speak more extravagantly about the church. The church, the Spirit-created fellowship
of believers, is nothing less than "the fullness of Him who fills all in
all." What does Paul mean? It is tempting to agree with the apostle Peter, who writes, "Our beloved brother Paul…has written…
some things hard to understand" (2 Peter 3:15–16). Paul's language
is soaring. He says the church is the "fullness" of Christ. There are
essentially two ways to understand Paul.

First, he could mean that the church completes Christ. This
would be the more normal meaning of the word in its grammatical
form in the New Testament, and this would make sense in the context.[2] The church is Christ's body, and what is a head without a body?
A body gives completion to a head, and vice versa. This was John Calvin's understanding: "This is the highest honor of the Church, that,
unless he is united to us, the Son of God reckons himself in some

---

2. "Fullness" ($\pi\lambda\acute{\eta}\rho\omega\mu\alpha$) can have an active or a passive meaning. In the New
Testament, "fullness" invariably has an active meaning, "that which fills." Charles
Hodge argues, "In every other case in which it occurs in the New Testament it is
used actively—that which doth fill.… The common usage of the word in the New
Testament is…clearly in favour of its being taken in an active sense here" in Ephesians 1:23. The idea, then, would be that the church fills up Christ; that is, in some
sense completes Him. Charles Hodge, *Ephesians* (1856; repr., Edinburgh: Banner
of Truth Trust, 1991), 53–54.

measure imperfect. What an encouragement it is for us to hear, that, not until he has us as one with himself, is he complete in all his parts, or does he wish to be regarded as whole."[3] As context, immediate and wider, ultimately governs translation, however, it seems more likely that Paul means here that Christ fills the church. However attractive it is to say that the church completes Christ, nowhere does the New Testament make that assertion. On the contrary, it is Christ who is said to indwell His church (Eph. 2:21–22; 3:19; Col. 1:27). Christ is not merely the church's Head; He is its "fullness," its life. His is the life that flows through and animates the church (John 15:1–5). Just as Christ fills "all in all" (v. 23), so, in a uniquely redemptive way, He fills His church as its Lord and life (John 14:6; Col. 3:4).

Paul's astonishing description of the church is a rebuke to the atomized individualism that has scarred evangelical Christianity in the last half century. If we are not thinking individualistically, we often think denominationally. Christ's deep concern that His church "all may be one, as You, Father, are in Me, and I in You" (John 17:21) does not seem to be shared by many. Paul later urges the Ephesian church to "[endeavor] to keep the unity of the Spirit in the bond of peace" (4:3). The unity of Christ's body, which He fills with His exalted presence in the Spirit, was a matter of concern to the apostle. Yes, a united church would give weight to its gospel testimony. But there is a deeper, more foundational reason why unity (not uniformity) should be a passion for all Christians. Christ fills His church. In Ephesians 3:18–19, Paul tells the Ephesians that it is only "with all the saints" that they will begin to "comprehend… what is the width and length and depth and height—to know the love of Christ which passes knowledge; that you may be filled with all the fullness of God." The church is the "fullness of Him who fills all in all" (v. 23), but the reality, power, grace, and glory of that fullness will not be known apart from "all the saints" (Eph. 3:18).

In a letter to Archbishop Thomas Cranmer, Calvin expressed his passionate commitment to help heal the divided body of Christ:

---

3. Calvin, *Galatians, Ephesians, Philippians and Colossians*, 138.

This other thing also is to be ranked among the chief evils of our time, viz., that the churches are so divided, that human fellowship is scarcely now in any repute among us, far less that Christian intercourse which all make a profession of, but few sincerely practice.... Thus it is that the members of the Church being severed, the body lies bleeding. So much does this concern me, that, could I be of any service, I would not grudge to cross even ten seas, if need were, on account of it.[4]

Calvin would have been mystified to see how evangelical, Reformed Christians today could appear to be so indifferent to Christ's "bleeding" body. More than ever the church needs to recover the covenantal and collegial nature of its life. This is not a plea to play down doctrinal or denominational distinctives. It is a plea for the true church of Christ to express the unity that is native to it as the one body of Christ.

---

4. John Calvin, *Tracts and Letters*, ed. Jules Bonnet (Edinburgh: Banner of Truth Trust, 2009), 5:347–48.

6

What We All Once Were

EPHESIANS 2:1–3

And you He made alive, who were dead in trespasses and sins, in which you once walked according to the course of this world, according to the prince of the power of the air, the spirit who now works in the sons of disobedience, among whom also we all once conducted ourselves in the lusts of our flesh, fulfilling the desires of the flesh and of the mind, and were by nature children of wrath, just as the others.

Sometimes Christians need to be reminded of their past. They need not wallow in it, be crushed by it, or be nostalgic over it, but they should highlight how blessed and privileged they are in Christ. John Newton (1725–1807), the famous English clergyman and hymn writer, was a captain of slave ships for several years even after his conversion. He never allowed himself to forget that the Lord had wonderfully converted him and eventually rescued him from that hideous and iniquitous trade. His memorable hymn "Amazing Grace" was his personal testimony to the saving and transforming mercy of God. It is easy for us to forget what we once were apart from Jesus Christ and the transformation the gospel has accomplished in our lives. When we forget who and what we are in Christ, we slowly lose our sense of love and gratitude to God for His saving love and grace to us in Christ.

Paul is going over old ground in these verses. He is highlighting gospel basics and reminding us what the gospel of God's love and grace has done for us, the tragedy it has rescued us from, the transformation it has accomplished in us, and the surpassingly glorious future it has secured for us.

The writer to the Hebrews urges his readers to leave "the elementary principles of Christ…[and] go on to perfection" (6:1). He is not, however, calling them to forget the elementary doctrine of Christ. We cannot hear too often what the gospel of God's grace in Christ has saved us from. We need regularly to "remember" what we once were (Eph. 2:11), that we might never lose our sense of indebtedness to God for His overflowing grace to us in Christ.

In 2:1–3 Paul reminds the Ephesians of what they once were apart from Christ. The Bible's description of men and women outside Christ is dark and deeply humbling. Its anthropology is deeply offensive to the modern world, though its truth stares the world in its face. The foundational truth that lies at the heart of the Bible's doctrine of man is that humanity is fallen in Adam (Rom. 5:12). The reality is not that we are essentially good with a few occasional blemishes. It is that we are, as our Lord Jesus taught, essentially evil (see Luke 11:13). Our nature is fallen from its original purity. We all need nothing less than a total renovation of our nature.

Apart from Christ We Are Dead

Paul writes that we are "dead in trespasses and sins" apart from Christ (v. 1). Our eyes blink, our hearts beat, our feet walk—but we are dead! He is clearly speaking here of spiritual death. God promised Adam that if he ate from "the tree of the knowledge of good and evil," he would "die" (Gen. 2:17). Adam sinned and died in his relationship with God. But Adam was more than an individual; he was a divinely appointed covenant head (Rom. 5:12; 1 Cor. 15:21–22). In Adam we all died spiritually, and our relationship with God was broken. The fact is that we sin because we are sinners (see Ps. 51:5). It is not our sinning that makes us sinners. Our sinning merely accentuates and makes visible our fallen state in Adam. The Westminster Confession of Faith 6.3–4 succinctly highlights this basic biblical truth: "They being the root of all mankind, the guilt of this sin was imputed; and the same death in sin, and corrupted nature, conveyed to all their posterity descending from them by ordinary generation. From this original corruption, whereby we are utterly indisposed, disabled, and made opposite to all good, and wholly inclined to all evil, do proceed all actual transgressions."

In verse 1, Paul uses two descriptive words to highlight the tragedy of the Ephesians' spiritual state outside of Christ. "Trespasses" (παράπτωμα; false step, wrongdoing, offense) contains the idea of crossing over a known boundary, of taking false steps. This is what Adam did in the garden of Eden. He deliberately crossed a God-defined boundary. Sin is walking out on God, living with no heart regard for His graciously defined boundaries. The root meaning of "sins" (ἁμαρτία) is missing the mark. Because our natures are fallen, no matter how hard we try, no matter how many resolutions we make, we miss God's mark, His holy standard, the perfection of His law (1 John 3:4). The hymn writer puts it well: "I aim at Thee but from Thee stray." We miss the mark because there is a fatal flaw within every one of us that we are powerless to remedy.

Both these words tell us that before God we are rebels and failures. Our problem before God is not that we are wrong at the edges, but that we are all wrong. You might be cultured, educated, religious, and respectable yet still be a rebel and a total failure in the sight of God. This is the human condition. This is what we all are, apart from Jesus Christ. John Stott captures well what Paul means by "dead in trespasses and sins": Such people "are blind to the glory of Jesus Christ and deaf to the voice of the Holy Spirit. They have no love for God, no sensitive awareness of his personal reality, no leaping of their spirit toward him in the cry, 'Abba, Father'; no longing for fellowship with his people. They are as unresponsive to him as a corpse."[1]

Apart from Christ We Are Dominated

Paul's description of how these Ephesian Christians "once walked" is damning (v. 2). "Walk" is a key word in this section. In verse 2 Paul tells the Ephesian believers that they "once walked according

---

1. Stott, *God's New Society*, 72.

to the course of this world," and in verse 10 he tells them that they have been redeemed in Christ in order to "walk" in good works. The gospel comes to transform how we walk—that is, how we order the whole course of our lives.[2] Paul highlights a trilogy of dominating powers that shaped the whole order of the believer's pre-Christian experience.

The Course of This World

The Ephesians once followed "the course of this world" (v. 2). The New Testament has essentially two ways of thinking about this world. First, the world is the wholly undeserved object of God's love (John 3:16). As such, this world is to be pitied and evangelized. But this world is also viewed as something to separate from, to avoid, to abhor, and not to love: "Do not love the world or the things in the world. If anyone loves the world, the love of the Father is not in him. For all that is in the world—the lust of the flesh, the lust of the eyes, and the pride of life—is not of the Father but is of the world. And the world is passing away, and the lust of it" (1 John 2:15–17). Outside of Christ we do not follow the course or ways God has set before us in His Word; rather, we follow the course of this fallen world. We follow its patterns of thinking, behavior, and expectations. Our lives are dominated by a lifestyle that has an earthly horizon. By nature we are more concerned to keep in step with the world around us than with the Word of God.

The Prince of the Power of the Air

They followed "the prince of the power of the air" (v. 2; see also John 8:34). There is little doubt that Paul is thinking about Satan. Later he will alert the Ephesians to the "wiles of the devil" (6:11). The New Testament is full of warnings against the subtle and malignant activity of the devil (Luke 22:31–32; Eph. 4:27; 1 Peter 5:8). Unconverted men and women follow the prince of the power of the air.

---

2. See Richard B. Gaffin, *Resurrection and Redemption: A Study in Paul's Soteriology* (Phillipsburg, N.J.: Presbyterian and Reformed, 1987), 43.

Many are unwitting dupes of the devil; others are willing disciples of the devil. But because our trespasses and sins have killed our relationship with God, until God makes us alive in Christ (Eph. 2:5), we are prisoners of God's implacable enemy. The tragedy of humanity outside of Christ is that it is dominated by a hate-filled spiritual power and doesn't know it. Sin not only corrupts us morally; it corrupts our intellects as well. We don't think straight, and we deceive ourselves. We measure ourselves by others and usually come off quite well. This is Satan's doing. He "now works in the sons of disobedience" (v. 2). Disobedient defiance is the hallmark of men and women outside of Christ. Their disobedient defiance may be cultured and even religious, but ultimately they are refusing to bow their knees and embrace in their hearts the lordship of God in His Son. Paul told the Corinthian church that unbelievers are those "whose minds the god of this age has blinded, who do not believe, lest the light of the gospel of the glory of Christ, who is the image of God, should shine on them" (2 Cor. 4:4).

The Lusts of the Flesh

They lived dominated by "the lusts of [their] flesh" (v. 3). Paul belonged to the covenant people of God. He had an impeccable religious pedigree (Phil. 3:4–6), and he belonged to a people on whom God had lavished spiritual privileges (Rom. 9:4–5). But here he identifies himself, and by implication everyone everywhere, with the tragic spiritual condition of the Ephesians in their pre-Christian days: "among whom also we all once conducted ourselves in the lusts of our flesh" (2:3). Israel was a vastly God-privileged people. In their bodies they bore the mark of circumcision, which was "a sign of the covenant" God had established with Israel (Gen. 17:11). But the sign of circumcision did not itself effect inward spiritual renewal. God looked for heart circumcision in His covenant people (Deut. 10:16; 30:6). It took the Damascus road experience finally to persuade Paul that he, with all his covenant privileges, needed a new heart (Acts 9:1–18). By the "lusts of our flesh" Paul means a lifestyle shaped by life in Adam. The "flesh" is unrenewed

Adamic humanity. To live in the "lusts of our flesh" is to live hostile to the law of God (Rom. 8:5–8). What controls the unconverted life is not the revealed wisdom and grace of God but "the desires of the flesh and of the mind" (2:3). These desires have one purpose: self-gratification. They are desires that cannot see beyond the horizon of this world.

Children of Wrath

Outside of Christ, we are children of God's wrath. The Bible's witness to God's righteous wrath is unambiguous, especially in the New Testament (Rom. 1:18; 5:9; Col. 3:6; 1 Thess. 5:9; Rev. 6:16; 14:19). It is important to understand that God's wrath is not arbitrary or irascible; rather, it is His holy, just, and righteous response to sinful rebellion. God holds out His hands all day long to sinners and takes no pleasure in the death of the wicked (Rom. 10:21, quoting Isa. 65:2; see Ezek. 33:11). But He is true to who He is. Just as He is a God "merciful and gracious, longsuffering, and abounding in goodness and truth," so He is also a God "by no means clearing the guilty" (Ex. 34:6–7).[3]

This is the tragic predicament that has engulfed humankind in its fallen state in Adam. The horror of sin is not that it messes up my life, though it does; nor that it dismantles and debases the moral fabric of society, though it does; but that it is against God (Ps. 51:4). Some ancient Christian writers called sin *decidium* (God killing). This is the word of God's solemn description of every human being outside of Jesus Christ. It was this dark reality that, in part, motivated the early Christians to give their all to making Christ and His gospel known. John the Baptist confronted the gospel-resisting Pharisees and Sadducees: "Brood of vipers! Who warned you to flee from the

---

3. Leon Morris, *The Apostolic Preaching of the Cross* (Grand Rapids: Eerdmans, 1956), has an exhaustive examination of the wrath of God in the New Testament (125–85), where he subjects to a searching analysis the view of C. H. Dodd that the ἱλάσκομαι word group means only to "expiate"—that is, remove sin—and not "propitiate," which is to remove sin by appeasing God's wrath.

wrath to come?" (Matt. 3:7). In his sermon at Pentecost, Peter urged his hearers, "Be saved from this perverse generation" (Acts 2:40).

The Bible's anthropology is dark and solemn, but realistic. This is what humankind is outside Jesus Christ. This is the living God's true description of our fallen state. That this world is not consumed in an unending conflagration of sin is only due to the mercy of God, who restrains the evil of sin from its native corruption.

7

But God!

EPHESIANS 2:4–7

> *But God, who is rich in mercy, because of His great love with which He loved us, even when we were dead in trespasses, made us alive together with Christ (by grace you have been saved), and raised us up together, and made us sit together in the heavenly places in Christ Jesus, that in the ages to come He might show the exceeding riches of His grace in His kindness toward us in Christ Jesus.*

Paul could hardly have described the human condition outside of Christ more darkly in Ephesians 2:1–3: dead toward God; dominated by the world, the flesh, and the devil; "children of wrath, just as the others." Christians always need to remember the darkness and hopelessness of what they once were apart from Jesus Christ. There is, of course, the danger that we spend too much time looking back. Samuel Rutherford wrote, "For every one look at yourself, take ten looks at Christ." Paul wants to remind us of what the gospel of God's grace in Christ has saved us from. He is not seeking to make us feel bad but to help us appreciate more the greatness of God's salvation in Christ.

The need to remember who God is and the grace of His goodness toward His people is accented regularly throughout the Old Testament (Ex. 20:24; Deut. 8:2, 11, 18; Judg. 8:34; Isa. 17:10; Jonah 2:7; Zech. 10:9). Israel's abject failure to remember that continually catapulted them into sin and rebellion against the Lord. We fail to remember at our own peril.

In verses 4–7, Paul's focus dramatically changes. The change is signaled by two words that immediately bring light into the darkness and hope into the hopelessness: "But God" (v. 4). Paul is accenting the sovereign intervening grace of God that alone could bring transformation to the spiritual darkness and hopelessness that our sin brought into our lives.

The Richness of God's Mercy

Paul never tires of celebrating the mercy of God that is the fountainhead of the great salvation that has come to us in Christ: "But God, who is rich in mercy" (v. 4). We owe everything to the God who is "rich in mercy." When Moses asked the Lord to show him His glory, the Lord descended in the cloud and proclaimed His name to His servant, "The LORD, the LORD God, merciful and gracious" (Ex. 34:6). Mercy is not an arbitrary attribute of God; He is a merciful and gracious God. He never needs to be persuaded to be merciful, because He is merciful. The root meaning of "mercy" is generous kindness. Here God manifests His generosity and kindness to sinners by not pouring out on them His just and righteous wrath. He does not treat us as our sins deserve.

The Greatness of God's Love

Next, Paul reminds his readers of "His great love with which He loved us" (v. 4). The New Testament struggles to convey the greatness of God's love. From one perspective, the greatness of God's love is seen in the objects of His love. He loved us "even when we were dead in trespasses" (v. 5). Paul says something similar in Romans 5:8: "But God demonstrates His own love toward us, in that while we were still sinners, Christ died for us." There is, however, another deeper perspective from which to view the greatness of God's love. It was God's love that gave to us a Savior: "For God so loved the world that He gave His only begotten Son" (John 3:16). "In this is love, not that we loved God, but that He loved us and sent His Son to be the propitiation for our sins" (1 John 4:10). The incalculable magnitude of God's love can begin to be measured only by the cross of

Calvary. God "did not spare His own Son, but delivered Him up for us all" (Rom. 8:32). The cross, as nothing else, placards the sovereign, undeserved, overflowing, unfathomable love of God for sinners.

There was not an iota of deserving in any one of us. It is the wonder of the gospel of Jesus Christ that judgment-deserving sinners are the objects of almighty God's mercy and love. But why did God set His love upon us when we were dead in trespasses? The biblical answer is simply because it pleased Him to do so. God is not obliged to show mercy, yet He is pleased to show mercy to whomever He is pleased to show mercy and compassion to whomever He is pleased to show compassion (Deut. 7:6–8; Rom. 9:15). No one anywhere at any time has had a claim on God's mercy. By nature, through our union with Adam, our first head, and by practice, we are children of wrath like the rest of humanity. The wonder is not that God is pleased to save some and not others. The wonder is that He is pleased to save any.

Alive, Raised, and Seated with Christ

Because of His rich mercy and great love, God did not leave us dead in our trespasses but "made us alive together with Christ...and raised us up together, and made us sit together in the heavenly places in Christ Jesus" (vv. 5–6). The union of believers with Christ is so intimate that what happened to Him happened to them (see Romans 6). The three phrases "made us alive," "raised us up," and "made us sit" are all in the aorist tense, signifying past, completed acts. This is what God, through the gospel of His grace, has done for every believer in Christ. The three verbs refer to the three successive historical events in the saving work of Christ: His resurrection (the seal and public vindication of His atoning work on the cross), His ascension, and His present heavenly session at the Father's right hand.

Alive with Christ

When Christ was made alive, we were made "alive together with Christ" (v. 5). Paul is referring to Christ's resurrection from the dead. The resurrection is not merely an event we believe in; it is an event in which we shared. In His resurrection, Christ triumphed over sin and death and hell, and we triumphed together with Him. This is the gospel! In Christ we died to sin, to its guilt and dominion (Rom. 6:1–11). In Christ we were made alive, raised with him to "walk in newness of life" (Rom. 6:4). The heart of this "newness of life" is fellowship with God (John 17:3; 1 John 1:3–4). No wonder Paul cannot refrain from saying again, "By grace you have been saved" (v. 8). We can never be reminded too often that we are debtors to mercy alone. Godly gratitude is nourished in the soil of gospel grace. When grace becomes just another evangelical commonplace, Christian worship becomes devalued and debased. It is the wonder of grace that results in radically God- and Christ-centered worship and that keeps the human heart humble and thankful.

Raised with Christ

When Christ was raised, we were raised with Him. Paul is referring in verse 6 to Christ's glorious, bodily ascension into heaven (Luke 24:51; Acts 1:9–11). Christ's ascension is a much-neglected truth. His resurrection was a prelude to His ascension, His return to the glory He had with the Father before the world existed (John 17:5). For a time God's Son laid aside that glory as He embraced the saving servanthood committed to Him by His Father (Phil. 2:5–8). For a time His glory was veiled. But with His ascension, God's Son returned to His sphere and to the glory that was natively His. And God has "raised us up together" (v. 6). We presently share in, as sinners saved by grace, the ascended glory of God's incarnate Son. He is our Head, and we are His body. Where He is, there we are.

Seated with Christ

The writer to the Hebrews tells us that after Christ had made purification for sins, He "sat down at the right hand of the Majesty on high" (1:3). It is a picture of redemptive accomplishment. All that needed to be done for the salvation of sinners, Jesus did. Now He is seated in regnant, redemptive splendor at the right hand of His Father. The staggering thing is, as Paul tells us, we can "sit together in the heavenly places in Christ Jesus" (v. 6). Characteristically, Paul foregoes grammatical niceties to highlight theological wonders. The phrase "in Christ Jesus" appears at first to be redundant. Paul has already told us that all the rich blessings we enjoy by God's grace are in Christ. It is clear, however, that the apostle cannot get over the wonder of union with Christ and the grace of God that has effected that federal, personal, spiritual union.

There are deep implications arising from these truths. First, Christians no longer belong to this world. Our foundational identity is in Christ. We live here, but we do not belong here (Phil. 3:20). We live in this world, but we are not of this world (Col. 3:1–3). Second, because of our union with Christ, we no longer belong to Satan's kingdom and are not subject to his thralldom (Col. 1:13). Third, because we have been made alive with Christ, have been raised with Him, and are now seated with Him in the heavenly places, we presently reign with Him (1 Cor. 15:20–28; Eph. 1:20–22). Christians truly are "more than conquerors through Him who loved us" (Rom. 8:37).

Public Exhibits

The question that might be asked at this point is, why has God so astonishingly blessed us in Christ? The answer is, "That in the ages to come He might show the exceeding riches of His grace in His kindness toward us in Christ Jesus" (v. 7). The transformed lives of believers, here and now, and later in the new heaven and the new earth, are to be exhibits of the transforming grace and love of God: we are "His workmanship" (Eph. 2:10). The redeemed people of God, united to the enfleshed Son of God, will be an endless display to the whole creation of the grace and kindness of God. Just as famous artists' paintings are immediately recognizable, so the church is to display the workmanship of its divine Artist. What will be perfectly true and evident in the ages to come is now true, if less evident. Jesus said to His disciples, "Let your light so shine before men, that they may see your good works and glorify your Father in heaven" (Matt. 5:16). God has united you savingly to His Son to display to this fallen world the transforming riches of His grace and kindness in you. What does this world see of the divine Artist in your life? Christians are to be "spiritual masterpieces," works of art who manifest the workmanship of the triune God.

8

Amazing Grace

EPHESIANS 2:8–10

For by grace you have been saved through faith, and that not of yourselves; it is the gift of God, not of works, lest anyone should boast. For we are His workmanship, created in Christ Jesus for good works, which God prepared beforehand that we should walk in them.

Paul had a deep jealousy for God's glory. Whenever he detected God's glory being imperiled in any way, he immediately responded with godly vigor (e.g., Gal. 1:6–10). It was imperative to the apostle that God's people understand that they owed everything they possessed in Christ to the grace of God. The great issue about grace is not that we talk or sing or preach about it, but that we understand what it is. Judaism is a religion of grace. How could it be otherwise when it originated in God? Roman Catholic writings say much about grace; the word "grace" is everywhere in Roman liturgies and catechisms. But ask a Jew, ancient or modern, or a Romanist to spell "grace," and the response invariably will be "w-o-r-k-s." It is necessary that we understand grace and not just confess it, sing it, or preach it.

By Grace

Salvation, in its totality, is of grace. From inception to consummation, God's undeserved, forgiving kindness has secured our salvation. Grace is God acting in Christ to secure our salvation and sanctification. Grace is not a spiritual blessing divorced from the person of Christ, as if the Savior dispensed grace from a treasury of merits (that is a picture of Roman Catholicism). Essentially, Jesus Christ Himself is the grace of God (2 Cor. 8:9). If God's "so great a salvation" (Heb. 2:3) were not by grace alone, no one would be saved. Sin has not merely disabled us; it has killed us (Eph. 2:1, 5). We can no more contribute to our salvation than fly to the sun on wings of ice.

It is little wonder that one of the Reformation watchwords was *sola gratia*, by grace alone. The Reformers had come to understand that the Roman Church had so profoundly corrupted the gospel that, while it spoke of salvation by grace, it actually taught that grace alone was not enough. This teaching was affirmed at the Council of Trent in the 1540s: "If any one saith that the sacraments of the New Law are not necessary unto salvation…and that without them, or without the desire thereof, men obtain from God, through faith alone, the grace of justification…let him be anathema."[1] Grace puts God where He belongs, uniquely and alone on the throne of the cosmos, and puts believing sinners where they belong, at His feet in humble adoration.

Through Faith

Paul never says that salvation comes to us *by* faith—that is, on the basis of faith—but always "*through* faith" (v. 8, emphasis added). Faith is the instrument by which we receive the grace of Christ. It is not faith as such, however, that brings to us God's salvation; it is faith in Jesus Christ. And it is not even faith in Jesus Christ that saves; it is Jesus Christ who saves sinners through faith. Faith's distinguishing feature is that it looks to Christ, not to self (Isa. 45:22).

It may be appropriate to ask, what is so special about faith? Why not salvation through love, the preeminent Christian grace (1 Cor. 13:13)? For one great reason: faith is a receiving and resting grace. By its very nature, faith has no constructive energy. Faith relies completely on another.[2] It is Christ-reliant, not self-reliant.

---

1. "The Canons and Decrees of the Council of Trent," in *The Creeds of Christendom*, by Philip Schaff (Grand Rapids: Baker, 1919), 119 (canon 4).

2. Murray, *Redemption, Accomplished and Applied*, 123.

Faith involves the abandoning of self, not the congratulating of self (Rom. 3:27). Faith kills all human boasting. And even the faith we believe with is God's gracious gift (1 Cor. 4:7)!

In his sermons on Isaiah 53, John Calvin highlights the gracious character of faith:

> Let us know that faith is not given to all, but is a singular gift that God keeps as a treasure for those he has chosen; and let us know that our duty is to cleave to Him, knowing the while that none of us gains faith by his own effort, but God has enlightened us and given us eyes by His Holy Spirit, and in so doing has declared His power…so that we know that the Gospel comes, not from men, but from Him.[3]

Faith draws everything from Christ and contributes nothing to Him. Faith is a receptor, not a contributor. Therefore, "he who glories, let him glory in the LORD" (1 Cor. 1:31).

The Gift of God

It is straightforward to show from God's Word that salvation in all its parts is the gift of God (Rom. 11:36; 1 Cor. 4:7–8). The question we need to answer in this passage is, however, what is the antecedent to the phrase "and that not of yourselves; it is the gift of God" (v. 8)? What exactly is this "that"? Paul could be saying that faith is the gift of God, which it is. He could also be saying that the grace by which we are saved is the gift of God, and it certainly is. Or, he could even be saying that salvation by grace, through faith, is God's gift, which it assuredly is. The grammar does not really help us come to a decisive conclusion. The demonstrative pronoun "that" is neuter in the Greek text, while "salvation" ("saved"), "grace," and "faith" are all feminine gender. Theologically, nothing of any great significance is lost whichever way we link and explicate "that." It seems best to take the embracive view, and see "that" as qualifying the totality of verse 8: the salvation of God, which has its origin in God alone and is

---

3. John Calvin, *Sermons on Isaiah's Prophecy of the Death and Passion of Christ* (London: James Clark, 1956), 50.

received through faith alone, is not our own doing. We have nothing to boast about. It is wholly and alone "the gift of God, not of works."

Paul never tires of demolishing all human boasting before God (1 Cor. 1:27–30). One of the principal marks of any life united to Jesus Christ is no boasting. The Christian's only boast is Jesus Christ (Gal. 6:14). The history of the Christian church is littered with attempts to smuggle some kind of self-effort and self-righteousness into the gospel way of salvation. In God's kindness and mercy, whenever those heretical attempts surfaced, He had His watchmen on hand to oppose and refute those attempts. Augustine in the fourth century, Luther and Calvin in the sixteenth century, and the Princetonians in the nineteenth century defended the gospel of sovereign grace with biblical integrity and passion. The church in every generation should remember the debt it owes to faithful men and women of previous generations. We truly do stand on their shoulders.

God's Workmanship

Alongside a "no-boasting" spirit, the saved life is marked by a transformed lifestyle: "For we are His workmanship, created in Christ Jesus for good works, which God prepared beforehand that we should walk in them" (v. 10). Martin Luther wrote that "faith is a busy little thing." He meant that where saving faith was present, it would show itself in a life of good works. Faith without works is dead (James 2:17). Because faith unites us to Christ, who went about "doing good" (Acts 10:38), it is inevitable that every life of faith is committed to good works. Notice the precision of Paul's language: "created in Christ Jesus for good works." Everything that is good comes from Christ. Only as we are in Christ can we do good works to the glory of God (Matt. 5:16). Moreover, the Christian's good works are to be as extensive as humanity. We are to "do good to all, especially to those who are of the household of faith" (Gal. 6:10). Just as God in Christ has exerted Himself to do good to this lost, rebellious, perishing world, so His children are to manifest in their good works the family likeness.

Christians are God's "workmanship." He is the master workman who shapes and styles our lives by the grace of Christ and the truth and wisdom of His Word (Ps. 119:105; John 17:8, 17; 2 Tim. 3:16–17). As God's workmanship, Christians exhibit His love and grace to a world shrouded in darkness. What does the world see when it looks at your life? At your church's life? Our Lord Jesus Christ went about "doing good" (Acts 10:38). Wherever He saw need, He went out of His way to minister to that need. The gospel of God's grace has come to make us like our Savior (Rom. 8:29). Does your life remind anyone of Jesus?

9

Transforming Unity

EPHESIANS 2:11–16

Therefore remember that you, once Gentiles in the flesh—who are called Uncircumcision by what is called the Circumcision made in the flesh by hands—that at that time you were without Christ, being aliens from the commonwealth of Israel and strangers from the covenants of promise, having no hope and without God in the world. But now in Christ Jesus you who once were far off have been brought near by the blood of Christ.

For He Himself is our peace, who has made both one, and has broken down the middle wall of separation, having abolished in His flesh the enmity, that is, the law of commandments contained in ordinances, so as to create in Himself one new man from the two, thus making peace, and that He might reconcile them both to God in one body through the cross, thereby putting to death the enmity.

The ancient world, much like our modern world, was deeply divided. The Greeks considered the rest of the known world barbarians, and the Romans, like the Greeks, thought themselves superior to every other culture. The Jews looked on the Gentiles as dogs. Racism, social snobbery, political elitism, and religious superiority deeply divided Paul's world. Paul has already told us that God has a "dispensation of the fullness of the times," a plan to "gather together in one all things in Christ, both which are in heaven and which are on earth" (Eph. 1:10). The thought is breathtaking in its comprehensive extensiveness. One day, God will remove all divisions and restore an unblemished unity to His creation. What Paul tells us in these verses is that this ultimate cosmic purpose has begun to be realized through the "blood of Christ" (v. 13) and is made visible in the world through Jews and Gentiles worshiping together as the one people of God (vv. 15–16, 19–22).

Remember

The Ephesian church was made up mostly of Gentiles, whom the Jews dismissively and derisively called the Uncircumcision (v. 11). Circumcision had a deep religious significance for the Jews. In Genesis 17, God commanded Abraham, with whom He had entered into a unique covenant relationship, to circumcise his descendants, including himself. This mark in the flesh, said God, "shall be a sign of the covenant between Me and you" (Gen. 17:11). The significance of the covenant sign was dramatized when God identified it as "an everlasting covenant" in Abraham's and his offspring's flesh (Gen. 17:13). Tragically, the Jews failed to understand, perhaps willfully, that this sign of God's covenant in their flesh was no substitute for the circumcision of their hearts (Deut. 10:16; 30:6). This is in Paul's mind when he speaks of "the Circumcision made in the flesh by hands" (v. 11).

Notwithstanding, the Jews were God's uniquely privileged people (Deut. 7:6–8). To them, as Paul reminded the Romans, belonged "the adoption, the glory, the covenants, the giving of the law, the service of God, and the promises." To them also belonged "the fathers…from whom, according to the flesh, Christ came, who is over all, the eternally blessed God" (Rom. 9:4–5).

This is why Paul commands the Ephesians in verse 11 to "remember." Before they came to Christ, before God in His grace found them, they were "without Christ" (v. 12). Paul could simply be stating the obvious: "Before you were converted, you were separated from Christ." Or, in the following statements, Paul could be explaining why and in what sense the Ephesians had been separated from Christ before their conversion to Him. They were separated from Christ because they were "aliens from the commonwealth of Israel and strangers from the covenants of promise" (v. 12). They were alienated from God's covenant people and were strangers to God's special, saving revelation.

The covenants are the covenants of promise because they hold out the promise of communion with God and the hope of eternal life. God promised, "I will be their God, and they shall be My people" (2 Cor. 6:16). To these covenants of promise the Ephesians were "strangers" (v. 12). Outside of God's special revelation, people languish in hopelessness and godlessness. The creation witnesses to God and His glory, but men and women hold down that revelation in unrighteousness and are therefore without any excuse (Rom. 1:18–20). But God gave the Jews a special revelation—His Torah, His teaching, which was His instruction about Himself, His promised Messiah, and life and faithfulness, making the Jews more accountable to God for the splendor of their privileges. The Ephesians had not been so privileged. They were without hope and without God. Paul could hardly have described the darkness of their life outside of Christ more comprehensively: Christless, friendless, hopeless, and godless.

But Now!

Against this dark background of separation and alienation, God in Christ acted to bring transforming hope into the heart of Christless, godless, divided humanity. This is why the Christian message, the message of Jesus Christ, is called the gospel—good news. This good news has a horizontal as well as a vertical dimension. Vertically, the gospel of Christ deals with our alienation from God and restores us to His fellowship and friendship. But when the gospel—or better, Christ who is the gospel—restores us to God's fellowship and friendship, individual believers are united to one another. Union with Christ is union with Christ and His body, the church (1 Cor. 12:12–13). You cannot be vitally united to Christ and not be vitally united with His body, the church. This is what Paul is telling the Ephesians in verse 13: "In Christ Jesus you who once were far off have been brought near by the blood of Christ." What overcame the Ephesians' separation from Christ and their alienation from the covenant people of God was the blood of Christ. In Christ Jesus, God had done something to overcome their separation from Him and His people and made the Ephesians "fellow citizens with the saints and members of the household of God" (2:19). The something God provided in His grace to bring the Ephesians near was the blood of Christ (v. 13).

"The blood of Christ" is biblical shorthand for Christ's penal, substitutionary, atoning sacrifice on Calvary's cross. Christ's death was a sacrifice. In the Old Testament, the sacrifices offered were essentially expiatory and propitiatory. John Murray captures the significance of the sacrifices: "The sacrifice was the divinely instituted provision whereby the sin might be covered and the liability to divine wrath and curse removed."[1] The offered sacrifice symbolically bore the sin and judgment of the offerer. Our great need before God is not only that our sins are expiated, but that God's holy wrath against our sin is removed. This is what the Lord Jesus Christ did for us on the cross. He Himself bore, as our covenant Head (Rom. 5:12–19), the penalty our sins deserved, and in doing so endured God's just and holy wrath against our sin (Rom. 3:25; Heb. 2:17; 1 John 2:2; 4:10).

Unlike the Old Testament sacrifices, however, Christ offered Himself in our place, freely and willingly, to bear the condemnation our sin against God deserved (Heb. 9:14). It was this humanly unimaginable transaction that Isaiah prophesied:

> He was wounded for our transgressions…
> And by His stripes we are healed….
> And the LORD has laid on Him the iniquity of us all….
> Yet it pleased the LORD to bruise Him;
> He has put Him to grief. (Isa. 53:5, 6, 10)

Isaiah places the Lord's action in the foreground of his exposition of the Messiah's sufferings. Christ's sacrifice on the cross was the will of the heavenly Father. It was the Father who "made Him

---

1. Murray, *Redemption, Accomplished and Applied*, 18.

who knew no sin to be sin for us, that we might become the righteousness of God in Him" (2 Cor. 5:21). "The blood of Christ"—His sin-bearing, sin-atoning death—was the result of the Father's love for sinners (1 John 4:10). It must never be thought that by His sacrifice Jesus secured, far less won, the Father's love for sinners. God's love for sinners is the fountainhead of the gospel and the reason why God's Son became flesh; lived His sinless, spotless life; and died His sin-bearing, sin-atoning death.

Embedded in the language "the blood of Christ" is the solemn fact of God's holy opposition to and wrath against human sin. We needed our sin removed, because God hates sin and will by no means clear the guilty (Ex. 34:7). In the sacrifice of His obedient Servant-Son (Isa. 53:4–12; Phil. 2:8), God found a way to punish sin justly, remove the enmity that separated Him from us and us from Him, and restore us to His fellowship and friendship.

It should be a source of wonder and unceasing praise that the persons of the Trinity were willing to go to such lengths to rescue sinners from God's righteous wrath and restore them to His fellowship. It is not surprising that Paul began his exposition of the gospel of God's grace with the exclamation, "Blessed be the God and Father of our Lord Jesus Christ" (Eph. 1:3). Unceasing thankfulness to God—Father, Son, and Holy Spirit—should be one of the birthmarks of the twice-born. In a way, the gospel is unfathomable. Paul writes about this in Romans 11:33: "Oh, the depth of the riches both of the wisdom and knowledge of God! How unsearchable are His judgments and His ways past finding out!" Before anything else, the blood of Christ should fill our hearts with doxology, not controversy.

Christ Is Our Peace

Paul now explains in verse 14 just how the blood of Christ brought the Gentile Ephesians near to God and His covenant people: "For He Himself is our peace, who has made both one." "Peace" is one of the Bible's big words. It means so much more than the cessation of hostility. To have peace (shalom) is to have wholeness and fullness of life. When Adam sinned, enmity with God and alienation from Him replaced peace and fellowship with God. Remarkably, Paul tells us that Christ "Himself" is our peace (2:14). Paul is using the reflexive pronoun to impress on us that gospel peace is not a blessing that Christ dispenses. He Himself is our peace. The peace God gives to believing sinners through the gospel is Jesus Himself. Believers enjoy gospel peace in fellowship with Jesus Christ, who is our peace. It is imperative that we understand that Jesus Himself is the gospel. This was Jesus's own understanding. Again and again in the Gospels, Jesus self-consciously set Himself forth as the good news of God. He is the "bread of God" who has come from heaven to give life to the world (John 6:33). He is the "light of the world" who gives to those who follow Him the light of life (John 8:12). He is the "door" through whom we enter into salvation (John 10:9). He is the "good shepherd" who lays down His life for His sheep (John 10:11). He is the "resurrection and the life" who guarantees the future for everyone who believes in Him (John 11:25). He is "the way, the truth, and the life" by whom we come to the Father (John 14:6). He is the "true vine" who shares His life with all who are united to Him through faith (John 15:1). Jesus saw Himself as the answer to the needs and burdens of broken sinners (Matt. 11:28–30). There is a striking, unavoidable, self-conscious egocentricity at the heart of Jesus's teaching.

Understanding the Epoch of the Law

Paul now explains how it is that Jesus is "our peace," the peace that unites Jew and Gentile in the one family of God (v. 14). Between the Jews, God's covenant people, and the Gentile world was a "middle wall of separation" (2:14). This was true literally and symbolically. Literally, there was a wall around the temple to keep Gentiles out. There was a sign on the temple wall that read, "Trespassers will be executed." Symbolically, the wall around the temple signified Jewish separation from the rest of the world. Gentiles were considered dogs, little better than fuel for the fires of hell. This wall of separation had been divinely instituted. It was God who had commanded the multiplicity of "commandments contained in ordinances" (2:15). He did so in order to differentiate His covenant people from the world outside His saving revelation.

Paul is not writing here about God's moral law, the Ten Words that had been deposited in the ark of the covenant. The "law of commandments contained in ordinances" that Paul has in mind here is the Mosaic administration of the covenant of grace. When God rescued Israel from its bondage in Egypt, He graciously imposed on them many rules and regulations regarding what they were to eat and not eat, the feasts and festivals they were to keep, the sacrifices they were to offer. These commandments and ordinances had a specific purpose in the history of redemption. In Galatians 3:19, 24, Paul explains why God gave these commandments to His covenant people: "What purpose then does the law serve? It was added because of transgressions.... Therefore the law was our tutor to bring us to Christ, that we might be justified by faith." This "law of commandments contained in ordinances" belonged to the church's infancy, as Paul goes on to explain in Galatians 4:1–7. It had a temporary function in the history of redemption. It was "added because of transgressions" (Gal. 3:19). That is, "the law of commandments contained in ordinances" served as a child's playpen, keeping the covenant people safe from hostile, outside influences and at the same time preserving their unique identity as the people of God.

It would be wrong to think that God intended His covenant people thereby to be isolated from the world. Israel had not been chosen and set apart by God to be self-righteous and self-absorbed. In Abraham "all the families of the earth [were to] be blessed" (Gen. 12:3). God sent Jonah to Gentile Nineveh as a messenger of His grace. But Israel had made these ceremonial boundary markers a wall of separation and isolation. God had called His people to be "a light to the Gentiles" (Isa. 49:6), but they became obsessively proud of their God-given, grace-given privileges and looked down in sinful disdain on the Gentile, uncovenanted world.

Breaking Down the Wall

How was this vast gulf, this "middle wall of separation," ever to be broken down? It was broken down "by the blood of Christ. For He Himself is our peace, who has made both one, and has broken down the middle wall of separation, having abolished in His flesh the enmity, that is, the law of commandments contained in ordinances, so as to create in Himself one new man from the two, thus making peace, and that He might reconcile them both to God in one body through the cross, thereby putting to death the enmity" (vv. 13–16). The wall of separation was killed, torn down, in Christ.

The whole Mosaic epoch had a predetermined "shelf life." It was to function as "our tutor to bring us to Christ" (Gal. 3:24). Paul's point here is not that the law as a dispensation convicts us of sin and sends us to Christ to be saved, though it does that. His point is that the law as an era or dispensation of God's grace had a "Christ purpose." It functioned as a temporary era of redemptive history, embodying in its types and ceremonies the promised Messiah King. When Christ came, the embodied fulfillment of all the old covenant types and sacrifices and ceremonies, the Mosaic dispensation was dismantled; its God-ordained time was over. It had acted like scaffolding around preplanned construction. When the construction was completed, the scaffolding was taken down; its temporary function was finished. The temporary scaffolding that was taken down and forever removed did not, however, include God's moral law. The moral law predated the Mosaic dispensation of the covenant of grace. God wrote His law on Adam's heart (Rom. 2:14–16). The enduring permanence of the moral law, summed up in the Ten Words, was signified by the placement of the Ten Words into the ark of the covenant. God's moral law had a creational and not a Mosaic origin and continues to mark out the shape of the believing life in Christ.

All that divided Jew from Gentile had been abolished "in His flesh" (v. 15). This is one of the great blessings of the gospel that speaks powerfully into our racially, socially, and economically divided world. In Christ, all the divisions that mark and mar our world have been abolished. The church of Jesus Christ is the one society under heaven where once inveterate enemies are now brothers and sisters, united to one another in their union with Christ. If our churches are not manifesting that countercultural oneness and harmony, we are debasing the gospel and making Christ's cross of no effect (1 Cor. 1:17).

10

Fellow Citizens

EPHESIANS 2:17–22

---

*And He came and preached peace to you who were afar off and to
those who were near. For through Him we both have access by one
Spirit to the Father.*

*Now, therefore, you are no longer strangers and foreigners,
but fellow citizens with the saints and members of the household
of God, having been built on the foundation of the apostles and
prophets, Jesus Christ Himself being the chief cornerstone, in whom
the whole building, being fitted together, grows into a holy temple
in the Lord, in whom you also are being built together for a dwelling place of God in the Spirit.*

In chapter 2, Paul has been emphasizing that those who were once
enemies, Jews and Gentiles, have now been brought together "in
one body" (v. 16)—the church. Verses 17–22 are a further explanation of how this is possible. Paul's statement in verse 17 that Jesus
"came and preached peace to you who were afar off and to those
who were near" seems at first to be impossible. We understand that
during His earthly life, Jesus preached "to those who were near"—
that is, to God's old covenant people, the Jews. But Paul says that
He has preached to the Gentiles as well. What can he mean when
he says that Jesus also "preached peace to you who were afar off"?

Jesus in Ephesus

Jesus never visited Ephesus, yet Paul can state that Jesus preached
God's gospel peace to the Ephesians. Paul is not indulging in flights
of poetic fancy. He has profoundly and biblically understood the

vital connection between Jesus and His church, which is His body (1 Cor. 12:12–31; Eph. 1:22–23). Isaiah 49:6 and Acts 13:47 highlight the rich theology lying behind Paul's statement that Jesus preached to the Ephesian Gentiles. In Isaiah 49:6, the covenant Lord says to His Servant, His Messiah, "I will also give You as a light to the Gentiles, that You should be My salvation to the ends of the earth." In Acts 13:47, Paul and Barnabas apply these words to themselves as Jesus's ambassadors:

> For so the Lord has commanded us:
> "I have set you as a light to the Gentiles,
> That you should be for salvation to the ends of the earth."

What the Lord applies to His Servant-Messiah in Isaiah 49:6, Paul and Barnabas apply to themselves. Did Paul and Barnabas misunderstand Isaiah 49:6? Did they misuse Scripture to suit their own ends? No, Paul in particular understood that just as a body is inseparably joined to its head, so the church, the body of Christ, is inseparably joined to its Head. Jesus preached peace to the Ephesian Gentiles through the ministry of His body, the church. In this instance, through Paul's preaching ministry, Jesus preached to the Ephesians. The Head spoke through the ministry of His ambassador. The church's Head, now risen and exalted to the right hand of His Father, makes His gospel appeals through the life and witness of His church (Rom. 10:14; 2 Cor. 5:20).

The church's ministry is superintended and informed by its Head, the Lord Jesus Christ. We are to take the gospel to the ends of the earth in His name, not preaching ourselves, "but Christ Jesus the Lord" (2 Cor. 4:5), so that it is the voice of the risen Savior that is heard as He proclaims Himself through His appointed servants.

What Jesus Preached in Ephesus

As we have seen, peace is one of the central notes of the gospel of Christ. It is through faith in Christ alone that we have "peace with God" (Rom. 5:1), the peace of being a justified sinner in Christ.

Earlier, in Ephesians 2:14, Paul told us that Christ Himself is our peace. The gospel message of peace is essentially about Jesus, the Prince of Peace. This is the force of verse 18: "For through Him we both have access by one Spirit to the Father." What is remarkable is that those who were near—God's covenant people, the Jews—were as much in need of peace as those "who once were far off" (v. 13). The weight of covenant privilege did not compensate for not having peace with God, the assurance of God's justifying grace.

In spite of the Jews' God-given covenant privileges, Paul had "great sorrow and continual grief" in his heart because they were not saved (Rom. 9:2; see 1–5; 10:1). Gospel privilege does not exempt us from needing God's salvation in Christ. Israel's great sin throughout the old covenant dispensation was covenantal presumption. They prided themselves in their privileges but not in the God of grace who gave them the privileges. God's answer to the sin that separated Him from the Gentile world and the sin that separated Him from His covenant people was His Son. It is "through Him" (v. 18) that both Jewish and Gentile sinners have access to the Father in one Spirit. Jesus is the "Mediator of the new covenant" (Heb. 9:15; 12:24). In that new covenant God has included both Jew and Gentile. In the new covenant, the nationalism and Jewish particularism of the old covenant have been replaced—brought to their gospel fulfillment. God's ultimate purpose was never intended to be exhausted in Israel. In Abraham, all the families of the earth were to be blessed (Gen. 12:3).

Christian Salvation Is Trinitarian

Paul continues to highlight the absolute centrality of Jesus Christ to the gospel of God's grace. It is "through Him" that both Jew and Gentile "have access by one Spirit to the Father" (v. 18). There is not one way of access for the Jew and another for the Gentile (see John 14:6). Because there is only one sin-atoning Savior, there can be only one way of access to the Father. The gospel of God cuts at the heart of everything in this world that erects divisions between people (Gal. 3:27–28). Before the cross of Christ, all racial, cultural, and historical barriers are brought to nothing. We don't stop being Scottish or Nigerian or Chinese. We don't stop being black or brown or white. We don't deny our history and heritage. But before the cross we stand with all fellow believers, united to Christ in the one family of God. All of this is the concerted purpose and work of the Holy Trinity—Father, Son, and Holy Spirit.

No Longer Strangers

The opening two words of verse 19, "Now, therefore," tell us that Paul is about to draw out the implications of this radical truth that in Christ Jew and Gentile are now "one new man" (Eph. 2:15). He uses three pictures to highlight the glorious inheritance the Ephesian Gentile believers have come to possess in Christ along with their fellow Jewish believers.

Fellow Citizens with the Saints

First, through the grace of God in the gospel, they are "no longer strangers and foreigners, but fellow citizens with the saints" (v. 19). All Christians have a dual nationality: they are citizens of the country they were born in, and citizens of the kingdom of God. Paul actually says "fellow citizens with the saints." Once again, he is highlighting the essential continuity of God's covenantal administrations. The new covenant church is not a separate entity from its old covenant counterpart (Rom. 11:17–24). God's church is one, though in the new covenant it has come into its most glorious and prophesied fullness. No longer is God's kingdom identified with a particular people or place. It is a kingdom found wherever people call upon the name of the Lord. It is an international, interracial, multicultural kingdom. Everyone who comes to the Father through the Son, in the Spirit, is a member of the "kingdom which cannot be shaken" (Heb. 12:28) that will endure forever (Dan. 4:3).

Members of the Household of God

Second, because of the peace-giving Jesus, the Ephesians are now "members of the household of God" (v. 19). Christians are not only citizens in God's kingdom but also children in God's family. The King is our Father in Christ. Paul's emphasis is, however, less on God's fatherhood than on the brotherhood into which believers are brought in their union with Christ. Just as we are fellow citizens with the saints, so also we are members together of God's household. When people come to faith in the Lord Jesus Christ, they are coming home. The church is God's family, His sons and daughters redeemed by the blood of His Son. By the new birth, the birth from above (John 3:3–6), we are born into God's family (John 1:12–13) and immediately become connected in Christ with everyone He has called brethren in the gospel (Heb. 2:11–12).

It is significant that God's household is singular. There is one divine family (Eph. 4:4–6). Nothing commends a family more than its loving unity. The reason Jesus commanded His disciples to love one another (John 13:34–35) and Paul exhorted the Ephesians to bear with one another in love (4:2) was to impress on God's people how seriously the heavenly Father took the unity and peace of His family. This should be sufficient for Christians to welcome one another as Christ has welcomed them, for the glory of God (Rom. 15:7). Nothing adorns the church's gospel witness more than its members loving one another (John 13:35).

A Dwelling Place for God by the Spirit
Third, because of their union with Christ, believers are "being fitted together…into a holy temple in the Lord" (v. 21). Christians are citizens in God's kingdom, children in His household, and living stones in His temple. In 1 Corinthians 6:19, the individual believer is called a "temple of the Holy Spirit." In 1 Corinthians 3:16–17, the local congregation is called "the temple of God." In Ephesians 2:21, however, the universal church is in view. The church in its transhistorical, transgenerational identity is "a holy temple in the Lord." In the Old Testament God's presence among His people was symbolically in the temple and especially in the Holy of Holies. The word Paul uses here for temple signifies the Holy of Holies (ναός). In this temple, this "dwelling place of God," believers are "being fitted together" (v. 21) as

living stones (1 Peter 2:5). Stone by living stone, God is building for Himself a dwelling place "in the Spirit" (v. 22).

Significantly, this temple-household is built on "the foundation of the apostles and prophets" (v. 20). Every meaningful building has a foundation; indeed, the foundation gives stability and strength to the building. God's temple, His spiritual dwelling place, is founded on "the apostles and prophets, Jesus Christ Himself being the chief cornerstone" (v. 20). The apostles are those uniquely called and appointed men who spoke in Christ's name and penned the new covenant Scriptures. The prophets Paul is referring to are not whom we might first think of—the old covenant spokesmen of God. They are the new covenant prophets who spoke God's new covenant word directly to God's people. The conjoining of prophets with apostles occurs again in Ephesians 3:5 and 4:11 and can refer only to the prophets of the new covenant era. The point is not that God's temple is a purely new covenant phenomenon, but that the apostles and prophets of the new covenant revealed and declared God's saving revelation in its covenantal fullness (Eph. 3:5).

Jesus Christ the Cornerstone

The cornerstone is the keystone or linchpin of a building. Everything hinges and depends on Jesus Christ (1 Cor. 3:11). He holds everything and everyone together. United to Him we stand. Without ever becoming weary of it, Paul reinforces the absolute foundational centrality of Christ. It is futile, however, to separate (as many have tried) the person of Christ from His work as Redeemer and Savior. He is the cornerstone of God's spiritual temple as the sin-atoning, sin-defeating Redeemer (Eph. 1:7; 2:13). It is when the church drifts from its sin-atoning, sin-defeating Savior that it unmoors itself and becomes prey to "every wind of doctrine" (Eph. 4:14). The present tragedy of the Christian church in the West is not that it is antiquated and unwilling to march with the times but that it has, by and large, walked in step with the times, abandoning the glory of the cross, the penal substitutionary atonement of God's incarnate Son. When you remove or tamper with a building's cornerstone, the building will collapse, unsurprisingly. The church is always at its most compelling when it unashamedly and boldly proclaims the message of the cross (1 Cor. 1:18, 23; 2:1–2).

The Growing Dwelling Place

Because God's temple, His dwelling place by the Spirit, is comprised of living stones, it has an organic rather than a static character. The "whole building…grows into a holy temple in the Lord" (v. 21). This growth is in both quantity and quality. As the Lord, by the grace of His Son, saves sinners, they are added, stone by living stone, to His temple. This adding to the church will continue until all of God's elect are gathered into its fellowship.

But Paul is clearly more concerned to highlight the qualitative growth of the "whole building" (v. 21). The growth that most pleases and honors God is growth in holiness. His temple is holy, set apart from everything common to be His unique possession and dwelling place. Paul will develop this thought later (Eph. 4:15–16). But it is vital that we understand that growth in numbers is no substitute for growth in holiness. It is not a question of either/or, but of both/and. Sadly, evangelicals have often been guilty of focusing on numerical growth to the virtual exclusion of laboring to make the church a fit dwelling place for God by the Spirit. We have a responsibility to do all we can to make God's temple a pure and welcoming dwelling place for Him to inhabit "in the Spirit" (v. 22). Now is the time for us to throw out all the garbage in our lives and fellowships that grieve the Spirit (Eph. 4:30)—our pride, our resentment, our bitterness, our complaining spirit, our lukewarmness and complacency—that our gracious God may have a fit and beautiful dwelling place among His saints.

11

The Mystery of the Gospel

EPHESIANS 3:1–13

For this reason I, Paul, the prisoner of Christ Jesus for you Gentiles—if indeed you have heard of the dispensation of the grace of God which was given to me for you, how that by revelation He made known to me the mystery (as I have briefly written already, by which, when you read, you may understand my knowledge in the mystery of Christ), which in other ages was not made known to the sons of men, as it has now been revealed by the Spirit to His holy apostles and prophets: that the Gentiles should be fellow heirs, of the same body, and partakers of His promise in Christ through the gospel, of which I became a minister according to the gift of the grace of God given to me by the effective working of His power.

To me, who am less than the least of all the saints, this grace was given, that I should preach among the Gentiles the unsearchable riches of Christ, and to make all see what is the fellowship of the mystery, which from the beginning of the ages has been hidden in God who created all things through Jesus Christ; to the intent that now the manifold wisdom of God might be made known by the church to the principalities and powers in the heavenly places, according to the eternal purpose which He accomplished in Christ Jesus our Lord, in whom we have boldness and access with confidence through faith in Him. Therefore I ask that you do not lose heart at my tribulations for you, which is your glory.

It is a striking feature of the Bible that often theology produces doxology, prayer, and our resolve to live worthy of our calling in Christ. The doctrines of God's Word are revealed truths that powerfully impact the minds and hearts of God's people into responses of thanksgiving, adoration, and obedience. This is the invariable grammar of God's Word: everything flows out of what God has done in grace in His Son for His people.

The opening words of chapter 3, "For this reason," link what Paul is about to write with what he has just written. He has just told the Ephesians that in fellowship with believing Jews they are "being built…for a dwelling place of God in the Spirit" (2:22). Now, in response to what God has done in uniting Jew and Gentile into "a holy temple in the Lord" (2:21), Paul desired either to pray with gratitude to the Father (3:14) or, if his digression stretches to 3:21, to summon the Ephesians to behave in a manner worthy of their high and holy calling in Christ (4:1). But Paul is interrupted in his train of thought. No sooner does he write "for this reason" when his mind is diverted further to explain his ministry as Christ's apostle to the Gentiles.

There is debate as to whether this digression occupies verses 2–13 or verses 2–21. In favor of the former, in 3:14 Paul reuses the identical words with which he began the section, "for this reason." In favor of the latter, in 4:1 Paul again speaks of himself as "the prisoner of the Lord" (cf. 3:1, "the prisoner of Christ Jesus"). On balance it seems better to see Paul's (necessary) digression ending at 3:13. While a series of exhortations to holy living would follow admirably from 2:22, the "mystery" (3:3–4), or wonder, of this truth would understandably provoke in Paul the desire to bow his knees before the Father (3:14).

Digression is a feature of Paul's letters. His mind and heart are so full and fertile that he easily pauses, or diverts, to amplify a truth or consider a related truth. Here Paul clearly feels the need to give the Ephesians further insight into what he calls "the dispensation of the grace of God which was given to me for you" (3:2).

A Prisoner of Christ

Verse 1 is the first time in his letter that Paul explicitly tells us he is in prison. In 6:20 he tells us that he is "in chains." Why does he mention his imprisonment at this point in his letter? Perhaps to remind the Ephesians that his care and concern for them transcended his care and concern for himself. He is in prison, in chains, and yet it is not his circumstances that dominate his thoughts. Helping the Ephesians to appreciate their privileges in Christ was the apostle's dominating concern.

Paul's care and concern for Christ's church was a creaturely analogue of the Savior's care and concern for His church. Pastors are called to seek the good of Christ's bride and, if need be, to lay down their lives for her good. They are to be examples to the flock (1 Peter 5:3) of self-denying love and selfless devotion.

Paul is a prisoner of Christ (v. 1). He is a prisoner of Caesar, but he is first a prisoner "of Christ Jesus." He is in prison not ultimately because of the Roman authorities but because of his faithfulness to Christ. He is in prison for Jesus's sake. It is gloriously liberating, as well as reassuring, to know that your life is governed by the sovereign, gracious, and wise will of God. Paul is in prison because the cause of the gospel will be best served by him being there (Phil. 1:12–13). Paul's imprisonment was also "for you Gentiles" (v. 1). It was Paul's undeviating resolve to bring the gospel of Christ to the Gentile world that landed him in prison. There is no trace of resentment in the apostle. Being in prison because of his commitment to the work of the gospel is almost a badge of honor for Paul. Suffering for the sake of the gospel was not something for him to resent or avoid; it was a badge of faithfulness and, remarkably, a sign of God's blessing (Phil. 1:29; Col. 1:24–26). These truths led Paul Gerhart to write,

> Why should cross and trial grieve me?
> Christ is near
> With his cheer;
> Never will He leave me.
> Who can rob me of the heaven
> That God's Son

For me won
When His life was given?[1]

The Stewardship of God's Grace

The word "dispensation," used in verse 2 of the NKJV, is better translated "stewardship." The idea contained in the Greek word οἰκονομίαν is that of a steward overseeing his master's domain. In his earlier first letter to the Corinthians, Paul described himself and Apollos as "stewards of the mysteries of God" (1 Cor. 4:1). A "steward" (οἰκονόμος) was a servant who had been entrusted with the care and oversight of his master's estate. His stewardship (οἰκονομία) of the estate was a huge privilege and responsibility. Paul's servant stewardship was especially to oversee the "grace of God" (v. 2). Why did Paul say "if indeed" they had heard of the stewardship of grace that God had entrusted to him? Paul had spent three years in Ephesus teaching night and day (Acts 20:31). Surely the Ephesian believers knew about the stewardship God had committed to Paul, didn't they? But Paul is thinking and writing as a pastor. He knows how easily and quickly truth can disappear from a church. So he reminds them of his stewardship of God's grace— and perhaps gently chides them in the process.

Paul cannot ever speak enough about God's grace. God had given to him the immense privilege of carefully and judiciously making known God's undeserved and overwhelming saving kindness in the gospel of Christ. Paul was a man with a message he had been "given," not one that he had devised (v. 2). It is possible that Paul had in mind his momentous encounter with Christ on the road to Damascus (Acts 26:16–20). Paul's entire life had been devoted to fulfilling this "dispensation of the grace of God."

What the apostle did in a uniquely redemptive-historical way, every gospel minister is called to do. In preaching the whole counsel of God (Acts 20:27), the gospel minister is to major on faithfully

---

1. Paul Gerhart (1607–1676), "Why Should Cross and Trial Grieve Me?," in the public domain.

managing, as a steward, the grace of God. This stewardship of God's grace will certainly include reasoning "about righteousness, self-control, and the judgment to come" (Acts 24:25), but it will always keep in mind that "God did not send His Son into the world to condemn the world, but that the world through Him might be saved" (John 3:17). In his commentary on Paul's words in 2 Corinthians 2:14–16, James Denney makes this striking comment: "When we proclaim the gospel, do we always succeed in manifesting its savour? Or is not the savour—the sweetness, the winsomeness, the charm and attractiveness of it—the very thing that is most easily left out?… We miss what is most characteristic in the knowledge of God if we miss this. We leave out that very element in the Evangel which makes it evangelic, and gives it its power to subdue and enchain the souls of men."[2]

The Revealed Mystery

In verses 1–13, Paul describes the message he had been commissioned to proclaim as a "mystery" (vv. 3, 4, 9). In particular, it is "the mystery of Christ" (v. 4). In the New Testament, a mystery is not a secret that only the spiritually initiated can understand; it is a truth that God has revealed for the salvation and sanctification of sinners. God made this particular mystery known to Paul "by revelation" (v. 3). The content of the mystery is highlighted in verse 6: "that the Gentiles should be fellow heirs, of the same body, and partakers of His promise in Christ through the gospel" (cf. Eph. 2:13, 19). Paul does not tell us when God revealed this mystery to him. The tense of the verb,[3] however, suggests that it happened at a particular point in Paul's history, quite possibly at his conversion on the road to Damascus (Acts 26:17–18). At that seismic moment in the history of the church, God revealed to Paul that His saving purpose embraced Gentiles as well as Jews. Paul had already "briefly written" about this

---

2. James Denney, *The Second Epistle to the Corinthians* (London: Hodder and Stoughton, 1894), 91–92.

3. $\dot{\epsilon}\gamma\nu\omega\rho\dot{\iota}\sigma\theta\eta$ (indicative aorist passive of $\gamma\nu\omega\rho\dot{\iota}\zeta\omega$).

(v. 3; see Eph. 1:8–10). Now he more fully and starkly makes known to the Ephesians what the Lord had made known to him.

This mystery was not something unknown to the church in the old covenant. Certainly it "in other ages was not made known to the sons of men, as it has now been revealed by the Spirit to His holy apostles and prophets" (v. 5). But it had been known. The foundational promise in God's covenant with Abraham was that in him all the families of the earth would be blessed (Gen. 12:3). Many of the psalms celebrate the covenant Lord's universal lordship. The prophets spoke of Israel being set apart to be "a light to the Gentiles," that the Lord's salvation might reach to the ends of the earth (Isa. 49:6). While we must never flatten the contours of the history of redemption, we must not so accentuate the privileges of the new covenant that old covenant Christianity is demeaned. The incarnation of the Lord Jesus Christ ushered in a new age of heightened blessing and more fully revealed truth; shadow gave way to substance, type to antitype, and promise to fulfillment. In Christ, truth does not replace error; rather, it comes into its fullest flowering.

The Mystery of Christ

Why does Paul call this gospel mystery of Gentiles being "fellow heirs, of the same body, and partakers of His promise in Christ" (v. 6) with the Jews "the mystery of Christ" (v. 4)? Because it is Christ "who has made both one," reconciling "both to God in one body through the cross" (Eph. 2:14, 16). It is in union with Christ that all human, fallen hostilities are abolished (Eph. 2:18). The gospel is centered and founded on Jesus Christ. He is the gospel's preeminent theme. It is in Him, as Paul reminded the Ephesians at the beginning of his letter, that God has blessed us with every spiritual blessing. It is not surprising that Paul told the church in Corinth, "I determined not to know anything among you except Jesus Christ and Him crucified" (1 Cor. 2:2). Christ, in His person and work, was the driving pulsebeat and supreme content of Paul's ministry.

It is perhaps difficult for us, at a distance of over two thousand years, to appreciate just how radical the division was between

Jew and Gentile. But in Christ this division (and all other human divisions) was obliterated. In Christ, as Paul tells the churches in Galatia, "there is neither Jew nor Greek, there is neither slave nor free, there is neither male nor female; for you are all one in Christ Jesus" (Gal. 3:28). The point is not that we stop being Jew and Gentile, male and female, slave and free, black and white, rich and poor, or whatever; it is that these cultural, social, racial, sexual divisions no longer demarcate our essential identity. In Christ we are all "Abraham's seed, and heirs according to the promise" (Gal. 3:29). In Christ, believers are first and essentially "children of the living God," the one family of God, members "of the same body [Christ's body], and partakers of His [same] promise in Christ through the gospel" (v. 6).

This foundational gospel truth must transform how we think and behave as Christians. The one place under heaven where racism, social snobbery, and all forms of sexism should never be found is within the church of the Lord Jesus Christ. Just as the Holy Trinity is a glorious diversity in unity, so must the church be. This is why the message of the cross must always be at the heart of the church's ministry and life. It is when the church drifts from the message of the cross that self rears its ugly head in any number of self-promoting enterprises, not least in magnifying differences of ethnicity, education, social origin, and much else. The church is called to display to a fallen world the transforming power of the gospel, a power that humbles us before God and unites us to fellow blood-redeemed sinners in the body of Christ.

The Greatness of the Gospel

Commonly, people have a stunted, truncated understanding of the gospel. Too often the gospel is explained atomistically, as if it had to do only with the salvation of individual men and women. In Ephesians 1:10, we saw that God's purpose is to "gather together in one all things in Christ, both which are in heaven and which are on earth." The gospel's purpose is ultimately to transform the cosmos. According to God's promise, as Peter tells his readers, we "look for new heavens and a new earth in which righteousness dwells" (2 Peter 3:13). This ultimate "cosmic harmony" is prefigured in the dismantling of the barriers that divided Jew and Gentile. This transformative, "manifold wisdom of God" is to be "made known by the church to the principalities and powers in the heavenly places" (v. 10). What God has done in Christ is to be made known, not kept hidden within the church.

The Gift of God's Grace

"Grace" is perhaps the most distinctive word in Paul's gospel vocabulary. The apostle never tires of tracing all his privileges in Christ back to the grace—the undeserved kindness and mercy—of God. The experience of the sovereign, undeserved kindness of God never produces complacency, far less indolence, in a believer's life. Rather, it stirs the believer to give himself and herself in glad surrender to the Lord's service (Rom. 12:1). Where such glad surrender is absent, the grace of God in Christ can hardly be present.

Paul's gospel ministry had been "given" to him as a gift of God's grace and "by the effective working of His power" (v. 7). He was a man under orders, a minister—that is, a servant. He was constrained by his heavenly calling to give himself heart and soul to making the gospel of Christ known. Paul is overwhelmed by the privilege God had given to him: "To me, who am less than the least of all the saints, this grace was given, that I should preach among the Gentiles the unsearchable riches of Christ" (v. 8). Paul is not engaging in hyperbole. He truly believes he is "less than the least of all the saints." What he actually says is, "Though I am the 'leaster' of all the saints."[4] There are times when the wonder of God's grace to Paul in Christ so overwhelms him that his grammar "goes out the window."[5] One of the distinguishing hallmarks of gospel grace

---

4. He uses the comparative, ἐλαχιστοτέρῳ (lesser), rather than the superlative, ἐλάχιστος (least).

5. The extended sentence that comprises Ephesians 1:3–14 is perhaps the best example of the grace of the gospel triumphing over Paul's sense of grammatical correctness.

is that it so magnifies God's sheer kindness to us in Christ that we
no longer compare ourselves to the people around us but to the God
who spared not His only Son but gave Him up for us all (Rom.
8:32). It is in the soil of such humility that usefulness to God in the
cause of the gospel is born.

The Unsearchable Riches of Christ

In verse 8b, Paul defines the gospel that God's grace had set him
apart to minister: "the unsearchable riches of Christ." It is characteristic of Paul that he understands the gospel as a bottomless deep
(Rom. 11:33–36). There is only so much that he can say. There are
depths to Christ that are and always will be unsearchable. Samuel
Rutherford knew what it was to be overwhelmed by the unsearchable depths of Christ. He wrote in one of his letters, "Christ is a
well of life; but who knoweth how deep it is to the bottom?...And
oh, what a fair one, what an only one, what an excellent, lovely, rav-
ishing one is Jesus! Put the beauty of ten thousand, thousand worlds
of paradises...in one.... It would be less to that fair and dearest
Well-beloved, Christ."[6]

It is possible that Paul is thinking generally about the unsearchable riches of Christ. If so, he is surely thinking about what he earlier
called "exceeding riches of [God's] grace in His kindness toward us
in Christ Jesus" (Eph. 2:7). These exceeding and unsearchable riches
are the riches of God's saving grace in Christ. They are the riches
that God displayed so unfathomably and yet so gloriously in the
blood atonement of Christ on Calvary's cross (Eph. 1:7). It is likely,
however, that Paul is thinking somewhat more narrowly here. In
the particular context of these verses, "the unsearchable riches of
Christ" are the riches that have specifically included uncovenanted
Gentiles in the salvation of God. This is what the risen Christ commissioned him to proclaim on the Damascus road (Acts 26:17–18).
Paul's mission was to take the gospel of God's grace in Christ to "all

---

6. Samuel Rutherford to Lady Kilconquar, August 8, 1637, in *Letters of Samuel
Rutherford* (Edinburgh: Banner of Truth Trust, 1995), 264.

the nations" (Matt. 28:19), heralding the universal saving grace of God in Christ.

The Manifold Wisdom of God

In verse 9, Paul more explicitly identifies the core of the gospel message he had been commissioned by God to preach (3:8). He calls it "the fellowship of the mystery, which from the beginning of the ages has been hidden in God who created all things" (v. 9). The translation "fellowship" does not quite capture the essential root meaning of the word οἰκονομία. Paul is continuing to speak of the privileged stewardship that God had entrusted to him. The ESV translation "plan" may better capture the heart of Paul's meaning. He has already identified the essential content of this mystery in verses 5–6. Now he tells us that his ministry was "to make all see" that "mystery" (v. 9). It was no longer to remain in any sense hidden or locked up within the church. This is why Paul is in prison— because of his faithfulness to his calling to bring the unsearchable riches of Christ to light for "all" (v. 9).

When Paul speaks of "the fellowship [plan or stewardship] of the mystery, which from the beginning of the ages has been hidden in God who created all things" (v. 9), he is telling us that the gospel of the unsearchable riches of Christ was not put together hastily as an afterthought. It was God's plan from the beginning—even before the beginning—because it was "in God." The hiddenness of this plan must be understood relatively. It was not so hidden that it did not surface in the old covenant Scriptures, as we have seen (see comment on Eph. 3:5). Paul is thinking of the clarity of redemptive purpose and history that had come to pass in the incarnation, life, death, and resurrection of Christ. All the types and shadows had come to their redemptive fulfillment in Christ, although we await the full eschatological fullness of God's redemptive plan (cf. Rom. 8:22–25).

Why does Paul add at this point, "who created all things" (v. 9)? Perhaps he is reminding us that God's salvation in Christ is truly cosmic in its ultimate intention. Through Adam's sin, God's good creation was terminally corrupted. But God had One better than Adam ready to undo the cosmic tragedy of Adam's sin (Eph. 1:8–10).

By the Church

It is this "manifold wisdom" that God has purposed to be made known "by the church to the principalities and powers in the heavenly places" (v. 10). Paul uses a striking adjective to highlight just how rich and multiform God's saving wisdom in Christ is. "Manifold" has been translated from πολυποίκιλος, meaning variegated or marked with many colors. Just as a painting is made up of many colors, all contributing to the design of the artist, so God's wisdom is multicolored, each color adding to the perfection of God's design.

This "manifold wisdom," which is disclosed in the unsearchable riches of Christ, is to be "made known by the church" (v. 10). The church is to display in its life of gospel unity God's manifold wisdom "to the principalities and powers in the heavenly places" (v. 10b). Who are these "principalities and powers in the heavenly places"? Later, in Ephesians 6:12, Paul uses a similar expression to denote the spiritual forces of evil, the kingdom of darkness that rules in the lives of sin-blinded men and women. In and by Christ's church, Satan and his kingdom of darkness are to be brought face-to-face with the transforming power of the gospel. The church is to showcase to this world and to the unseen world of spiritual darkness the power of the gospel of the grace of God in Christ. This is what the cross was all about. This was God's plan from the beginning and has been realized "in Christ Jesus our Lord" (v. 11).

The gospel of Christ is in no sense God's "plan B." God has had only one plan from the beginning, and it is in the cross of Christ that we see the glory and grace of God's plan of manifold wisdom (see 1 Cor. 1:24). This saving and transforming wisdom is not something that the sin-darkened human mind can begin to comprehend. It is utter folly to the unsaved man and woman (1 Cor. 1:18; 2:14–16). It is the ultimate tragedy that sin has so darkened our minds that by nature we are utterly blind to the multiform and multicolored saving and life-transforming wisdom of God. We all need to be born from above, inwardly enlightened by the Spirit of God, before we can begin to see and appreciate God's wisdom in Christ.

Boldness and Access

Paul had earlier spoken of the access that both Jews and Gentiles have through Christ to the Father (Eph. 2:18). In verse 12 he states this glorious truth again. Why does he say it again? Surely because Paul simply wanted to highlight the astonishing truth that "in Christ Jesus our Lord," all believers have unfettered, unhindered "access" to God with "boldness" and "confidence," "through faith in Him." What enables anyone, Jew or Gentile, to have access to God with boldness and confidence, rather than fear and shame, is "faith in [Christ]." Faith alone, in Christ alone, rooted in the grace of God alone enables us to draw near to God "in full assurance of faith" (Heb. 10:22). Paul never tires of accenting the significance of God's grace, but he is even more passionate about highlighting the absolute centrality of God's Son. "In Christ" is the dominant note in Paul's gospel proclamation (Eph. 1:3). Paul never severs Christ from His sending by the Father or His equipping by the Spirit (Isa. 42:1). But just as it is the Holy Spirit's new covenant ministry to glorify Christ (John 16:14), so it was Paul's new covenant ministry, and the new covenant ministry of all gospel preachers, to set forth the Savior, in whom God "has blessed us with every spiritual blessing" (Eph. 1:3).

Tribulations and Glory

In verse 13, Paul draws a remarkable conclusion from his exposition of the unsearchable riches of Christ. He urges the Ephesians not to lose heart over the tribulations he is suffering for them, his imprisonment in chains. Rather than lose heart over what Paul is suffering, he tells them that his tribulations are their "glory" (v. 13). If Paul had said that his tribulations were producing glory in him, we could in measure understand what he meant. God uses our tribulations to conform us more to the likeness of our Savior. In our tribulations, we are cast back on the Lord and find in all our suffering His promised grace. Paul speaks about that relationship between suffering and glory in Romans 5:3–5; 8:18; and 2 Corinthians 4:17. But here the connection between tribulations and glory is not personal. Paul's tribulations are the glory of the Ephesians!

The principial pattern of Christ's ministerial life was being overlaid on Paul's ministerial life. It was the Savior's tribulations that were the glory of His people. What He suffered in life and supremely in death brought present and eternal glory to every believer. Just as death worked in Him and life in us, so Paul could tell the Corinthians that "death is working in us, but life in you" (2 Cor. 4:12). This is the way of Christ.

Paul was in prison as an ambassador of Christ. It was his faithfulness to the stewardship of God's grace that God had given to him that led to him being chained in a Roman prison. But that gospel stewardship had brought the salvation of God into the heart of pagan Ephesus and had taken some out of their darkness into God's marvelous light (Col. 1:13). If we choose to avoid tribulations for the sake of Christ, we give the lie to our claim to be "joint heirs with Christ" (Rom. 8:17). God has inextricably joined suffering to glory. You cannot have one without the other. The servant is not greater than his Master (John 15:18–20).

What Paul writes here is deeply challenging. When we hear of believers in prison and suffering for the sake of the gospel, what is our first instinct? Is it not to cry to the Lord to rescue them and restore them to their loved ones and to the church? But should our first prayer not be to bless the Lord who works all things together for the good of His people, who is pleased in His gracious love to ordain suffering in order to bring glory to His children (Phil. 1:12–14)? This is easier said than done. But this is the life pattern we see modeled in the earthly life and ministry of our Savior. When the shadow of the cross began to penetrate His human soul, he said, "Now My soul is troubled, and what shall I say? 'Father, save Me from this hour'? But for this purpose I came to this hour. Father, glorify Your name" (John 12:27–28). It is our gospel privilege to reflect this mind in us which was first found in our Lord Jesus Christ (Phil. 2:5).

12

Prayer for Strength

EPHESIANS 3:14–19

For this reason I bow my knees to the Father of our Lord Jesus Christ, from whom the whole family in heaven and earth is named, that He would grant you, according to the riches of His glory, to be strengthened with might through His Spirit in the inner man, that Christ may dwell in your hearts through faith; that you, being rooted and grounded in love, may be able to comprehend with all the saints what is the width and length and depth and height—to know the love of Christ which passes knowledge; that you may be filled with all the fullness of God.

A remarkable feature of Paul's prison letters is that his mind and heart transcend his confinement. He assured the Philippians that his imprisonment had "turned out for the furtherance of the gospel" (Phil. 1:12). He told the Colossians that he rejoiced in his sufferings for their sake (Col. 1:24) and the Ephesians that his suffering was their glory (Eph. 3:13). He encouraged Timothy that though he had to "suffer trouble as an evildoer, even to the point of chains …the word of God is not chained" (2 Tim. 2:9). He assured the Philippians that they were partakers with him of God's grace, "both in my chains and in the defense and confirmation of the gospel" (Phil. 1:7). Paul's dominating concern and passion was never himself, but the spiritual good of the people of God. He was absolutely persuaded that "all things work together for good to those who love God" and are "called according to His purpose" (Rom. 8:28). It was this prevailing, God-centered perspective on life that liberated Paul from self-pity and set him free to seek, even in chains, the good of

God's people. So here he prays not that he will be rescued from his imprisonment but that God will establish the Ephesians, enrich them, and fill them "with all the fullness of God" (v. 19).

Why Paul Prayed

Paul begins this section, "For this reason I bow my knees to the Father" (v. 14). What is this reason that causes Paul to bow his knees before the heavenly Father? It is possible that Paul is picking up the train of thought that was interrupted in Ephesians 3:1. If so, then the reason he is referring to is the stupendous thing God has done in uniting Jew and Gentile in Christ, through the cross, "thereby putting to death the enmity" (Eph. 2:16). This is reason enough for Paul to bow his knees before the Father and to pray that He would root and ground this new, cross-created humanity in the love of Christ. It is possible, however, that Paul is referring more immediately to 3:7–13, where he reflected on his calling as the apostle to the Gentiles. God had given him the unspeakable privilege of preaching "among the Gentiles the unsearchable riches of Christ" (v. 8). The Ephesians were not to lose heart over Paul's suffering, because it was the result of his being a "minister according to the gift of the grace of God" (v. 7). The overwhelming sense of privilege of preaching to the Gentiles the unsearchable riches of Christ constrained Paul to pray for this Gentile church. While in prison he could not preach to them, but he could pray for them, and he did. Thankfully, we are not obliged to choose which one of these reasons motivated Paul to pray to the Father. In the overall thought of the apostle, these two reasons merge into one and provide the fuel that constrained him to pray.

The Father to Whom Paul Prayed

Paul almost always prayed to the Father, through the Son, in and by the Spirit (Eph. 2:18). We are not to think that it is wrong to pray to the Son or to the Spirit (Acts 7:59). The Holy Trinity is one, each person equal in glory and equally to be honored, loved, and praised. And yet the normal practice of the New Testament is to address prayer to the Father, in and through the Son, and in the power of the Spirit. This is not because the Father is intrinsically greater than the Son and the Spirit, but because it is the Spirit's delight to glorify the Son (John 16:14) and the Son's delight to glorify His Father (John 17:1). Within the Holy Trinity there is absolute equality of dignity, but a revealed order of mutual love in which the Father initiates, the Son accomplishes, and the Spirit applies.

Paul follows verse 14 with, "from whom the whole family in heaven and earth is named" (v. 15). Paul could mean one of two things. He could be saying that every family owes its origin to the purpose and will of the heavenly Father. The Father is the originator of every family. Or he could be saying that the whole family in heaven and earth—that is, the totality of the redeemed—bears the Father's name. However we understand Paul, it is the Father's fatherhood that he is accenting. Paul is not simply making a pious introductory statement as he prepares to pray for the Ephesians. He is a caring pastor, and he knows that there is nothing that will give security and stability to these believers more than the conviction and sense that God is their Father. Jesus impressed this foundational but often neglected truth on His disciples. In Matthew 6 He speaks again and again of "your Father" (vv. 1, 4, 6, 8, 15, 18) and of "your heavenly Father" (vv. 14, 26, 32). Jesus wants His disciples to understand that their fundamental relationship with God is familial. And because the heavenly Father is the best of all fathers, He is always committed to doing what is good and best for His children.

The assurance that God is a Father to His believing people who loves them with an everlasting love is a truth the whole Bible labors to burn into God's people's hearts and minds. In his High Priestly Prayer in John 17, Jesus again and again tells His disciples that His Father is their Father. He assures them that "the Father Himself loves you" (John 16:27). John Owen, the English Puritan pastor-theologian, well understood how slow God's people are to take to heart the love of the heavenly Father: "How few of the saints are experimentally acquainted with this privilege of holding immediate communion with the Father in love! With what anxious, doubtful thoughts do they look upon him! What fears, what questionings are there, of his good-will and kindness! At the best, many think there is no sweetness at all in him towards us, but what is purchased at the high price of the blood of Jesus."[1] Owen never wearies of impressing on his readers that the Father's love "ought to be looked on as the fountain from whence all other sweetnesses flow."[2] It is to such a Father that Paul prays.

Paul Bows His Knees

Jews normally stood to pray, but as a sign of exceptional earnestness they would kneel. In the garden of Gethsemane, Jesus "fell on His face, and prayed" (Matt. 26:39). In his posture (v. 14), Paul is acknowledging the greatness and glory of his heavenly Father. He is doing what one day all "of those in heaven, and of those on earth, and of those under the earth" will do (Phil. 2:10, echoing Isa. 45:23). While there is no more intrinsic excellence in one prayerful posture than another, our bodies are not incidental to the life of faith. We are to present our bodies as living sacrifices to God (Rom. 12:1). It matters what you and I do with our bodies, because the life of faith is concrete and physical (Rom. 6:19). How we use and dress our bodies should reflect that we are not our own and that we are the bondservants of the living God (1 Cor. 6:19–20).

The Riches of God's Glory

Paul is asking that the Father will give of Himself, in Christ, to the Ephesian church, that He will bless the Ephesians with the overflow of His glory (3:16). God's glory is everything that He is, or perhaps a better way to put it is His glory is the outshining of all that He is. This glory has not been hidden from us. Jesus is the revelation of God's glory, and His glory is "full of grace and truth" (John 1:14, 18; 14:8–11). We see the riches of God's glory in Jesus, and we are blessed as God grants us "the riches of His glory" (v. 16). It is never

1. Owen, *Works*, 2:32.
2. Owen, *Works*, 2:22.

right to dislocate God's blessings from God Himself. When He blesses His people, He blesses them with Himself. All God's blessings come to us in Christ and are the overflow of His love for us.

Strengthened with Might

Verses 6–19 are a tightly packed series of explanatory clauses, climaxing in "that you may be filled with all the fullness of God" (v. 19). Paul initially asks that the Father may grant them "to be strengthened with might through His Spirit in the inner man" (v. 16). These Ephesian Christians lived out their faith in a deeply hostile environment. They were no longer to walk as the Gentiles did (4:17). They were to "put on the new man which was created according to God, in true righteousness and holiness" (4:24). They were not to "give place to the devil" (4:27). They were to "put on the whole armor of God" in order "to stand against the wiles of the devil" (6:11). If ever a people needed "might," these believers in Ephesus did. They especially needed to be strengthened with power in their "inner man" (v. 16). Why does Paul add, "through His Spirit"? The multifaceted blessings of the gospel never come to us unmediated. The Holy Spirit is the person in the Godhead through whom all God's blessings come to His people. In God's gracious work of redemption, the Holy Spirit is uniquely the Spirit of Christ. He indwells God's people as the Spirit of the crucified, risen, and ascended Jesus. In John 14:16, Jesus says the Holy Spirit is "another Helper."

The Indwelling Christ

Paul's prayer for power is not an end in itself; it has a particular point or purpose: "that Christ may dwell in your hearts through faith" (v. 17). By God's grace in Christ, the Savior already dwelt in the hearts of these believers. How then can he pray that Christ will dwell in their hearts through faith? The following phrase explains: "that you, being rooted and grounded in love" (v. 17). Paul longed to see Christ dwelling more rootedly, more securely, in these Ephesians. Charles Hodge wrote, "The indwelling of Christ is a thing of degrees."[3] Christ can dwell in us and yet dwell more fully in us. This is highlighted by the word "dwell." In New Testament Greek there are two words for "dwell," παροικέω and κατοικέω. The former is weaker and means "to inhabit." The latter means "to settle down and make a permanent abode." It is this word, κατοικέω, that Paul uses here. He is praying that Christ will settle down and be at home in the hearts of His people. Before my wife and I married, she lived in a one-room temporary apartment called a "bed-sit" in the United Kingdom. But when we married, we set up home and settled down to dwell together for the rest of our lives.

Through Faith

Once again, in verse 17, Paul highlights the pivotal centrality of faith in the believing life. It is "through faith" that Christ will "dwell," or settle down, in our hearts. His ever-deepening indwelling will not just happen. It will not come about by any so-called crisis experience. As we rest the weight of all that we are, moment by moment, on the grace and sufficiency of Christ, He increasingly takes root within our lives. Faith in Christ (He is always the true object of faith) is the operative spiritual reality in the believer's life. Without faith we cannot please God (Heb. 11:6) nor experience the rich blessings in Christ that can be "dug up" only by faith.

Rooted and Grounded in Love

It is not easy to follow the flow of Paul's argument. The thought seems to be, "When God grants you to be strengthened with power through His Spirit in your inner being, so that Christ dwells in your hearts through faith, then, as a result, you will be rooted and grounded in love." As Christ, who is Himself love, takes root within our hearts, so our lives, by faith, take ever-deepening root in Him. God is love (1 John 4:8, 16). We can only truly love God and one another as we are rooted and grounded in God's love in Christ. Paul

---

3. Charles Hodge, *A Commentary on Paul's Letter to the Ephesians* (New York, 1860), 186.

uses an agricultural metaphor, "rooted," and an architectural metaphor, "grounded," to stress the importance of the lives of the believer and the church being securely established in love (v. 17).

Paul's words pose a searching question: Do we sufficiently take to heart the New Testament's insistence that the presence of love most evidences the reality of our Christian profession (John 13:34–35; 1 John 3:14, 16–18; 4:20–21)? The absence of love and its practice, of self-denying service to God and His people, is a sure indication that we yet remain in darkness and do not have the life of God within us (1 John 4:12, 16). If we are strangers to love, we must be strangers to the God who is love. The principal evidence that Christ truly is dwelling in our hearts by His Spirit is the presence and overflow of love in our lives, first to God and then to His people. The New Testament insists that heart heresy is as serious as head heresy. Love for God and love for one another are among the indelible marks of an authentic Christian church. But when was a professing Christian last disciplined in a church for lovelessness?

Comprehending Christ's Love

Paul's prayer comes to its climax in verse 19. Paul desires that the Ephesian church know experientially "the love of Christ which passes knowledge." He first prays that the church "may be able to comprehend with all the saints what is the width and length and depth and height" of Christ's love (v. 18). Here is a four-dimensional love that is truly out of this world. It is broad enough to embrace the world (John 3:16). It is long enough to last for eternity. It is high enough to lift us to heaven. It is deep enough to reach the most degraded of sinners. Paul wants the church to "comprehend" ($\kappa\alpha\tau\alpha\lambda\alpha\mu\beta\acute{\alpha}\nu\omega$) this love. The word essentially means "to seize or to overtake." The thought is that we so apply our renewed minds and love-rooted hearts to the immensities of God's love in Christ that we pursue it until we overtake it and make it our own. But we will only ever do this "with all the saints." The life of faith is at heart a corporate or communal life. We were never meant to live the Christian life in atomized isolation. Christians are members together of Christ's body (1 Cor. 12:12–27). We are living stones, "built together for a dwelling place of God in the Spirit" (Eph. 2:22). This is one vital reason why all Christians should prize the local congregation of Christ and commit themselves to its life, worship, and service. We need one another. When one member suffers, all suffer; when one member rejoices, all rejoice (1 Cor. 12:26). Too often Christians see the church and its fellowship like a watering hole, a place to be spiritually replenished, not as a family to love and cherish and belong to. If we are members together of the body of Christ, then our growth in Christ is dependent on us belonging with great commitment to the life of the body. Without one another we will spiritually die. "With all the saints" is the default of the life of faith. Growth in grace, in understanding, and in love is impossible without it.

Knowing Christ's Love

There is a vast difference between knowing the truth and knowing the power of the truth. Paul wants the Ephesians to "know," personally, experientially, "the love of Christ which passes knowledge" (3:19). The love of God in Christ is not merely a truth Christians believe and confess; it is a truth that we are to experience. For example, there is a world of difference in believing that marriage is a good thing and being married. The love of Christ is most and best seen in His giving Himself as the Father's obedient Servant-Son on Calvary's cross. John writes, "In this is love, not that we loved God, but that He loved us and sent His Son to be the propitiation for our sins" (1 John 4:10). This is why Paul says that Christ's love "passes knowledge." No matter how long and hard and deep you think about and meditate on Christ's love, you will never begin to plumb its length and breadth and height and depth. At the end of his exposition of God's saving love in Christ in the gospel, Paul has to exclaim, "Oh, the depth of the riches both of the wisdom and knowledge of God! How unsearchable are His judgments and His ways past finding out!" (Rom. 11:33). Who can think—far less speak—adequately about the love that brought the Son of God from the glory of His Father to the cursed death of a cross? There is a point at which all our ponderings must cease and adoring wonder must take over.

The Fullness of God

Here Paul reaches both the conclusion of his prayer and its climax: "that you may be filled with all the fullness of God" (v. 19). Filled with all the fullness of God! What can Paul possibly mean? The New Testament tells us again and again that God by His Spirit dwells in the lives of His people (2 Cor. 6:16; Eph. 2:22; Col. 1:27). Jesus encouraged His disciples, "If anyone loves Me, he will keep My word; and My Father will love him, and We will come to him and make Our home with him" (John 14:23). And yet here is Paul praying that the Ephesian believers will be "filled with all the fullness of God." It is best to understand these words in light of verse 3:19a. God indwelling His people is not a static reality. He indwells us so that He might increasingly fill us. The more we know—that is, experience the love of Christ, love that surpasses knowledge—the more we will be filled with all the fullness of God.

Since God is love (1 John 4:8, 16), the fullness of His presence in us will be seen in the growing presence and practice of love in our lives. The life of faith is organic, not static. Every Christian is called to attain "to the measure of the stature of the fullness of Christ" (Eph. 4:13). We are to "grow up in all things into Him who is the head—Christ" (Eph. 4:15). The Christian life is to be an ever-increasing experience and practice of the love of God. The "love of God [that] has been poured out in our hearts by the Holy Spirit" (Rom. 5:5) is not for our private and personal pleasure alone. God fills us with His fullness so that we might "shine as lights in the world" (Phil. 2:15) and be love-fueled ambassadors of the Lord Jesus Christ.

Ineffable Language

The language God's Word uses to describe the state and privilege of a Christian is staggering. What God has done for His people in Christ and is continuing to do through the Savior's high priestly ministry (Heb. 7:25) is ultimately beyond all human telling. The gospel cannot fully, or even fitly, be explained in all its divine grandeur and glory. That was Paul's conclusion as he reflected on the grace of God in the gospel in another of his soaring doxologies, Romans 11:33–36. He is lost for words and out of his depth. He has said much, but his conclusion is, "Oh, the depth" (Rom. 11:33)! All our expositions of the gospel of Christ should leave us and our hearers thinking, "Oh, the depth!"

13

Soaring Doxology

EPHESIANS 3:20–21

Now to Him who is able to do exceedingly abundantly above all that we ask or think, according to the power that works in us, to Him be glory in the church by Christ Jesus to all generations, forever and ever. Amen.

Martyn Lloyd-Jones said, "Our greatest trouble in the Christian life is our failure to realize that God is not man." Nearly five hundred years ago, Martin Luther said to Erasmus, the great humanist and Greek scholar who resisted joining the ranks of the Reformation, "Your God is too small." In Ephesians 3:20–21, Paul highlights in stunning language the immeasurable greatness of God. The verses are really a doxology, an outburst of praise. Paul has been expounding the gospel of the "exceeding riches of [God's] grace" (Eph. 2:7) and praying that the Ephesians would be "filled with all the fullness of God" (Eph. 3:19). As he does so, his heart and mind overflow with praise to God. Doxology is the first resting place of true theology. Where doxology is absent, true theology can hardly be present. Before we contend for the gospel of grace, we must first praise and bless God for the gospel of grace. One of the tests of the genuineness of any profession is that the Christian joyfully praises God. We should regularly ask ourselves, does the gospel of Christ continue to move my heart and lips to praise?

Paul's prayer in 3:16–18 is magnificently expansive. The climax in verse 19 all but defies exposition: "that you may be filled with all the fullness of God." Is it possible such a prayer could be answered and not just be a pious hope? Absolutely—"Now to Him who is able," Paul continues in verse 20. John Newton captures the heart of Paul's prayer in one of his well-known hymns:

> Thou art coming to a King,
> Large petitions with thee bring;
> For his grace and power are such,
> None can ever ask too much.[1]

Paul heaps superlative on superlative to impress on us that God is able to answer any prayer that His people bring to Him. There are a number of ascending stages in Paul's doxology, each stage expanding on the one before.

God Is Able to Do What We Ask

God is the living God who is neither inactive nor unconcerned. Elijah's taunting of the prophets of Baal on Mount Carmel focused on the utter inability of their gods to answer prayer (1 Kings 18:27–39). In dramatic contrast, the "LORD God of Abraham, Isaac, and Israel" was the God who heard and responded in power to the prayer of His servant (v. 37). God's ability to answer the prayers of His children is not limited by anything or anyone. His power is limitless. There is nothing He cannot do. He spoke the cosmos into being. He deluged the world in the days of Noah. He opened up the Red Sea to rescue His people from the Egyptians. God manifested his "mighty power" supremely when he raised Christ from the dead and "seated Him at His right hand in the heavenly places" (Eph. 1:19–20). The whole Bible is punctuated with demonstrations of God's power to subdue nature, overwhelm nations, help His trusting children, and manifest His might. It is not surprising that Moses sang,

> Who is like You, O LORD, among the gods?
> Who is like You, glorious in holiness,
> Fearful in praises, doing wonders? (Ex. 15:11)

---

1. John Newton, "Come, My Soul, Thy Suit Prepare," in the public domain.

God Is Able to Do All We Ask

There is nothing God cannot do for His people. He hears and is able to do all we ask, nothing excepted. Because He is the living God and because His power is limitless, His ability to answer our every cry is unquestioned.

God Is Able to Do More Than All We Ask

The God and Father of our Lord Jesus Christ delights to answer His children's prayers above and beyond all their asking. Jesus taught this truth to His disciples in the Sermon on the Mount: "If you then, being evil, know how to give good gifts to your children, how much more will your Father who is in heaven give good things to those who ask Him!" (Matt. 7:11). Paul is magnifying the grace and goodness of God, but he is also seeking to minister that grace and goodness to encourage the hearts of God's children.

God is able to do abundantly above all that we ask or think. There are some things we dare to think but dare not speak. But the apostle wants us to know that God is able to answer even our most extravagant prayers. He is not limited in any way. The problem is that we ask for little because we have such small views of who our God is. Our faith is cramped by our failure to take to heart all that the Lord reveals of Himself in His Word. The church's great needs in our day are a re-centering of its life in the majestic greatness of God and a reawakened sense of God's power and joy to bless His people.

God Is Able to Do Exceedingly Abundantly Above All That We Ask or Think

Paul takes his language to the edge and beyond. He uses a "super superlative"[2] to highlight the sheer limitlessness of God's ability to answer the prayers of His people. There are no limits or boundaries to what our God can do. Remember, Paul is not writing a textbook on Christian doctrine; he is writing as a concerned pastor. The pastoral implications of this truth are immense for individual believers

---

2. ὑπερεκπερισσοῦ.

and for the church in general. Because God is such a God, we need never lose heart. There is no one beyond His power to save; there is no enemy He cannot vanquish; no temptation He cannot help us to overcome; no indwelling, troublesome sin we cannot put to death with His enabling help (Rom. 8:13). In Psalm 81:10 God commanded His people, "Open your mouth wide, and I will fill it." It was a staggering promise of unparalleled blessing if only His people would open wide their mouths and allow Him to fill them with His covenant love. The Lord says, "Oh, that My people would listen to Me" (Ps. 81:13). Unbelief hindered the Lord from blessing His people. One of the saddest and most challenging verses in the Bible is Matthew 13:58: "Now [Jesus] did not do many mighty works there because of their unbelief." God is sovereign in all He is and does. But it has pleased Him to link His saving and sanctifying blessings to the faith of His people.

If ever the church needed to be reacquainted with the truth of God's limitless power and limitless commitment of love to His people, it is today. We do not have because we do not ask (James 4:2). And when we do ask, are we not guilty of asking timidly?

Power in Us

Paul wants the Ephesians to be in no doubt about God's power to respond to any and every need and further tells them that this limitless power "works in us" (v. 20). It is not an alien power. This God of limitless power dwells within His church (Eph. 2:22), and His power in Christ is "toward" or "in" us who believe (Eph. 1:19). The power that raised Christ from the dead and exalted him over all things (Eph. 1:20–22) and that transforms children of God's wrath into His adopted sons through Jesus Christ—this Christ-exalting, sin- and Satan-conquering power—"works in us." Every Christian is a walking testimony to divine omnipotence. Perhaps our backwardness in prayer is because our minds and hearts are not as overwhelmed and captivated by God's greatness and goodness as they might be. When Peter had his eyes fixed on Jesus, he walked on water, but when he took his eyes off Jesus and became aware of the wind, he was afraid and began to sink. Jesus reached out to Peter and said, "O you of little faith, why did you doubt?" (Matt. 14:29–31). Faith is nourished and deepened only when it fixes its gaze on the grace and power of God.

As the church today finds itself hard pressed on every side, it needs to sink into the limitless power and grace of its Savior, who promised that He would build His church, and the powers of hell would never prevail against it (Matt. 16:18).

To Him Be Glory

How else could Paul conclude his doxology than by extolling God: "to Him be glory in the church by Christ Jesus to all generations, forever and ever. Amen" (v. 21). The church exists for God's glory in Christ Jesus. "Glory" is one of those often-used and not always well-understood biblical words. There is no one synonym for glory. To give God glory is to give Him the praise, honor, worship, and service that alone belong to Him as God. God—Father, Son, and Holy Spirit—is to be the supreme focus of the church's attention when it gathers for worship and when it engages in its mission of service to the world. We need to be reminded afresh that our highest joy is tied to His glory. It is when God is most glorified that His people are most satisfied. The quest by many professing Christians for satisfaction and joy is often misdirected. Satisfaction and joy are the inevitable overflow of lives that give glory to God alone. This is why Jesus said, "Seek first the kingdom of God and His righteousness, and all these things shall be added to you" (Matt. 6:33).

God-Glorifying Worship

If God's glory in Christ was the goal of our worship services, services would be transformed. Our first concern would be, Will this song, this prayer, this sermon, or this activity bring glory to God in Christ? The concern for seeker sensitivity in worship can be laudable. The church should always aim to receive seekers warmly and openheartedly when they come to a worship service. But the greatest good we can ever do seekers is to center our worship on God, extolling and declaring His greatness, grace, and love in Christ. The gospel of God's grace in Christ manifests its presence "in the church" (v. 21) in God-glorifying worship.

Worship is the response of redeemed sinners to the sovereign electing kindness and mercy that delivered them from the domain of darkness and brought them into the kingdom of God's beloved Son (Col. 1:13). Within the Reformed tradition, there has been a right and necessary emphasis upon the regulative principle. Worship, indeed the entire Christian life, is to be shaped by God's revealed Word alone, in precept and principle, and not by human fancies. There is the danger, however, that we so stress the elements of biblical worship that we fail to stress with no less vigor the essence of biblical worship (cf. Mark 7:6). God looks on the heart. The worship God seeks from us is worship "in spirit and truth" (John 4:24). This verse is probably one of John's double entendres. He is thinking about worship that is in spirit and truth, heart worship shaped by God's revealed Word. But he is also thinking about worship that is in "Spirit and Truth," that is animated by the Spirit and in Christ. The glory the church gives to God is "by Christ Jesus to all generations, forever and ever. Amen" (v. 21). God's glory has been revealed to us in Christ (John 1:14, 18).

It is increasingly common today to hear people say that when Christians gather together on the Lord's Day, their purpose is not to worship but to edify. The argument goes like this: in the new covenant, worship is all of life, not what we do on one specific day of the week. It is absolutely true that worship is not what the Christian does only on Sundays or on other specified occasions. Worship is all of life; it is the offering up in worshipful devotion of all that we are to the God who has, in Christ, saved us and made us His own sons and daughters (Rom. 12:1). But—and it is a huge but—this in no way means that when Christians gather on the Lord's Day that they do not gather to worship. Christian worship has a weekly, concentrated focus. On the Lord's Day, the Christian Sabbath, the church gathers to make melody "to the Lord," giving thanks to God the Father for everything (Eph. 5:19–20). It is striking that it was as the church in Antioch was worshiping the Lord that Paul and Barnabas were set apart for the work to which the Lord had called them (Acts 13:2). Worshiping the triune God, the God of our salvation, is the church's highest and holiest privilege in this life and in the life to come.[3]

3. See Revelation 4–5, where we are shown the present activity of God's redeemed and glorified people.

14

The Unity of the Spirit

EPHESIANS 4:1–6

I, therefore, the prisoner of the Lord, beseech you to walk worthy of the calling with which you were called, with all lowliness and gentleness, with longsuffering, bearing with one another in love, endeavoring to keep the unity of the Spirit in the bond of peace. There is one body and one Spirit, just as you were called in one hope of your calling; one Lord, one faith, one baptism; one God and Father of all, who is above all, and through all, and in you all.

Many "how to" books are published for Christians today. Christians rightly want to know how to honor God with their lives in a fallen world. Many times, however, these "how to" books on the Christian life fail to appreciate that how we live the Christian life flows out of how we think about Jesus Christ and the great salvation He has won by His life, death, and resurrection. This is why Paul spends the first three chapters of his letter introducing us to the width, length, depth, and height (Eph. 3:18) of the gospel of God's grace in Christ before he details the practical features of the God-pleasing life.

In the broadest terms, chapter 4 begins the practical section of Paul's letter. Although it is somewhat artificial to divide the letter into doctrinal (Eph. 1:1–3:21) and practical or applicatory (4:1–6:24) sections, the opening words of chapter 4, "I, therefore," signal Paul's intention to draw practical implications from the rich theology he has been expounding, though he punctuates his practical applications and exhortations with rich theology, just as he punctuates his theology of grace with inevitable applications and exhortations. It was said of Jonathan Edwards that his theology was all application and his application was all theology; he learned that from the apostle Paul. Paul's pastoral method, rooting exhortations to holiness of life in the gospel of God's grace in Christ, defines the shape and style of the Christian life. Application that is not rooted in the gospel of God's grace is inevitably metallic and clinical, not Christ-magnifying and compelling.

A Prisoner of the Lord

Paul describes himself as "the prisoner of the Lord" (v. 1). He is in prison, probably in Rome, "an ambassador in chains" (Eph. 6:20). Paul refused, however, to be intimidated or depressed by his circumstances. He was persuaded that "all things work together for good to those who love God, to those who are the called according to His purpose" (Rom. 8:28; see also Phil. 1:12–14). He may be in prison, but he is still Christ's ambassador, His loyal and faithful emissary. It is possible that in describing himself as the prisoner of the Lord, Paul is adding moral authority to his apostolic authority. Who are the people you are most likely to listen to when they urge you to a certain course of action? Surely those who are exemplifying what they are urging you to do. Living worthy of the gospel had cost Paul great personal suffering. And yet he is undaunted. Godly example gives spiritual weight and credibility to the words you speak.

Walking Worthily

Although he is in prison, Paul's great concern is not for himself but for the Ephesian church. Only at the end of the letter does Paul ask the Ephesians to pray for him, and even then his request is that he might declare the gospel boldly (6:19–20). Here he urges the church to "walk worthy of the calling" with which God had called them (v. 1). In Christ, through the gospel, God had called these believers to a high and holy calling (Eph. 1:18). They had been called, sovereignly and effectually, into the fellowship of God's Son (1 Cor. 1:9). That initial, regenerative calling initiated them into a lifestyle in which they were to reflect in their congregational and personal lives the "exceeding riches" of God's grace (Eph. 2:7). They were the children of God (Rom. 8:21), called to reflect in the manner of their life together as Christ's church the family likeness. The Christian life is a calling. The gospel of God's grace in Christ not only changes our status before God but also transforms our state. We become new creations in Christ (2 Cor. 5:17), and the life of the new creation is shaped and styled by loving unity, the essential mark of the Holy Trinity.

Foundational Spiritual Unity

The "unity of the Spirit" (v. 3) is the unity that the Holy Spirit creates and inhabits. Paul is not thinking here about organizational unity, far less denominational or broader ecumenical unity. He is thinking about the foundational spiritual unity that unites all true believers in Christ (1 Cor. 12:12–13). He calls this the "unity of the Spirit" because men and women do not and cannot create it. By the grace of the new birth from above that only God the Holy Spirit can effect (John 3:3–8), God enables us to repent and believe the gospel and become members of the one body of Christ, His church. The supernatural nature of true Christian unity must be at the heart of all God-honoring ecumenical endeavors. The church is called to manifest its unity to a watching world. The Lord Jesus Christ prayed for this (John 17:20–26). Pursuing visible, public unity is not a luxury Christians can ignore; to do so is to treat the Lord's High Priestly Prayer as unrealistic or even undesirable. But God-honoring ecumenism is absolutely rooted in this "unity of the Spirit." Christian unity is a Spirit-wrought fact. The new birth leading to a personal embrace of Jesus Christ as Savior and Lord is the nonnegotiable basis of Christian unity. Merely to unite around the great ecumenical creeds is to repeat the tragedy of God's old covenant people who, said Jesus, honored Him with their lips while their hearts were far from Him (Mark 7:6, quoting Isa. 29:13). True Christian unity is animated by the pulsebeat of the Holy Spirit's life-renewing, life-transforming presence and power.

Keeping the Unity of the Spirit

This unity cannot be manufactured, but it must be maintained and not neglected. Christian unity is a spiritual given. All Christians everywhere are one in Christ. Our unity is rooted in the Spirit, who is Himself our bond of union with Christ. This unity can no more be created than it can be destroyed. If every Christian is indissolubly united to Christ, then our foundational unity cannot be harmed. This is the Bible's starting point for thinking about the church (vv. 4–6). Sadly, however, this unity of the Spirit can be fractured, marred, and even defaced by sin. Paul told the church in Rome that ungodly living by professing believers can cause the name of God to be blasphemed among the Gentiles (Rom. 2:24) and render the church's witness to the world incredible. Paul uses strong language to impress on the Ephesians his concern that they "walk worthy" of their calling in Christ, a walk that will manifest itself in maintaining "the unity of the Spirit in the bond of peace" (v. 3). He beseeches them and calls them to endeavor[1] (v. 3) to pursue this "walk" or lifestyle (vv. 1, 3). Maintaining the church's unity is to be pursued eagerly. This eagerness will depend in large measure on how much we prize the church's unity and, more significantly, how much we prize the church's Lord and Savior.

The worthy life that Paul is urging his readers to pursue is to reflect their calling as men and women who have been called, through the gospel, into the fellowship of God's Son (1 Cor. 1:9). One vital, foundational aspect of this gospel-worthy life is cultivating an eagerness to "keep the unity of the Spirit in the bond of peace" (v. 3). This unity is to be a public reflection of the unity of the Godhead (John 17:20–26). Paul is not urging the Ephesians to create the unity of the Spirit but to keep it. God in Christ, by the ministry of the Spirit, has created this unity. But it is the church's responsibility to keep—that is, give public expression to—this

---

1. It is difficult to translate the Greek verb simply (σπουδάζοντες, a plural participle). It has the root idea of hastening eagerly, of giving yourself determinedly in pursuing some goal.

Spirit-created gospel unity. The language Paul uses tells us that this maintenance will not just happen. It requires effort. Our Reformed forebearers greatly prized the church's unity. John Calvin famously wrote that he would cross ten seas if only he could help heal Christ's bleeding body.[2]

Lowliness, Gentleness, Longsuffering

Paul proceeds to tell us how eagerness for the church's unity will evidence itself in our lives. Maintaining the unity of the Spirit amid the stresses and strains of indwelling sin, the allurements of the world, and the wiles of the devil (2 Cor. 2:11) requires that we live "with all lowliness and gentleness, with longsuffering, bearing with one another in love" (v. 2).

If the unity of the Spirit is to be maintained, it will only be, first, "with all lowliness." *Lowliness* (or humility) is a primary Christian grace. When Augustine, the great early church father, was asked what the chief Christian graces were, he replied, "*Humilitas, humilitas, humilitas.*" Jesus drew personal attention to this grace in His own life (Matt. 11:29). The humble are those who do not seek their own good but selflessly seek the good of others. The humble are not self-promoting or self-advertising (Isa. 42:2). The humble may be bold, courageous, and strong-minded, but they are always looking beyond themselves, esteeming other believers as better than themselves (Phil. 2:3) and never insisting on their own way (1 Cor. 13:5). The disunity that marks so much of evangelical Christianity has its roots in pride and selfishness, a refusal to practice the generosity of God toward fellow blood-bought believers. Humility does not mean ignoring differences, and certainly not turning a blind eye to error. It does mean treating fellow believers as the brothers and sisters they are and loving them and respecting the different gospel traditions they come from. This can sound naive, but it is the naiveté of the gospel. But neither does humility mean naively accepting everyone who professes the gospel of Christ. Jesus said that by their

---

2. Calvin, *Tracts and Letters*, 5:347–48.

fruits we would know false teachers, however loudly they proclaim their orthodoxy (Matt. 7:15–20). Where "gospel" teaching produces a greater concern for miracles than for holiness, a greater desire for wealth than for conformity to Christ, a greater appetite for celebrity than service, the gospel of Christ has been completely lost.

A second necessary ingredient of gospel unity is *gentleness.* Sadly, gentleness has not often been readily associated with an evangelical, Reformed Christian profession. And yet our Lord Jesus also personally drew attention to the presence of this grace in His own life (Matt. 11:28). In classical Greek, this word[3] was used to describe strength under control, sometimes of a horse under the harness. It has nothing to do with weakness—indeed, the opposite. The gentle are the strong who have found in union with Christ the grace of self-control (it is interesting that in Galatians 5:23, Paul juxtaposes gentleness and self-control within the fruit of the Spirit). If the unity of the Spirit is to be maintained, gentleness is greatly needed. Believers are always tempted to assert themselves and not listen generously and humbly to the views of others. The gentle are strong in their convictions concerning the truths of the gospel but hold those strong convictions within hearts that love the saints. Paul counsels Timothy to correct his opponents with gentleness, in the hope that God may grant them repentance leading to a knowledge of the truth (2 Tim. 2:25). The first Servant Song (Isa. 42:2–3) pictures God's Messiah Savior dealing gently and forbearingly with the fragile and weak among God's flock. Earlier, in Isaiah 40:11, the prophet tells us that the sovereign Lord

> will feed His flock like a shepherd;
> He will gather the lambs with His arm,
> And carry them in His bosom,
> And gently lead those who are with young.

This is a stunning picture of the gentle grace that marks all God's dealings with His children, and even His chastening rebukes are

---

3. πραΰτης.

the tokens of His gracious love (Heb. 12:5–6). Where this grace is present in believers' lives, the unity of the Spirit will be maintained in the bond of peace.

A third necessary quality is *longsuffering*. God's longsuffering (or patience) with His people is legendary. When Moses begged the Lord to show him His glory, the Lord hid His servant in the cleft of the rock and passed before him proclaiming, "The LORD, the LORD God, merciful and gracious, longsuffering, and abounding in goodness and truth" (Ex. 33:18–34:6). "Longsuffering" essentially means, as Paul tells us here, "bearing with one another in love" (v. 2). The root meaning of patience is the idea of being "long-souled."[4] The church is a fellowship of saved but not yet perfected sinners. We all battle with indwelling sin, what the Westminster Confession of Faith 13.2 calls "remnants of corruption." We all are prone to disappoint and even fail one another, sometimes badly. We therefore greatly need the Christlike grace of patience with one another. The explanatory phrase "bearing with one another in love" captures precisely the defining feature of gospel patience. In his exposition of truly Christian love in 1 Corinthians 13, Paul tells us that love is patient and kind, never insists on its own way, and is not irritable. Without this generous grace, it would be impossible to maintain the unity of the Spirit. And patience, like all other Christian graces, is a grace gift. All we have, we have by the kindness and mercy of God (1 Cor. 4:7).

In such gospel soil the church's unity takes root and grows. For Paul, as indeed for the whole Bible, such grace is only the overflow of the grace we have first received from God. Christians are to treat one another with humility, gentleness, and patience because God in Christ has so treated them (Eph. 4:32). A failure to practice these gospel graces puts a huge question mark over our Christian profession. Jesus warned us that if we do not forgive the sins of others

---

4. Sinclair B. Ferguson, *Let's Study Ephesians* (Edinburgh: Banner of Truth Trust, 2005), 100.

against us from our hearts, we can be sure that God will not forgive our sins against Him (Matt. 6:14–15).

Christian unity is not essentially structural; it is radically Spiritual. But the church's Spirit-ual unity is to be visible (John 17:21, 23). God wants the world to see the "unity of the Spirit in the bond of peace." He wants His church to reflect in its life on earth the perfect unity that defines the life of the Holy Trinity. This is our high and holy calling. The church is more than an aggregate of saved sinners. It is the family of God. It is the bride of Christ. It is the one body of Christ. It is the "dwelling place of God" (Eph. 2:22). Public, visible unity is not a luxury Christians can ignore; it is a gospel imperative they are to pursue and spare no effort to maintain. God our Father desires, like all fathers, to see His children living peaceably and harmoniously one with the other. Jesus's words to His disciples should never be far from our thoughts: "By this all will know that you are My disciples, if you have love for one another" (John 13:35).

Sevenfold Unity

Verses 4–6 are among the most significant verses in the New Testament. Seven times Paul uses the word "one": "one body," "one Spirit," "one hope," "one Lord," "one faith," "one baptism," "one God and Father of all." It would be difficult for Paul to accent the vital importance of maintaining the unity of the Spirit more than he does here. There are few things more tragic and distressing than a disunited, fractured family. Such a family becomes an object of pity, perhaps even derision, not a model to emulate and cherish. As this sevenfold oneness highlights, the essential identity of the church as one body arises out of the essential identity of God's oneness. God is Trinity. He is Father, Son, and Holy Spirit, one God in three persons. God Himself is the perfect model of diversity in unity. There is nothing He desires more than to see His blood-bought children reflect in their diversity the unity that is natively theirs because they belong to Him.

One Body

There is "one body" (v. 4). God's church is one. There may be many individual churches and denominations, but there is only one church, the one body of Christ (1 Cor. 12:12–20; Eph. 1:22–23). There can't be more than one church any more than there can be more than one Christ. All who are joined by the Spirit through faith to Christ belong to His body and are kin to everyone else so joined to Christ. What an incentive to maintain the unity of the Spirit and so publicly placard the harmony of Christ's body.

One Spirit

There are many spirits (1 John 4:1–3), but there is only one Holy Spirit, the third person of the Godhead (v. 4). The Spirit brings us to the new birth from above (John 3:3–8), upheld the Lord Jesus Christ during His earthly life and mission (Isa. 11:1–2; 42:1–2), and in His chief new covenant ministry is to glorify the Savior (John 16:14). Because there is only one Spirit, it is His indwelling, binding presence that gives the church its essential oneness. What an incentive to maintain the unity of the Spirit and so help the Spirit bring glory to Christ.

One Hope

The church's essential unity means that it has "one hope" (v. 4; see also Eph. 1:18)—the "hope of the glory of God" (Rom. 5:2). Every Christian is traveling in the same direction, whether we are aware of it or not. Our ultimate destination is the consummation of our Spirit-wrought union with Christ to be forever with the Lord. Is this not a further incentive eagerly to maintain the unity of the Spirit, locking our spiritual arms with our brothers and sisters in Christ as we make our pilgrim way through this world to the nearer presence of our God?

One Lord

The Lord Jesus Christ is one (v. 5). He is the one Lord who reigns over and rules all His believing people. He is not one Lord for the Baptists and another for the Presbyterians. He is the Father's one and only Son, the one Savior of the world, the one way, truth, and life (John 14:6). Everyone who owns Jesus as Lord, who bows before the grace and sovereignty of His saving lordship, not only has an obligation to acknowledge as family all such believers but also to recognize openly that they are family. Jesus sternly rebuked His disciples for trying to stop a man casting out demons "in [His] name" "because he does not follow us" (Mark 9:38–41). They could not see beyond themselves. They were denying that this unknown man truly belonged to Jesus, denying that their Lord was his Lord. They were, in effect, defining Jesus's lordship by their own categories, limiting it to their own little circle. But if there is only "one Lord," then Jesus is Lord of everyone who serves God in His name, whether they belong to us or not. If they are Christ's, then they are family and must be treated as family—the one Lord Jesus Christ insists it be so.

One Faith

There is "one faith" (v. 5) because there is one Lord. The one Lord Jesus Christ, as the Sent One of the Father, is the sole object of saving faith. In the church tradition I belong to and serve in, we promote what is called the Reformed faith. I personally believe that the Reformed faith, as expressed in, for example, the Westminster Confession of Faith, is the purest and most biblical expression of "the faith which was once for all delivered to the saints" (Jude 3). But there is the ever-present danger of thinking that everyone who does not heartily embrace the Reformed faith can hardly be a Christian. Not all Christians are confessional Calvinists. This is simply a fact. The "one faith" Paul is highlighting here is the saving faith that has the Lord Jesus Christ as its foundation, epicenter, and omega point. It is the faith that glories in the cross of Christ alone for salvation (1 Cor. 1:23; 2:2; Gal. 6:14). Where this faith is present, true Christianity is present.

One Baptism
Christian baptism is the sealing sign of cleansing from sin and union with Christ (Matt. 28:19; Rom. 6:1–4). Baptism is into the one name of the Holy Trinity, marking us out as those on whom God has placed His name. Our baptism is intended to mark us out publicly as belonging to God and His church. It does not and cannot effect that belonging, but it is the divinely commanded sign to publicize that we are not our own. It is surely a tragedy that the sign that God commanded to be placed on all who belong to His covenant people should have become such a storm center of controversy within the church. This is not the place to judge the relative merits of covenant baptism and credo-baptism. It is perhaps enough to say that there is "one baptism" (v. 5). If we cannot agree with our fellow blood-bought believers as to who should be baptized, at the very least we should respect the godly, scriptural convictions of those we differ from. If our Christian profession cannot rise above the waters that divide so that we tell the world that despite our differences we are brothers and sisters who love one another and are bound together in the fellowship of Christ, it is deeply flawed.

One God
Paul concludes and climaxes his sevenfold oneness of the church by reminding the Ephesians of the "one God and Father of all, who is above all, and through all, and in you all" (v. 6). The church is not only the body of Christ; it is the family of God (Eph. 2:19). In that divine family there is one Father. Paul could hardly more effectively and dramatically accent the church's essential oneness. The one Father is "above all, and through all, and in you all." How can there be a Jewish church and a Gentile church, a church for blacks and a church for whites, a church for the cultured and a church for the uncultured, a church for the haves and a church for the have-nots? There is one God and Father who is "above all, and through all, and in you all." The theology of the Bible compels us to refuse every attempt to divide the church on the basis of race, culture,

color, education, wealth, or anything else. God is one. The Father is one, not many.

God's church is natively one. And yet Paul is compelled by the Spirit to urge us to "keep the unity of the Spirit in the bond of peace" (v. 3). Indifference to the visible, public unity of the body of Christ is a mark of spiritual immaturity at best and spiritual ignorance at worst. The one Father, the one Lord, and the one Spirit require all Christians to do all they can to promote the church's Spirit-wrought, Christ-bought unity. This will not just happen. It will take the greatest effort, allied to the resolve to be to other believers what God in Christ has been to us.

We cannot avoid the obvious question: What practical steps can we take to promote and strengthen the unity of the Spirit? We first need to be persuaded that the visible, public unity of Christ's church is a gospel imperative. It should weigh heavily with us that as the Lord Jesus Christ faced the unimaginable darkness of Calvary, He prayed that His church would all be one (John 17:21). Second, we need to grasp that public, visible gospel unity has a compelling evangelistic power (John 17:21, 23). Third, we need to be much in the main things. Richard Baxter expresses this point well:

> The work of conversions is the first and great thing we must drive at; after this we must labour with all our might. Alas! the misery of the unconverted is so great, that it calleth loudest to us for compassion.... I confess I am frequently forced to neglect that which should tend to the further increase of knowledge in the godly, because of the lamentable necessity of the unconverted. Who is able to talk of controversies, or of nice un-necessary points, or even truths of a lower degree of necessity, how excellent soever, while he seeth a company of ignorant, carnal, miserable sinners before his eyes, who must be changed or be damned? Methinks I see them entering upon their final woe.[5]

---

5. Richard Baxter, *The Reformed Pastor* (Edinburgh: Banner of Truth Trust, 1974), 95.

Baxter is making an important point. There are doctrines that Christians disagree over and will continue to disagree over until Christ returns. But if we were as persuaded as Baxter was about the solemn fate of the unconverted, would that not help us to focus on those fundamental gospel truths that lie at the heart of a true, evangelical confession of faith? Gospel unity is not an option we can commit to if we choose. It is the express will and purpose of our Savior, the Lord Jesus Christ.

15

Christ's Gifts

EPHESIANS 4:7–11

But to each one of us grace was given according to the measure of Christ's gift. Therefore He says:

> *"When He ascended on high,*
> *He led captivity captive,*
> *And gave gifts to men."*

(Now this, "He ascended"—what does it mean but that He also first descended into the lower parts of the earth? He who descended is also the One who ascended far above all the heavens, that He might fill all things.)

And He Himself gave some to be apostles, some prophets, some evangelists, and some pastors and teachers....

The visible unity of Christ's church weighed heavily with Paul. He could hardly have impressed this burden more tellingly and persuasively on the Ephesians than he did in 4:1–6. The oneness that characterizes the church is native to its constitution and existence; there is "one Lord, one faith, one baptism" (v. 5). But for Paul, unity did not mean uniformity. Just as within the oneness of the Holy Trinity there is a glorious diversity, so within the oneness of the church there is a diversity that is to be appreciated and practiced. This truth leads Paul to highlight the diversity and range of gifts that the risen, ascended Lord has bestowed on His church.

Spiritual Gifts Are Sovereignly Given

The gifts that God has blessed the church with are "grace gifts." They are His gifts to the church. They have not been earned; rather, "to each one of us grace was given" (v. 7). As we have seen, grace is God's undeserved kindness to judgment-deserving sinners. Whatever spiritual gift we possess (and gifts have been given to each one of us) we have because of the good pleasure and kindness of Christ. Paul further underlines the sovereign disposition of spiritual gifts in the phrase "according to the measure of Christ's gift" (v. 7). To envy another Christian's grace gifts is to question the wisdom of Christ. Rather than envy another's gifts, we should seek prayerfully to develop and mature whatever gifts the Lord has been pleased to give to us. Jealousy does not only introduce a devilish attitude into the life of the church fellowship (Was it not jealousy that motivated Satan in his rebellion against God?) but it is a frontal attack on the goodness and wisdom of God, a heart rebellion against His sovereign disposition of spiritual gifts. It is little wonder Paul tells Timothy that "godliness with contentment is great gain" (1 Tim. 6:6). We should rightly admire another's gifts and thank God for His grace in blessing the church with those gifts.

A Mistaken Exegesis?

The mention of Christ giving gifts to His church brought Psalm 68:18 to Paul's mind. There is an initial problem when we compare what Paul writes in 4:8 with Psalm 68:18, which says,

> You have ascended on high,
> You have led captivity captive;
> You have received gifts among men,
> Even from the rebellious,
> That the LORD God might dwell there.

In 4:8, however, as Paul quotes Psalm 68 he writes not that Christ received gifts but that He gave gifts. Much has been made of Paul's supposed misquotation or deliberate mishandling of the psalm. For some this is a clear example of how fallible the Bible is. Others argue that Paul is simply manipulating a text that nearly said what he wanted to say. Was Paul mistaken? Did he treat Scripture to suit his own purpose? A careful reading of the text, however, elucidates Paul's faithful, Spirit-inspired exegesis of the biblical text. In verse 9 Paul draws a logical conclusion from the fact that Christ ascended, and that if He ascended, He must also first have descended. Similarly, in Psalm 68:18, if the ascended Lord received gifts, He did so in order that He might give gifts. This is how Peter understood the relationship between Christ receiving gifts and giving gifts in Acts 2:33: "Therefore being exalted to the right hand of God, and having received from the Father the promise of the Holy Spirit, He poured out this which you now see and hear." Paul is not playing fast and loose with the inspired text of Holy Scripture. He is, under the sovereign overruling of the Holy Spirit, elucidating the compacted meaning of the Scripture.

The Ascended Christ

Christ's ascension is a significant moment in the history of redemption. Too often Christians do not give attention to the New Testament's clear emphasis on the saving significance of Christ's continuing work as our ascended high priest. This emphasis on the finished work of Christ belongs at the heart of the Christian faith. When Jesus cried, "It is finished," He was signaling the completion of His sin-bearing, sin-atoning death on the cross. But the continuing work of Christ as our Great High Priest at the right hand of His Father is no less essential for our salvation. Jesus's continuing work as our unfailing intercessor, protecting us from all our enemies and ministering to us the blessings of His grace, is as integral to the work of salvation as His definitive, once-for-all oblation on Calvary's cross as our sin-bearing substitute. Christ's ascension not only sealed the triumph of His once-for-all work of atonement but signaled the beginning of His present reign as the King-Priest who unfailingly watches over, cares for, and defends His people. For Paul, Christ's ascension necessarily implied His incarnation, His descent "into the lower parts of the earth" (v. 9). Paul could be thinking simply about the fact of Jesus's incarnation, or he could be thinking about the deep humiliation that accompanied His incarnation (Phil. 2:5–8). It was as the once deeply humiliated One that Jesus ascended as the risen and glorious One, "that He might fill all things" (v. 10). Paul has already used this expansive language in Ephesians 1:23. It would miss the point to think of Paul's language in spacial terms. His point is simply, but astonishingly, this: the incarnate, crucified Jesus is now the risen, ascended Lord who has "all authority…in heaven and on earth" (Matt. 28:18). He fills all things—that is, He reigns and rules over all things and, as the cosmically regnant Jesus Christ, gives grace gifts to His church.

Gifts from the Risen Christ

The New Testament mentions spiritual gifts in five clusters (Rom. 12:3–8; 1 Cor. 12:1–11, 28–30; Eph. 4:11; 1 Peter 4:11–12). In all, at least twenty gifts are mentioned, but there is no suggestion that these are the only gifts that the risen, ascended Christ has given to His church. Here Paul highlights five of the gifts Christ gave to enrich, mature, and equip His people for "the work of ministry" (v. 12). A common feature unites these five grace gifts: they are all identified with the ministry of teaching. Christ's principal way of building up His body, the church, is to instruct it in the rich truths of God and the gospel. If "the church…[is the] pillar and ground of the truth" (1 Tim. 3:15), it needs the constant instruction of God's Word to keep it faithful to the truth that God has "once for all delivered to the saints" (Jude 3).

It should be noted that the Lord has not given these gifts to all but to "some" (v. 11). As was noted earlier, we should have no trace of envy of another's gifts, because it is the Lord who distributes His grace gifts to whom He chooses.

Paul mentions apostles first (v. 11), as he does in 1 Corinthians 12:28. Paul has earlier mentioned apostles in 2:20 and 3:5. The word "apostle" means someone who has been sent (ἀπόστολος). In John's gospel Jesus says that He was "sent" by His Father into the world (17:18; 20:21). The writer to the Hebrews describes Jesus as "the Apostle and High Priest of our confession" (3:1). Jesus is the church's prototypical apostle who exemplifies all that it means to be a faithful and a true Sent One of the Father. In a general sense, all Christians are apostles because of our union with Christ and because we have all been sent out by Him to be His witness bearers. The word is also used in a more restricted sense in 2 Corinthians 8:23, where Paul describes the various Christian churches' missionaries, as "messengers of the churches." But here Paul is clearly thinking about himself and the Twelve chosen and sent out by Christ as His authoritative eyewitnesses (in Acts 1:21–26 Matthias replaced Judas, and Paul writes that he was commissioned as "one born out of due time" in 1 Corinthians 15:8). The apostles belong to the church's foundation (Eph. 2:20). As such, the church no longer has apostles to shape its life and witness, except in the sense that they continue to do so through their foundational inscripturated witness. Jesus promised these men that the Holy Spirit would teach them all things and bring to their remembrance all that He had taught them (John 14:26). When Luke describes the new activities of the three thousand converted to Christ through Peter's preaching, he tells us first that they "continued steadfastly in the apostles' doctrine and fellowship" (Acts 2:42). Apostles have a unique, unrepeatable redemptive-historical role and function in the life of the church.

Second, Paul mentions "prophets" (v. 11). He mentioned prophets earlier in 2:20 and 3:5. It is clear that Paul is not thinking about the prophets of the Old Testament epoch but the prophets of God's new covenant revelation (3:5 makes this clear). With Christ's apostles, these prophets and their directly inspired ministry are embedded in the church's foundation (Eph. 2:20). In the Old Testament, prophets were men who received directly from God His inspired and authoritative word and then declared that word to His people. They declared, "Thus says the Lord." Like the apostles, the church no longer has or needs prophets. God's written revelation is complete (2 Tim. 3:16–17). God has spoken His final word in His Son (Heb. 1:1–2). This does not mean that preachers do not preach "prophetically"—that is, relevantly and powerfully, as the Holy

Spirit enables them. It does mean that no preacher, however gifted, is a prophet, someone who speaks new words from God. God has spoken, and preachers are to proclaim the exposition and application of that final and authoritative word.

The third gift the ascended Christ gave to His church is "some evangelists" (v. 11). That only some were given this gift suggests that Paul is not thinking about the calling of every Christian to tell the good news. Who were or are these evangelists? As John Stott has observed, the "noun occurs only three times in the New Testament [here, in Acts 21:8, and in 2 Timothy 4:5]."[1] It has been suggested that this gift, like apostles and prophets, had a foundational, unique role in the life of the church. It is impossible to be dogmatic, however. Timothy was to do "the work of an evangelist," a work that coincided with his calling to shepherd and teach the church in Ephesus (2 Tim. 4:5). It is possible, then, that while every Christian is called to be an evangelist, to share with others the saving good news of Christ (Acts 8:4), the risen Lord has especially gifted some in His church to give themselves, full time as it were, to the "work" of evangelism. We see something similar in 1 Timothy 5:17, where Paul writes of some elders who "labor in the word and doctrine." All elders must be "able to teach" (1 Tim. 3:2), but some elders have been called and set apart to "labor in the word and doctrine." The church today greatly needs Spirit-gifted evangelists, men especially talented to proclaim the good news of Jesus Christ to a lost and dying culture.

Finally in verse 11, Paul mentions the "pastors and teachers." There has been great discussion as to whether Paul is thinking of two categories, or whether there is only one, the pastors who teach. Both the grammar[2] and the New Testament's teaching regarding the ministry of pastors suggest that Paul is thinking about one category. Nowhere in the New Testament do we find men who are set apart to teach but not to pastor. Indeed, one of the essential

---

1. Stott, *God's New Society*, 163.
2. The words τοὺς δὲ (and the) are not used before "teachers."

qualifications of a "bishop" is the giftedness to teach (1 Tim. 3:2). It also seems clear that within the eldership, some men would devote themselves wholly to the ministry of the Word (1 Tim. 5:17). It is principally by the means of teaching the Word that the church's undershepherds feed and pastor God's flock (1 Peter 5:1–4).

The Lord Jesus Christ is the prototypical Shepherd-Teacher. He models what it means to be a shepherd-teacher for the church and for those men especially set apart by the church. In John 10, two striking features of the Lord's ministry are especially highlighted.

First, as the church's Shepherd-Teacher, Jesus knows His sheep (v. 14). Like the shepherd of the sheep in the analogy, Jesus knows his sheep "by name" (v. 3). The church's shepherd-teachers are never to minister the Word in isolation from personal, intimate contact with God's flock. In the church today, pastors, especially in larger churches, can minister like CEOs rather than as men who are personally involved in the lives of those to whom they minister the Word. In this regard, the near demise of pastoral visitation is much to be regretted. Luke tells us that when Paul ministered in Ephesus, he taught both in public and from "house to house" (Acts 20:20). Richard Baxter attributed much of the success of his ministry in Kidderminster to his diligent pastoral visitation. Reflecting on his lengthy ministry in Kidderminster, Baxter wrote, "I have found by experience, that some ignorant persons, who have been so long unprofitable hearers, have got more knowledge and remorse of conscience in half an hour's close discourse, than they did from ten years' public preaching."[3]

Second, as the church's Chief Shepherd (1 Peter 5:4), the Lord Jesus Christ laid down His life for His sheep (John 10:15). Selfless, sacrificial love was the hallmark of the Shepherd-Teacher's life and ministry. How the church's shepherd-teachers live among God's precious sheep will either powerfully commend their ministry or render their ministry disreputable. Just as husbands are to love their wives as Christ loved the church, selflessly and sacrificially

---

3. Baxter, *Reformed Pastor*, 196.

(Eph. 5:25), so the church's pastors are similarly to lay down their lives if necessary to secure the good of God's flock. Like the apostle Paul, every shepherd-teacher is called to fill up what is lacking in Christ's afflictions for the sake of His body, the church (Col. 1:24).

16

Perfect Manhood

EPHESIANS 4:12–16

...for the equipping of the saints for the work of ministry, for the edifying of the body of Christ, till we all come to the unity of the faith and of the knowledge of the Son of God, to a perfect man, to the measure of the stature of the fullness of Christ; that we should no longer be children, tossed to and fro and carried about with every wind of doctrine, by the trickery of men, in the cunning craftiness of deceitful plotting, but, speaking the truth in love, may grow up in all things into Him who is the head—Christ—from whom the whole body, joined and knit together by what every joint supplies, according to the effective working by which every part does its share, causes growth of the body for the edifying of itself in love.

What do you look for in the ministry you receive in your church? In recent years many evangelical churches have become so seeker sensitive in their approach to worship that the ministry of God's Word has ceased to have the central significance it has had since the recovery of the gospel in the sixteenth-century Reformation. Music and drama have replaced the ministry of the Word in many professedly evangelical churches. It should not surprise us that when the centrality of preaching is eclipsed in the life of a church, it only too easily becomes a prisoner of the ever-changing societal and theological currents that swirl around it. To resist the world's diet of false illusions, the church needs to be rooted and grounded in God's unchanging truth.

The exposition of the Word that signally marks the ministries of apostles, prophets, evangelists, pastors, and teachers has, therefore, a divinely ordained purpose. In verses 12–16 Paul spells out in some detail the risen Lord Jesus's purpose in giving these ministries of the Word to His church. What can hardly be missed is that Christ gives spiritual gifts not for personal enjoyment but for serving one another (1 Peter 4:10).

In summary terms, God's purpose was to bring His church "to a perfect man, to the measure of the stature of the fullness of Christ" (v. 13). Jesus Christ is the perfect man. It is God's purpose to make His church like His Son, filling it with the presence, grace, and glory of His Son. He does this by the indwelling ministry of the Holy Spirit as the word of God dwells richly in us (Col. 3:16). If we follow carefully Paul's unfolding exposition, we can see that this purpose had first a general and then a specific dimension.

Equipping the Saints

The overall purpose of the ministry of the Word in the life of the church is "for the equipping of the saints for the work of ministry, for the edifying of the body of Christ" (v. 12). To use modern analogies, Paul is not comparing the church to a train, where all the passengers sit comfortably and passively until they arrive at their destination, brought there by the giftedness of their spiritual leaders. Rather, he is likening the church to an orchestra, where all the members play their part and contribute to the melodic symphony of service to God. In order for the saints to have such a "work of ministry," they need to be equipped.[1] The verb "equip" is used in Matthew 4:21, where James and John are "mending their nets," repairing them to make them fit for service. The word was used in medicine for repairing broken bones and reconnecting dislocated limbs. Paul is vividly describing the healing, restorative, powerful ministry of God's Word. The ministry of God's Word is never merely to inform, enlighten, and expand our minds. God has given

---

1. The noun καταρτισμός occurs only here in the New Testament. The verb καταρτίζω, which is found more frequently and expresses the general idea of making complete, is used in the sense of repairing (e.g., nets in Matt. 4:21) and of restoring in a spiritual or disciplinary sense (Gal. 6:1).

the ministry of His Word to His church in order to transform it, to heal it of its various spiritual sicknesses, make it whole, and restore it to a fit working order, thereby enabling it to exercise a "work of ministry" (v. 12) that will build up the body of Christ.

The "work of ministry" that God's Word equips us for is to be carried out by men and women whose lives are being made whole and restored to the image of God that sin had defaced. The gospel of God's grace in Christ will come credibly to a fallen world only when it is delivered by those whose lives are mastered and transformed by the grace of God's truth. This is something our Lord Jesus prayed for: "Sanctify them by Your truth. Your word is truth" (John 17:17). The transformation into the likeness of Christ that God has predestined for all His children (Rom. 8:29) is not achieved passively or automatically. It is achieved as God's Word impacts our lives and shapes and styles us into the likeness of Christ, who was Himself shaped and styled by the Word of God. The building up— that is, the maturing, strengthening, establishing, and beautifying of the body of Christ—is effected as the saints engage as gospel-transformed men and women in the work of ministry.

In verses 13–16, Paul unpacks in a number of specifics what the building up of the body of Christ is to look like. A spiritually healthy church will first evidence in its life "the unity of the faith" (v. 13). How many churches give their best energies to cultivating the unity of the faith? Sadly, the default in many Christian churches is the saving and sanctifying of the individual, not the God-honoring unity of the faith that gives luster and power to the church's gospel witness. These two are, of course, not mutually exclusive. The church, however, is not to exist in the world as an aggregate of saved sinners but as the body of Christ, the family of God. As the shadow of the cross began to pierce the human soul of our Lord Jesus, He prayed that His church would exhibit oneness, "that the world may know that You [Father] have sent Me, and have loved them as You have loved Me" (John 17:23). Attaining to the unity of the faith is not an optional extra that Christians and Christian churches can pursue as opportunity and inclination coalesce. While this unity will not be fully—that is, visibly—manifested until Christ returns, the day-by-day ministry of the Word should, and must, have woven through it the revealed will of God that the body of Christ be marked, visibly, by "the unity of the faith." This is not first a matter of organizational unity, though that should never be dismissed. Principally and principially it is a matter of manifesting our unity in Christ, the Head of the church. The faith is one because the triune God on whom the faith rests is one (see 4:1–6).

A second evidence of a spiritually healthy church is a growing "knowledge of the Son of God" (v. 13). The ministry of the Word will have failed calamitously if it is not bearing the priceless fruit of a growing knowledge of Christ in the life of the church. As God's Word is ministered week by week, the exposition of Jesus Christ should be its epicenter and manifest passion. The gospel exposes us to "the love of Christ which passes knowledge" (Eph. 3:19). Throughout eternity the church will be endlessly exploring the immensities and infinities of the knowledge of the Son of God.[2] As God's Word is ministered and as God's people serve one another to the "edifying of the body of Christ" (v. 12), there will be a growing and deepening knowledge of the Savior.

It is surely striking that unity in the faith and knowledge of the Son of God is what the ministry of the Word, equipping the saints for the work of ministry, is intended to produce in the church. How do you measure the present state of your personal faith and the faith of the church you belong to? It is sadly possible to be notionally

---

2. George Herbert's (1593–1633) hymn "King of Glory, King of Peace" wonderfully captures the eternal exploration of Christ's glory that will engage the redeemed in heaven:

> Seven whole days, not one in seven,
> I will praise thee;
> In my heart, though not in heaven,
> I can raise thee.
> Small it is, in this poor sort
> To enroll thee:
> E'en eternity's too short
> To extol thee.

orthodox and yet live disunited from other believers and ignorant of the rich, experiential knowledge of the all-glorious, all-lovely Mediator and Savior, Jesus Christ.

God's Goal for His Church

The Lord Jesus Christ's ultimate purpose in giving spiritual gifts to His church reaches its omega point when "we all [finally] come to the unity of the faith and of the knowledge of the Son of God, to a perfect man, to the measure of the stature of the fullness of Christ" (v. 13). The ministry of the Word in the life of the church is to be its principal ministry "till" (v. 13) we attain to that unity and knowledge. The "till" is a significant marker, calling and challenging us to persist diligently and undistractedly in making the ministry of the Word central and never peripheral in the life of the church. It is because the church has lost confidence in the truth, authority, wisdom, and sufficiency of God's Word that it is a sad shadow of a perfect man. Only the ministry of the Word, in the power of the Spirit, can produce churches of spiritual depth and maturity.

It seems likely that what Paul means by "a perfect man" is explained in the following phrase, "to the measure of the stature of the fullness of Christ." Paul is adept at using language that all but defies explanation (Eph. 1:23). Perhaps he is saying simply this: God's purpose in establishing the ministry of His Word in the life of His church is to make His people like His Son (Rom. 8:29). Jesus is the perfect embodiment of "a perfect man," and God's predestined purpose is to conform each of His children, and all of them together, into the likeness of His Son. In other words, God purposes that the church should reflect the likeness of its Head.

No Longer Children

The "that" introducing verse 14 is a significant grammatical and theological connective. Paul highlights two features of the "perfect man" (v. 13) that the ministry of the Word seeks to produce in the life of the church. Spiritually, a perfect man will evidence himself first in doctrinal stability. As a pastor, Paul is concerned to see God's people established in the faith and not blown about "with every wind of doctrine." He understands that what will best guard the church from being easily impressed immature children and protect her from being "tossed to and fro" is becoming "a perfect man," which is conformity to the likeness of its Head and Savior. Such conformity to Christ includes having the mind of Christ, which detects the presence and influence of error no matter how cunningly and craftily it is disguised. Paul uses vivid language and paints a vivid picture to impress on us how vulnerable immature spiritual believers can be. Paul likens immature, unstable believers to little children tossed about like boats in a stormy sea. They are at the mercy of the waves and the wind, blown this way and then that way with no anchor to keep them safe and secure. False doctrine is sometimes blatant and is easily detected. Often, however, it comes dressed in clothes of "cunning" and "craftiness," aiming to deceive gullible and immature believers. Today this cunning and craftiness is most blatantly seen in the exponents of the so-called prosperity gospel. Gullible men and women are deceived by slick showmen offering a life of comfort, free from the ills and trials of this present life. But the cunning and craftiness can often be less obvious. Scholars with impressive academic credentials can seek to undermine the authority, sufficiency, and absolute truthfulness of God's written Word. They write with erudition, but their aim is to do what the devil has been doing from the beginning, to question and challenge the authority of the Bible. Faced with such cunning, we must do what the Word of God bids us do: test all that we hear and read by the infallible touchstone of the word that cannot be broken (Isa. 8:20; John 10:35).

Following Paul's logic, what will protect the church from being taken in by this cunning and craftiness is a perfect man. A perfect man roots believers deeply in the soil of the gospel and gives them a spiritual sensitivity to unsound doctrine. The Spirit of Christ gives us a relish for Christ and the truth of God's Word. As we allow the word of Christ to dwell richly in our hearts (Col. 3:16), our minds develop a distaste for teaching that is not absolutely shaped and styled by God's infallible Word, however charismatically and passionately presented.

False teaching is deadly and deeply dishonoring to God and the gospel. Paul's vehement blast against the false teaching on justification that had infected the churches of Galatia (Gal. 1:6–9) was considered and deliberate. Not only was Paul concerned that this false teaching was imperiling the eternal good of sinners but it was denying that salvation was wholly of grace, and so was gravely dishonoring God. Heresy is grievously wicked as well as doctrinally aberrant. It is a fact of history that gospel truth—truth that exalts God and humbles sinners—will be opposed in every age. Paul writes here of "the cunning craftiness of deceitful plotting" (v. 14). False teaching often comes clothed in fine words, spoken and written by theologically well-educated men. In the history of the church, error infiltrates its way first into the church's seminaries and then into its pulpits. One striking example of this was the introduction of German higher critical thought into the life of the Free Church of Scotland seminaries in the 1870s and 1880s. In 1843, over 450 ministers seceded from the Church of Scotland to form the Church of Scotland Free. Charles Hodge considered the Free Church the purest church in Christendom. Forty years later it was as theologically liberal as the national church it had left. What had happened? The church had failed to guard the teaching in its seminaries. Often, sadly, it is the desire to be thought credible by the Academy that causes men to abandon "the faith which was once for all delivered to the saints" (Jude 3).

The unchanging gospel of God is to be proclaimed and taught relevantly in every generation. We live in the twenty-first century, not in the sixteenth or seventeenth century. But the content of God's saving revelation does not change, however much it runs counter to the society and culture of the day. Paul writes in Romans 6:17 of believers becoming obedient from the heart to "that form of doctrine" to which they had been delivered. "Form" conveys the idea of a mold, a definite and defined shape that contours the minds and lifestyles of believers. God's truth is not malleable. For Paul the truth of the gospel of God's grace was worth fighting for and, if need be, dying for.

Second, a perfect man will show itself spiritually in a lifestyle that speaks the truth in love (v. 15). In contrast to the cunning, craftiness, and deceit that are native to a fallen world and are hallmarks of false doctrine, Christ's church is to speak the truth in love. The translation "speaking the truth in love" is, literally, "truthing in love."[3] Paul is reminding us first that speaking the truth in love is the overflow of a life lived under the ministry of the Word—a life invaded, captured, and captivated by God's love and truth in Christ. Second, he is impressing on us that truth, not hypocrisy and deceit, is to be a public feature of the church's life in a fallen world. It is difficult to know whether Paul means by truth the "faith which was once for all delivered to the saints" (Jude 3)—the revealed truth of the Christian religion—or the Christian's commitment to speak truly and unambiguously, come what may. Perhaps we need not choose between these two as they belong to the new life and perfect man that is produced by the ministry of the Word in the life of the church. The increasing absence of gospel truth and unvarnished integrity in the visible church (and sadly in professing evangelical churches) is the result of the ministry of the Word being shifted from the center and replaced by the "fads and fashions" of a passing culture.[4]

Third, we can hardly miss the connection between truth and love. Speaking the truth is never to be clinical or arrogant. The truth, whether the doctrine of the gospel or the truth in general, is always to be maintained, defended, and declared in love. God is never content that we merely speak the truth. He is concerned that we do so

---

3. ἀληθεύοντες δὲ ἐν ἀγάπῃ. The force of the present participle contains the related ideas of maintaining, practicing, and living the truth.

4. C. S. Lewis wrote, "Fads and fashions come and go but they mostly go. Our business is to present that which is timeless (the same yesterday, today, and tomorrow) in the particular language of our own age. The bad preacher does exactly the opposite.... The core of his thought is merely contemporary; only the superficies is traditional. But your teaching must be timeless at its heart and wear a modern dress." "Christian Apologetics," in *God in the Dock* (Grand Rapids: Eerdmans, 1998), 91–94.

in a spirit and with motives that commend the gospel of His grace in Christ. Truth and love are never mutually exclusive. They belong together because they are found united in Christ. When truth is distanced from love, it loses its grace and becomes pharisaic, clinical, cold, and hard-edged. When love is distanced from truth, it loses its moral character and becomes supine and little more than an excuse for unfettered indulgence. Paul's counsel to Timothy to "pursue righteousness, faith, love, peace" and to be "gentle to all," correcting his gospel opponents with "humility," applies to every defender of the faith, clerical or lay (2 Tim. 2:22, 24–25).

Growing Up into Christ

"Truthing in love"—maintaining, defending, and living in Christ-like love—has a deeply maturing purpose. In verses 15b–16, Paul further develops his colorful and dramatic picture of the church as the body of Christ. Paul is not out to teach us anatomy but to impress on us further the way the church grows into a perfect man. As the church corporately and believers individually practice, maintain, and speak the truth in love, they will "grow up in all things into Him who is the head—Christ" (v. 15). In 1 Corinthians 8:1, Paul tells the self-inflated Corinthian church that "love edifies." The priority and practice of love in the life of the church is spelled out in searing, self-deflating clarity in 1 Corinthians 13. What is often called a hymn to love is actually a sledgehammer indictment of the pride, selfishness, and thoughtlessness that was disfiguring the life and destroying the gospel witness of the church in godless Corinth. The whole chapter is an escalating proclamation of the priority and superiority of self-denying, Christ-imitating love in the life of the church. Love edifies. This is the principal focus of the apostle as he brings this section of his letter to a conclusion. The "growth of the body" is "for the edifying of itself in love" (4:16b). Love for one another in the body and love to those outside the body reflect "the measure of the stature of the fullness of Christ" (4:13b).

The metaphor inevitably draws us to see it is the connection of the body, the church, with its Head, Jesus Christ, that provides the growth in grace, the perfect man that is to characterize the church's life in a fallen world. Paul's primary emphasis is on the Head, Christ, who "causes growth of the body for the edifying of itself in love." But the spiritual growth and maturity that flow from the Head, Christ, does not happen automatically. Growth into a perfect man happens only with "the effective working by which every part does its share" (4:16). All Christians have a responsibility to do their utmost with the gifts and capacities given to them by the risen Lord to help build up the body of Christ, His beloved church. There are to be no passengers in the church, just as there are no redundant joints and ligaments in the body. Everyone is needed. Everyone has a significant part to play in the church's growing into a perfect man (cf. 1 Cor. 12:12–27).

Throughout this section of his letter, Paul has set before us the church's native unity and its manifest diversity—unity and diversity, unity in diversity, and diversity in unity. It should always challenge and humble us that as our Lord Jesus Christ faced the unimaginable prospect of dying, the just for the unjust to bring us to God, He prayed to His Father "that they [His disciples, the church] may be one just as We are one: I in them, and You in Me; that they may be made perfect in one, and that the world may know that You have sent Me, and have loved them as You have loved Me" (John 17:22–23). Indifference to the church's visible unity in the world is to live in defiance of Jesus Christ. Refusing to give yourself heart and soul to serving in the church, to the end of building it up in love, is to live in defiance of Jesus Christ. The church is one church; let us do all we can to manifest that. The church, Christ's body, is made up of many members (1 Cor. 12:27); let us be the healthy members that enable the body to "grow up in all things into Him who is the head—Christ" (v. 15).

17

New Life in Christ

EPHESIANS 4:17–24

This I say, therefore, and testify in the Lord, that you should no longer walk as the rest of the Gentiles walk, in the futility of their mind, having their understanding darkened, being alienated from the life of God, because of the ignorance that is in them, because of the blindness of their heart; who, being past feeling, have given themselves over to lewdness, to work all uncleanness with greediness.

But you have not so learned Christ, if indeed you have heard Him and have been taught by Him, as the truth is in Jesus: that you put off, concerning your former conduct, the old man which grows corrupt according to the deceitful lusts, and be renewed in the spirit of your mind, and that you put on the new man which was created according to God, in true righteousness and holiness.

Hostility and opposition provide the context of the church's life in this world. This is seen dramatically today where the church in the Middle East finds itself persecuted, often unto death, by the hostility and intolerance of Islam. But the hostility is also increasingly evident in the West, where secular intolerance is seeking to marginalize and even penalize Christians who seek to live out and promote the saving gospel of the Lord Jesus Christ, especially proclaiming Jesus as the one and only way to the Father.

Jesus warned His disciples that because the world hated Him, it would certainly hate them (John 15:18–25). The only way the church of Christ can avoid the world's relentless antagonism is to do what it has tragically often done, seek to accommodate the truth of the gospel to the prevailing thinking and prejudices of the world. How then are gospel-faithful Christians to live in a fallen, hostile world? The answer Paul gives in these verses is the answer the New Testament in its totality gives: "according to God, in true righteousness and holiness" (v. 24). Paul wants the Ephesian believers to understand what it means to be a Christian in a fallen world.

A Christian is a believer in Jesus Christ, who was crucified for our sins and raised for our justification (Rom. 4:25). But the Christian faith that unites us to Christ is not a bare, notional faith. Saving faith is transformative. Believers have been "created in Christ Jesus for good works, which God prepared beforehand that [they] should walk in them" (Eph. 2:10). Later, in Ephesians 5:1–2, Paul will tell the church to be "imitators of God as dear children. And walk in love, as Christ also has loved us and given Himself for us." This is the big picture that is to shape and style the life of faith. But this big picture is filled with specifics. What does it mean in our daily lives to be like God "in true righteousness and holiness" (v. 24)? The Christian life is not nebulous. It involves what we do with our "members" (Rom. 6:12–13, 19). There is concreteness to the believing life. Sanctification is not a theory to commit to; it is a lifestyle to be shaped by.

Godly Renunciation

The opening words of verse 17 highlight the importance Paul attaches to what will follow. He is not content simply to say, "This I say, therefore," but adds "and testify in the Lord." Paul is not in any sense saying that his apostolic authority is not sufficient for the strong injunctions that he is about to press upon the Ephesians. Rather, by adding, "and testify in the Lord," Paul is doubly impressing on his readers the seriousness of what he is about to say to them.

Paul begins his description of the God-pleasing life with an emphatic negative: "This I say, therefore, and testify in the Lord, that you should no longer walk as the rest of the Gentiles walk" (v. 17). The word "walk" is not merely a synonym for "live." Rather, it highlights the deliberate, step-by-step character of our lifestyle choices. The Christian has a distinctive walk—that is, a distinctive, deliberate, thought-through pattern of life (Eph. 5:2, 8, 15). The church in Ephesus was composed mostly of Gentiles (Eph. 2:11–12). But by God's grace in Christ, its members had been saved and reconciled to God, and had become "fellow citizens with the saints and members of the household of God" (2:19). Now, through the gospel, the deepest truth about them is not that they are Gentiles but that they are "a dwelling place of God in the Spirit" (2:22), united to Christ, and members of His body, the church (4:15–16). So Paul appeals to them to live up to their new identity in Christ. Significantly, this would involve first a renunciation of the lifestyle that dominated their culture and that once dominated them (2:3). Paul's description of the prevailing lifestyle of the Gentile world is all embracing.

Futile Mind

The lifestyle of the Gentile world is the result of "the futility of their mind" (v. 17). How you think determines how you behave. What you think inevitably shapes how you live. One of the slogans of our time is, "You are what you eat." The much deeper truth is that you are what you think. When Adam and Eve sinned in the garden of Eden, their first thought was to hide from God (Gen. 3:8). Sin mangled their minds and caused them to think that the good and gracious God was someone to hide from. Their thinking became futile. Paul defines the essential character of this futility in verse 18: "having their understanding darkened." Sin darkens our understanding in every way. God is an enigma to us, and He becomes someone to hide from. God's world is a closed book to us; we don't know why it is there and what it is for. We cannot understand ourselves. We don't know that God has put eternity into our hearts (Eccl. 3:11) and that nothing "under the sun" can satisfy the relentless quest of our hearts for life.

The centrality of the mind in determining how we live is an idea that is found throughout the New Testament. In Romans 12:2, Paul recognizes that the life pleasing and acceptable to God requires believers to be "transformed by the renewing of [their] mind[s]." He strikes the same note in Colossians 3:2: "Set your minds on things above, not on things on the earth." Christians face a lifelong battle for control of their minds. What you think will shape how you live. The psalmist understood this: "Your word I have hidden in my heart, that I might not sin against You" (119:11). God's living Word, filled with truth, is the Christian's great weapon in guarding the mind against the lies and seductions of the world, the flesh, and the devil. A Scripture-saturated mind helps us to see through the wiles of the devil (2 Cor. 2:11; Eph. 6:11) and keeps our minds fixed on God.

Alienated from the Life of God

In verse 18 Paul traces the pathology of the Gentile world's mental futility to its "being alienated from the life of God, because of the ignorance that is in them, because of the blindness of their heart." Paul is highlighting the Gentile world's personal culpability for its spiritual darkness. The Gentiles did not have to be alienated from the life of God. Their ignorance of God and His ways is "because of the blindness of their heart." Ignorance of God is not because of lack of education or opportunity; it is the willful choice of men and women determined never to relinquish their imagined autonomy. Paul told the church in Rome that "what may be known of God is manifest in them" (Rom. 1:19). But rather than embrace what God has revealed of Himself in His creation, "His eternal power and Godhead," they choose to "suppress the truth in unrighteousness" (Rom. 1:20, 18, respectively). Consequently, the Gentile world is "without excuse" (Rom. 1:20).

God's unconditional, unabridged sovereignty in no way excuses sin. We sin not because we are programmed to sin but because we inherit from Adam a fallen nature with a predisposition to sin. We sin because we are sinners. Like Pharaoh, we willfully harden our hearts against God and His word.

Spiraling Ungodliness

The fruit of this "blindness of their heart" is a spiraling ungodliness. The hardness is "past feeling" (v. 19), or callous, and is increasingly impervious to the reproofs of truth and the pricks of conscience. This callousness reveals itself in the resolve to pursue "lewdness" (v. 19), a lifestyle in which the senses indulge themselves to the full without constraint. This lewdness in turn manifests itself in a voracious desire "to work all uncleanness with greediness" (v. 19). Paul is describing the general conduct of human society since the fall. He is making a connection that is throughout the Bible: immorality is the inevitable fruit of ungodliness. The moral free-for-all that is increasingly defining Western society has its roots in the West's resolve to abandon the God of the Bible. But when you turn your back on God and His Word, there are tragic but inevitable consequences.

The hope for the nations of our world does not lie in political renewal, societal regeneration, the overthrow of ISIS, or the imposition of tougher laws for crimes. The world needs to see and to hear from a renewed Christian church, a church freshly invaded by the power, grace, glory, and truth of the gospel. The world is the way it is not because of a lack of education or a failure in social manners but because people harden their hearts against God. The fundamental problem in every society is theological and spiritual. The Bible has a radical diagnosis of the ills that afflict our world. Humanity lives in active, willful rebellion against God. This is why the world's greatest need is the heart- and life-renewing power of the gospel of Christ. The heart of the human problem truly is the problem of the human heart. This is the dark but wholly realistic doctrine of total depravity. This doctrine has been much misunderstood. It simply means that there is "no soundness in it" (Isa. 1:6), that sin's presence in us is wholly pervasive and not episodic. It is this biblical truth that perhaps more than any other deeply offends unbelievers. But sin is not a tumor that can be cut out; it is a deadly disease that can only be remedied if we become "a new creation" (2 Cor. 5:17; see also John 3:3). Jesus told Nicodemus, "the teacher of Israel" (John 3:10), that nothing less than a new birth from above would restore him to God's friendship and fellowship. How radical is that?

Learning Christ

The life of faith in Jesus Christ is lived in mindful contrast to the earthbound, self-pleasing lifestyles that mark this fallen world. In verse 20, Paul characteristically marks this contrast with one of his "buts": "But you have not so learned Christ." The meaning of the phrase "learned Christ" is not immediately clear. Paul could simply but pointedly be reminding the Ephesians that the life of faith is a Christlike life. The gospel has come not merely to change our status before God but to transform our lives "according to God" (v. 24). But perhaps Paul's grammar suggests something more. He doesn't say, "learned *about* Christ" but "learned Christ." We learn Christ when we love Christ and live in all things to please Him. The gospel is absolutely concerned to teach us "about" Christ, but only in order to bring us to know, love, and serve Him.

In verses 21–24, Paul graphically pictures the foundational lineaments of the life that has "learned Christ." But before he spells out these lineaments, Paul adds, "if indeed you have heard Him and have been taught by Him, as the truth is in Jesus" (v. 21). These words reflect the pastoral care Paul had for this church that he had personally labored in for three years (Acts 20:31), teaching them the "whole counsel of God" (Acts 20:27), and doing so "with all humility, with many tears" (Acts 20:19). He wants to know that they have rightly grasped the truth in Jesus. Ministers of the gospel should never thoughtlessly assume that their congregations, however well taught, have grasped what it means to be a Christian and to live as a Christian.

Putting Off and Putting On

What then does it mean to learn Christ? That is, how will learning of Christ show itself in our lives? Paul is not writing a systematic theology, or even a treatise on biblical theology. He is addressing the vital question of how Christians are to live distinctive and Godlike lives in a fallen world (4:24). Possibly using baptismal language (Col. 3:5–17), Paul defines the life that has learned Christ in terms of putting off the "old man" (v. 22) and putting on the "new man"

(v. 24). In essence, Paul is summoning the Ephesians to be what they truly are in Christ. In Christ they had become new creations, united to Jesus Christ, God's New Man (Eph. 2:15). "New creation" (2 Cor. 5:17) does not so much highlight the internal change wrought by the gospel. Rather, the phrase expresses the change of sphere that the gospel has effected in the lives of believers. No longer are we in "the power of darkness"; we have been "conveyed… into the kingdom of the Son of His love" (Col. 1:13). In this new sphere of Christ's kingdom, a certain lifestyle is to prevail.

This new lifestyle will be marked first by believers putting off their "old man," the mind-set and behavior that once belonged to their "former conduct" (v. 22). In the Greek text, Paul's verbs are infinitives, not imperatives. That is, Paul is not issuing a series of new commands. He is reminding the Ephesians what it was that they learned from Christ. They had learned that they had put off their old man and had put on the new man. They truly were new creations in Christ. Now they needed to live as the new creations they assuredly were. This understanding is supported by the parallel passage in Colossians 3:8–10.[1]

Deceitful Lusts

All Christians have a unique story to tell about their redemption in Christ. But every Christian has an identical "former conduct." Before their conversion, every Christian lived a life "corrupt according to the deceitful lusts" (v. 22). This may seem extreme, but it is true. Not every unconverted man and woman lived a grossly ungodly life, but every unconverted man and woman lived a life "corrupt according to the deceitful lusts." The lives of all people who do not worship Jesus as Savior and Lord are marked by the great deceit that pursuing their own desires will bring them the fulfillment their hearts ache for.[2] This deceit does not die at conversion. Satan will seek

---

1. See the compelling argument in John Murray, *Principles of Conduct* (London: Tyndale, 1957), 214–21.

2. Augustine wrote memorably of this in his *Confessions*: "You stir man to take pleasure in praising you, because you have made us for yourself, and our heart is

untiringly to seduce believers into thinking that pursuing their own desires, rather than God's revealed will (His desire), is the recipe for a fulfilled life. This is the deceit Christians are to put off, resolutely and daily. John Owen made the pithy comment, "Be killing sin [daily] or it will be killing you."[3] This putting off is easier said than done. The key to its success in any measure lies in grasping the grace, blessedness, and power of union with Christ. It is only by the Holy Spirit's enabling help that sin in all its multivalent malignancy can be put off (Rom. 8:13, 26).

Recognizing that the old man has been put off at conversion is essential if we are to "be renewed in the spirit of [our] mind" (v. 23). The Gentile walk is marked by futility of mind (v. 17); the Christian walk is to be marked by Spirit-renewed minds. At the new birth, the birth from above, our minds are renewed. We have a new center of gravity in our thinking—God and His glory. We have a new considered resolve, to "seek first the kingdom of God and His righteousness" (Matt. 6:33). This, however, is but the beginning of a mind transformation that will take a lifetime and more! In Christ, God calls every Christian to bring "every thought into captivity to the obedience of Christ" (2 Cor. 10:5). This will not happen easily. Every inch of ground will be contested by Satan and the remnants of sin yet indwelling us (Rom. 8:13). But union with Christ means that all the resources of the risen, reigning Savior are ours to draw on by faith.

It is not enough, however, for Christians to remember that they had once "put off…the old man" (v. 22). More positively, Christians need constantly to be reminded that they have "put on the new man" (v. 24). Paul is encouraging them to remember who they are and to live accordingly. His language echoes the divinely revealed account of the creation of man in Genesis 1:26–27. What sin so tragically spoiled and defaced, the gospel of God's grace in Christ

restless until it rests in you." Trans. Henry Chadwick (Oxford: Oxford University Press, 1991), 3.

3. Owen, *Works*, 6.9.

comes to restore and repristinate, and more. In Christ, believers are "new creation[s]" (2 Cor. 5:17). Native to that new creation is a restored likeness "according to God, in true righteousness and holiness" (v. 24). God's ultimate purpose is to make His Son "the firstborn among many brethren" (Rom. 8:29b). His proximate purpose is to conform believers to the "image of His Son" (Rom. 8:29a).

Paul highlights the two defining, even comprehensive, features of that image or likeness, "true righteousness and holiness" (v. 24). God is righteous—that is, He is true to Himself and never acts or thinks contrary to His perfect nature. He is also holy—indeed, thrice holy (Isa. 6:3). Why does Paul say *true* righteousness? Perhaps simply to remind the Ephesians that the only righteousness that honors and pleases God is the righteousness that is exhibited in God Himself and in no other. God's holiness is His otherness, his absolute uniqueness as God. By union with Christ, believers have been made new in God's likeness. We don't become God, but we do become His image bearers and are called to reflect that image in our lives, as Paul will detail in the following verses. This is what all Christians are by virtue of their faith union with Jesus Christ.

Paul understood the need for his beloved Ephesians to be reminded once again of what the gospel had made them. Living in a fallen world and surrounded by a constant atmosphere of ungodliness can dull our sense of our new identity in Christ. One of the principal emphases in a pastor's preaching ministry will be recurring reminders to his hearers of the gospel-created new identity that is the possession of every Christian by God's grace in Christ. Loss of identity is a hugely dispiriting and debilitating crisis in a person's life. Constant exposure to "the truth [as it] is in Jesus" (v. 21) is imperative for healthy, God-honoring living.

18

Living the Life

EPHESIANS 4:25–32

Therefore, putting away lying, "Let each one of you speak truth with his neighbor," for we are members of one another. "Be angry, and do not sin": do not let the sun go down on your wrath, nor give place to the devil. Let him who stole steal no longer, but rather let him labor, working with his hands what is good, that he may have something to give him who has need. Let no corrupt word proceed out of your mouth, but what is good for necessary edification, that it may impart grace to the hearers. And do not grieve the Holy Spirit of God, by whom you were sealed for the day of redemption. Let all bitterness, wrath, anger, clamor, and evil speaking be put away from you, with all malice. And be kind to one another, tender-hearted, forgiving one another, even as God in Christ forgave you.

In a series of searchingly practical examples, Paul now illustrates the social, relational features of the God-pleasing life. The new life that believers have because of their union with Jesus Christ is as radically social and relational as it is doctrinal. Jesus pointedly told His disciples, "A good tree cannot bear bad fruit, nor can a bad tree bear good fruit. Every tree that does not bear good fruit is cut down and thrown into the fire. Therefore by their fruits you will know them" (Matt. 7:18–20; see also John 15:1–8). Jesus is speaking particularly here about false teachers, but the principle holds for everyone who professes to be one of God's redeemed children. Where the grace of God has truly invaded our lives and planted within us "His seed" (1 John 3:9), it cannot remain hidden. It is the grace of God "teaching us that, denying ungodliness and worldly lusts, we should live soberly, righteously, and godly in the present age" (Titus 2:12).

The opening word of verse 25, "therefore," is characteristic of Paul. Before he calls for effort, he first teaches the grace of the gospel. The commands of the gospel are rooted in and flow out of the grace of the gospel. Where God's commands are dislocated from the soil of His grace to us in Christ, they sound dispiritingly demanding, even clinical and metallic. But when God's commands come to us as from the One who spared not His own Son for us (Rom. 8:32) and who has blessed us in His Son with every spiritual blessing (Eph. 1:3), they sound pleasing and not burdensome (1 John 5:3).

Gospel Morality

The Christian life that has "learned Christ" (Eph. 4:20) and has been "created according to God, in true righteousness and holiness" (Eph. 4:24) is a morally and relationally transformed life. The gospel that makes us right with God plants within our lives the life of God. Not only do believers live their lives "in Christ," but God in Christ lives in them (Eph. 1:3, 20–22; see also John 14:20–24; Eph. 3:17; 1 John 3:9). The New Testament could not be more clear and more insistent that anyone who professes to be a Christian but does not keep God's commandments and does not love their fellow Christians is a liar, the truth is not in them, and God's love does not abide in them (1 John 2:3–4; 3:14–15). Rather than dismissing notions of duty and demand, the gospel of God's extravagant grace to us in Christ provides both the doctrinal rationality and personal desire to live a life of glad obedience to God's commandments.

It is not surprising, then, that Paul now spells out in the most practical ways the moral and relational contours of the life of faith. Throughout the Bible, the doctrines of God's revealed truth are always presented as giving birth to a lifestyle that gladly embraces God's commandments. The evidence of a new birth is a new life. Where there is no new life, there has been no new birth. By their fruits you will know them. In this section of Ephesians, then, Paul highlights the down-to-earth character of the "true righteousness and holiness" that is to shape the social lives of those who have put off, in Christ, the old man and have also in Christ put on the new man (4:22, 24).

Paul focuses on a number of areas that probably reflected the particular circumstances of life in Ephesus. Each of the six prohibitions is balanced by a positive affirmation. It is never enough for Christians not to sin. Our calling is to live "according to God, in true righteousness and holiness." Too often the Christian church has been defined by what it is against rather than what it is for. These two are, of course, not mutually exclusive. If our calling is to "be imitators of God as dear children" (Eph. 5:1), however, what we "put away" (v. 31) and "put to death" (Rom. 8:13) will be balanced—and more than balanced by what we "put on" (Eph. 4:24) and practice. Simply pulling up noxious weeds does not make a garden beautiful, nor is it enough simply to plant flowers among the noxious weeds to make the garden attractive. There is, however, a radical disconnect between the horticultural and the spiritual. In the world of gardens, before you plant good seed and pretty flowers, you must first prepare the soil by pulling out all the weeds. Only when the pulling up has been done will the gardener begin to plant. In the spiritual world, the pulling up and the planting are to be done simultaneously. Indeed, we can only meaningfully pull up the noxious weeds of sin in our lives when we do so putting on the Lord Jesus Christ (Rom. 13:14). John Owen makes the point well: "Set faith at work on Christ for the killing of thy sin. His blood is the great remedy for sin-sick souls. Live in this, and thou wilt die a conqueror."[1]

No Lies, Only Truth

In Christ, believers must "[put] away lying" (v. 25). In our union with Christ in His death and resurrection (Rom. 6:1–14), we have been rescued from the kingdom of darkness, where the father of lies ruled (John 8:44), and have been brought into the kingdom of light and love where Jesus Christ, the truth, is king (Col. 1:12–13;

---

1. Owen, *Works*, 6:79.

John 14:6, respectively). As new creations in Christ, we are to be "speaking the truth" (Eph. 4:15). Truth speaking is to be one of the hallmarks of our new life in Christ.[2]

The reason Paul gives for Christians speaking the truth with their neighbors is at first sight surprising: "for we are members of one another" (v. 25). We might have expected him to say, "For God hates lies," or, "for Jesus Christ is truth." But Paul reinforces the command to speak the truth by reminding the Ephesians that they are members together of the body of Christ (4:15–16). Not to speak the truth to a fellow believer is to despise Christ's body and, consequently, Christ Himself. Lies are like cancers that cause the body of Christ, His church, to putrefy and lose social credibility in its calling to proclaim Christ as Lord and Savior.

Be Angry but Don't Sin

Paul is not commanding the Ephesians to be angry. Rather, he is recognizing there is such a thing as righteous anger. Paul is quoting Psalm 4:4. He recognizes, however, that anger can easily and quickly give way to sin. But the danger of anger developing into sin must not distract us from the gospel virtue of anger that is righteous. Likeness to God will mean that we share His anger at what sin has done in His good creation. Where we see social and political injustice, the iniquity of abortion and euthanasia, the sexual exploitation of women and children, and the arrogance of power and wealth, we have a God-given right to be angry. Where we encounter hypocrisy and unbelief in the life of Christ's church, a lack of anger would be a sign of our indifference and perhaps complicity in those sins.

The Christian life is never to be stoically indifferent to the trampling of God's truth in society and in the church. The Gospels provide us with two striking examples of Jesus's righteous anger. In John 2:13–17, we read of Jesus entering the temple and seeing

---

2. Paul writes τὸ ψεῦδος (the lie or falsehood). It is possible he is thinking of the lie that worships and serves the "creature rather than the Creator" (Rom. 1:25). This lie would have been a marked feature of the pagan culture that prevailed in Ephesus.

people buying and selling "and the money changers doing business" (v. 14). The scene so incensed Jesus that He made a whip of cords and "drove them all out of the temple" (v. 15). Toward the end of His public ministry, Jesus excoriated the scribes and Pharisees, the spiritual leaders of God's church (Matthew 23). In a series of seven woes, Jesus poured out His righteous anger toward these "blind guides" (vv. 16, 24) who were disgracing their office and abandoning God's sheep to ignorance and deadly exposure: "Woe to you, scribes and Pharisees...blind guides...hypocrites! For you are like whitewashed tombs which indeed appear beautiful outwardly, but inside are full of dead men's bones and all uncleanness" (vv. 13, 16, 27). It is true that Jesus's anger was unblemished. He had no sin. But if we are to be like Him, the absence of godly, righteous anger can only accentuate our unlikeness to Him.

Because he is a concerned pastor, Paul recognizes the ever-present activity of the devil in the life of the church. So he cautions the Ephesians, "Do not let the sun go down on your wrath, nor give place to the devil" (vv. 26–27). The devil is always on the prowl, "seeking whom he may devour" (1 Peter 5:8). Paul will later warn the Ephesians to guard themselves "against the wiles of the devil" (Eph. 6:11). One of the ways the devil insinuates himself into the life of the church is when Christians allow righteous anger to breed a resentful spirit or when they nurse unrighteous anger so that it breeds an arrogant spirit in them. Both of these give the devil an opportunity to sow discord and division among the members of the body.

No Longer Steal but Work

Paul is summoning the Ephesian believers to be what they truly now are in Christ. It is nonetheless remarkable that he is so basic—perhaps surprisingly basic—in his exhortations to them. "Let him who stole steal no longer" (v. 28). Why does Paul feel the need to say this? Is the eighth commandment—"You shall not steal"—not plain enough (Ex. 20:15)? Paul understands well that when a man or woman is converted, they are not lifted out of their native environment, where the prince of this world continues to exercise his malignant presence and power (2 Cor. 6:4; 1 John 5:19). Nor has sin been totally removed from their lives. Within every Christian there is a hospitable landing ground for Satan's deceits and seductions. This means that the Christian believer must, with the help of the Holy Spirit, "put to death the deeds of the body" (Rom. 8:13). It may be that stealing was rife in Ephesian society, just as Internet pornography is rife in today's society. So Paul addresses the need for God's new creations to live differently—to live according to God's law, not the acceptable practices of a fallen world.

Again, Paul's prohibition is matched by a positive exhortation, "but rather let him labor, working with his hands what is good, that he may have something to give him who has need" (4:28). God has not saved us for lives of idleness but for lives of usefulness. Honest labor is to be one of the hallmarks of a Christian's life in society.

It is imperative that every Christian understand his or her daily work as a vocation, a calling from God. However seemingly mundane our work may be, we are to do that work *coram Deo*, before God's face and for His glory. In this sense, every Christian has a holy calling designed to honor and please God and to be a gospel testimony to a watching world. Christians live in the light because they are "children of light" (Eph. 5:8). More than that, the Christian is called to care for others. All that we have, we have as stewards (1 Cor. 4:7). Working only to provide for our own needs and desires reflects a self-engrossed life, not a Christlike life.

Work is one of God's creation ordinances (Gen. 2:15). God set Adam to work in the garden. He was not created for a life of indolence, far less hedonism. Adam was made to work. Paul's strong words, "If anyone [that is, any Christian] will not work, neither shall he eat" (2 Thess. 3:10), are not directed to those who would love to work but for whatever reason cannot but to those who are able to work but choose not to.

Use Your Mouth for Good

Paul has already exhorted the Ephesians to put away falsehood and to speak the truth (v. 25), but he needs to return to the way God's new creations in Christ are to use their mouths. Again, Paul begins with a negative, "Let no corrupt word proceed out of your mouth" (v. 29). "Corrupt" is another horticultural word, used of fruit that is rotten. Later (Eph. 5:4), Paul will return to the way Christians are to avoid using their mouths as instruments for spreading vulgar, morally corrupting speech. But it is never enough for Christians to avoid sin. The avoidance of corrupting talk is to be married to a desire to speak only "what is good for necessary edification, that it may impart grace to the hearers" (v. 29). Is it kind? Is it necessary? Is it true? These should be the questions that govern what we say to others. Paul is not suggesting that a Christian will never speak passionately or rebuke. He is saying that our words are always to be appropriate, "good for necessary edification," never thoughtlessly inappropriate. Everyone we speak to is made in God's image and should be respected, even honored.

It is remarkable how often the Bible tells us that what we say with our lips is a telling exposure of the state of our hearts (Ps. 15:2–3; 34:13–14; James 3:1–12). Jesus said to His Pharisee opponents, "How can you, being evil, speak good things? For out of the abundance of the heart the mouth speaks" (Matt. 12:34). Jesus warned His disciples that on the day of judgment we will all have to give an account for "every idle word" we have spoken (Matt. 12:36).

The importance of always speaking the truth is placarded in the ninth commandment: "You shall not bear false witness against your neighbor" (Ex. 20:16). The Westminster Shorter Catechism provides a searching exposition of what is entailed in the ninth commandment. First, the Catechism asks the question, "What is required in the ninth commandment?" The answer follows, "The ninth commandment requireth the maintaining and promoting of truth between man and man, and of our own and our neighbour's good name, especially in witness bearing." The Catechism proceeds to ask a second question, "What is forbidden in the ninth commandment?"

The answer follows, "The ninth commandment forbiddeth whatsoever is prejudicial to truth, or injurious to our own or neighbour's good name."

A church or society where truth and truth telling are not held in the highest regard sows the seeds of its own destruction. Christians are "light in the Lord" and must therefore "walk as children of light" (Eph. 5:8). The Lord Jesus Christ described Satan as the father of lies (John 8:44), while He described Himself as "the truth" (John 14:6). Part of the Christian family likeness is reflecting the integrity of the God who cannot lie (Titus 1:2).

Do Not Grieve the Holy Spirit

It is a deeply solemn thing that God's new creations in Christ can "grieve the Holy Spirit of God" (v. 30) by their un-Christlike behavior. It is not immediately clear why Paul should mention the Holy Spirit at this time. Perhaps he is making the point that when we use our mouths to harm rather than help fellow believers, the Holy Spirit who indwells us is grieved because we are dishonoring the Lord Jesus Christ who lives in us, just as we live in Him (John 15:6). The Holy Spirit indwells believers as their helper and sanctifier, working constantly to make us like God "in true righteousness and holiness" (Eph. 4:24). When we do not behave like God, not only do we provoke His fatherly displeasure but we actually grieve Him. The Holy Spirit is no mere influence or power. He is personal and capable of being grieved. He is the "Spirit of truth" (John 14:17) and is affected when God's people use their mouths ungraciously and ungenerously.

Sealed for the Day of Redemption

No right-thinking Christian would ever want to "grieve the Holy Spirit of God" (4:30), because it is the Holy Spirit who has sealed us for the day of redemption. This sealing, or authenticating, took place at conversion (Eph. 1:13). It is not a work of the Spirit subsequent to conversion. For the Christian, redemption is both a present experience (Eph. 1:7) and a future hope (Rom. 8:23). The Holy Spirit has set God's seal of ownership on our lives; indeed, He Himself is that seal of ownership. And God's ultimate purpose is to make every Christian like His Son, who was "gentle and lowly in heart" (Matt. 11:29) and who only spoke graciously and generously, although at times strongly, to His disciples.

Not only does Paul in his teaching precede imperatives with indicatives, he constantly punctuates, as here, exhortations to godliness with gospel grace. There is surely no more powerful incentive to pursue godliness than an ever-deepening awareness of the riches of God's grace to us in the gospel. The indwelling of the Holy Spirit and His sealing of us for the day of redemption is "grace, gospel-grace."[3] And nothing humbles believers more and quickens their desire to live to God's praise and honor than to be constantly reminded of the innumerable spiritual blessings that are theirs in Christ (Eph. 1:3).

More Dos and Do Nots

Paul concludes his exposition of the "true righteousness and holiness" (Eph. 4:24) that is to mark indelibly the lives of God's new creations by highlighting six un-Christlike attitudes that they are to put away (v. 31), and three Christlike attitudes they are to cultivate (v. 32).

"Bitterness" is a spirit soured by adverse providences. It is often directed at people, but at heart it is resentment against God. "Wrath" is anger that overflows, either into sullen hostility or into brawling, uncontrolled "anger." "Clamor" is characteristic of people whose wrath and anger explode into public abuse of others. "Evil speaking" is slander, or speaking evil of others to others. It has a malicious intent and belongs not to the new man but to the old man (Rom. 1:30; Gal. 5:19–21). Slander is the stock in trade of the devil.[4] "Malice" is wickedly plotting to do harm against enemies, real or imagined. Paul writes of "all malice"—that is, malice of all

---

3. John Owen, *Works*, 2:47.
4. διάβολος (the devil, the slanderer).

kinds. No trace of malice in any of its forms belongs to the lifestyle of those "created according to God, in true righteousness and holiness" (v. 24).

Again, Paul moves from the negative to the positive, from what we must put away to what we must put on. "Be kind to one another" (v. 32). Kindness is one of the fruits of the Spirit (Gal. 5:22). In Luke 6:35, Jesus tells us that "the Most High…is kind to the unthankful and evil." In his *Confessions,* Augustine tells how in his unconverted days he was deeply impressed by Bishop Ambrose of Milan: "I began to like him, at first indeed not as a teacher of the truth, for I had absolutely no confidence in your [God's] church, but as a human being who was kind to me."[5] Before Augustine heard the words "*tolle lege*" (pick up and read) and was in a moment converted to Christ, God had pierced his deeply immoral life by Ambrose's kindness. It is impossible to read the four Gospels and not be impressed with Jesus's kindness, especially to the poor and needy. In purposing to conform all His redeemed children to the likeness of His Son, the heavenly Father is seeking to impress His Son's kindness on their lives.

"Tenderhearted" is best understood by the words that follow, "forgiving one another, even as God in Christ forgave you" (4:32). Tenderheartedness is an attitude of generosity and sympathy to people who have fallen and failed. The tenderhearted do not treat people as their sins deserve, because God did not treat them as their sins deserved (Ps. 103:10). In Christ God has forgiven us freely and fully. Not to forgive others their sins against us would be to place a huge question mark over our Christian profession. In his postscript to the Lord's Prayer, Jesus impressed on His disciples the absolute necessity of forgiving others: "If you do not forgive men their trespasses, neither will your Father forgive your trespasses" (Matt. 6:15). Jesus is not saying that because we forgive others God will forgive us. He is saying that an unforgiving heart is a symptom of an unforgiven heart. Is it possible to receive God's gracious and costly

---

5. Augustine, *Confessions,* 88.

forgiveness in Christ and not ever be ready to forgive others who have sinned against us?

How transformed church life would be if we all treated one another as God in Christ has treated us! Every day we should meditate on the Lord's patient, longsuffering, kind, and generous love. The wonder of the Lord's unfailing love to us should surely shape and style our calling to love one another (John 13:34; 1 John 3:18). Love for the brethren is not an ideal for Christians to seek; it is a lifestyle they are to practice. Every time we meet a fellow believer it would transform our attitude toward them if our first thought was, "This is my brother, my sister, washed like me in the precious blood of our common Lord and Savior."

19

Be Like God

EPHESIANS 5:1–16

Therefore be imitators of God as dear children. And walk in love, as Christ also has loved us and given Himself for us, an offering and a sacrifice to God for a sweet-smelling aroma.

But fornication and all uncleanness or covetousness, let it not even be named among you, as is fitting for saints; neither filthiness, nor foolish talking, nor coarse jesting, which are not fitting, but rather giving of thanks. For this you know, that no fornicator, unclean person, nor covetous man, who is an idolater, has any inheritance in the kingdom of Christ and God. Let no one deceive you with empty words, for because of these things the wrath of God comes upon the sons of disobedience. Therefore do not be partakers with them.

For you were once darkness, but now you are light in the Lord. Walk as children of light (for the fruit of the Spirit is in all goodness, righteousness, and truth), finding out what is acceptable to the Lord. And have no fellowship with the unfruitful works of darkness, but rather expose them. For it is shameful even to speak of those things which are done by them in secret. But all things that are exposed are made manifest by the light, for whatever makes manifest is light. Therefore He says:

"Awake, you who sleep,
Arise from the dead,
And Christ will give you light."

See then that you walk circumspectly, not as fools but as wise, redeeming the time, because the days are evil.

In the opening of chapter 5, Paul seems to be summing up his exhortations from 4:25–32 and in the process giving them a familial pointedness. Christians are God's "dear children" (v. 1). Some years ago a friend of mine was interviewed for a teaching position in a seminary. One of the first questions he was asked was, "What is your default thinking as a Christian?" My friend's answer was immediate and instinctive: "I think of myself as the son of a loving heavenly Father." He could hardly have answered more accurately and beautifully. God has adopted us as His sons through Jesus Christ (Eph. 1:5). This is our fundamental status as believers. We were once children of God's wrath (Eph. 2:3), but in Christ we have been saved from His wrath (Rom. 5:9; 1 Thess. 5:9) and have been adopted as forgiven and newborn children into His family (John 1:12). "Therefore," Paul writes in 5:1, "be imitators of God." Paul longs to see the likeness of God etched in the lives of His children. But he knows that the power and effectiveness of his exhortation will only impact the Ephesians when they grasp what God has made them in Christ. They are "dear children." God in Christ has forgiven them all their sins (Eph. 4:32). They owe a debt of unceasing thankfulness to God for His great grace to them in Christ.

Walk in Love

But what does it mean to imitate God as a dearly loved and graciously forgiven child? It means to "walk in love, as Christ also has loved us and given Himself for us, an offering and a sacrifice to God for a sweet-smelling aroma" (v. 2). The Christian family likeness is a lifestyle of love patterned after the self-giving, sacrificial love of Christ. Paul commands the Ephesians to love. He is not suggesting this would be good if and when the mood suited and the circumstances were right. Like Jesus (John 13:34), Paul issues an unconditional command: "Walk in love."

In the gospel, every Christian is called to be like Christ. He is not only our Savior and King, He is our example (1 Peter 2:21). The example of Christ's love is a life given up in death for us and an offering given up to God in sacrifice. He gave Himself "for us," but

His sacrifice was "to God" (v. 2). Paul is highlighting two foundational features of Christ's love.

First, it was a self-giving, self-sacrificing love. In Jesus, love was not a mere sentiment; it was an unimaginably costly sacrifice. To rescue us from a fate worse than death, He died in our place, as our appointed substitute, bearing the righteous judgment and wrath of God that our sin deserved. "In this is love, not that we loved God, but that He loved us and sent His Son to be the propitiation for our sins" (1 John 4:10). To imitate God is to lay down your life for the good of your brothers and sisters in Christ (1 John 3:16; 4:11). This level of sacrificial love is not what we are to arrive at after so many years of discipleship. No, this is the level of love that all Christians are called to the moment they believe on the Lord Jesus Christ. This is why Jesus never wearied of telling would-be followers to count the cost involved in following Him. Perhaps not many reading these pages will be called to lay down their lives for their fellow believers, but some may be so called. This is why the apostle John wrote, "By this we know love, because He laid down His life for us. And we also ought to lay down our lives for the brethren" (1 John 3:16).

Second, it was a love that sought to please God. Jesus's giving of Himself for us was "an offering and a sacrifice to God for a sweet-smelling aroma" (v. 2). To "walk in love" (5:2) is to live unto God. This was the hallmark of Jesus's earthly life (John 6:38). He had not come from heaven to please Himself (Rom. 15:3; Phil. 2:5–8). He came to die, the just for the unjust, to bring them to God (1 Peter 3:18). Sacrificial love for others is a sacrifice pleasing to God.

The emphasis we find in the New Testament on love is both striking and challenging. Heresy of the heart is condemned as much as heresy of the head. Love for fellow Christians is considered one of the distinguishing marks of authentic discipleship to Jesus (John 13:34–35), and the absence of love is a sure sign that we do not truly love God (1 John 4:20–21). Paul's "eulogy" (it is actually a searing indictment of the Corinthian church) on love in 1 Corinthians 13 expresses what it means for God's beloved children to walk in love: "Love suffers long and is kind; love does not envy; love does not parade itself, is not puffed up; does not behave rudely, does not seek its own, is not provoked, thinks no evil; does not rejoice in iniquity, but rejoices in the truth; bears all things, believes all things, hopes all things, endures all things" (vv. 4–7). Does this define the tenor and style of your life? If not, what should you conclude? The gospel of God comes to transform every aspect of our lives. It brings the life of God into our souls. How then can Christians not reflect something of that life in their relationships with other Christians?

Live Differently

The ancient world into which God planted His fledgling church was immersed in sexual immorality. Much like our world today, sexual permissiveness was the default, not the exception. Paul feels the need to spell out in detail what God's new creations in Christ must no longer indulge in and why such behavior is absolutely inappropriate for God's "dear children" (v. 1), redeemed by the precious blood of God's Son (Eph. 1:7). When the Bible tells us that the Lord Jesus Christ came into the world to win salvation for us, it means salvation in all its fullness. God's salvation in Christ is double-edged: we are saved from the just judgment and condemnation of God, and we are saved for lives of righteousness and holiness (Eph. 4:24). Christians are citizens of a kingdom that reflects the righteousness and moral purity of its King. This means that God's dear children are to live differently, not according to the thinking and behavior of this passing world but according to the unchanging character of the thrice holy, pure, and righteous God. This sets the Christian and the church on an inevitable collision course with the world and its values.

Countercultural

We should not be surprised that Paul initially focuses on "fornication and all uncleanness or covetousness" (v. 3) as he further develops the distinctive features of the God-pleasing life (4:1). Ephesus was notorious for sexual indulgence of every kind. The two Greek words

Paul uses[1] embrace every conceivable sexual sin. It is not that Paul, or the Bible for that matter, is in any sense prudish. The Bible celebrates sexuality in general (in the Song of Songs, for example) and the particular sexual intimacy that belongs to marriage. But it is unequivocal in condemning all expressions of sexuality that go beyond and are contrary to the revealed will of God, heterosexual and homosexual. For the Bible this is never a matter of culture but of God's will. What is at issue is the Christian's calling to live a God-pleasing life. Fundamentally, the Christian's refusing to engage in sexual immorality is not as much a matter of obedience as a matter of trust. Will we trust the heavenly Father, who spared not His only Son for us, who has redeemed us by His blood, who has made us His dear children, to seek only our best? He has blessed us in Christ "with every spiritual blessing" (Eph. 1:3) and has promised, with Christ, graciously to give us "all things" (Rom. 8:32). He can be trusted absolutely, particularly when He commands us to put off sexual immorality, all impurity, and covetousness.

The pressure to resist the times we live in today is no more than it was for Christians in first-century Ephesus. Perhaps Christians today will experience increasingly the cost of living differently, of living to please and honor God in a world that denies and defies Him. Sexual purity is a reflection of our confidence in God's goodness and love. This is why the wisest pastoral response to a Christian who faces sexual temptations, particularly Internet pornography, is to go back to basics and explain afresh the grace of God in the gospel.

It is striking that Paul links "covetousness" with "fornication and all uncleanness" (v. 3). He does so because much sin is rooted in our desire to possess what we do not have. In this context the desire is to possess the bodies of others for sexual gratification. This sin is addressed specifically in the tenth commandment (Ex. 20:17). Paul has already highlighted self-aggrandizing greed as one of the defining features of Ephesian society (Eph. 4:19). What was true of first-century Ephesus is true of every great city in the twenty-first

---

1. Πορνεία δὲ καὶ πᾶσα ἀκαθαρσία.

century. The pursuit of self-gratification, whatever the cost, is one of the defining sins of our age. The increasing sexual abuse of women and children is almost a hallmark of Western society in particular. When people stop believing the Bible, they not only start believing anything but they start behaving abominably. There are tragic consequences, personal and societal, when men and women turn their backs on the God of Holy Scripture.

Holy Speaking

Not only are God's people to have nothing to do with such sexually promiscuous lifestyles but these sins must "not even be named among you, as is fitting for saints" (v. 3). Paul once again joins moral exhortation to gospel grace. Christians are saints, men and women set apart for God, to live as His dear children in a fallen world. Just as our outward lifestyle is to reflect the moral purity of God, so also is the way we speak. It is never enough for Christians to abstain from the practice of sin; we are to abstain from the language of sin. Filthiness of speech, foolish talk, and crude joking "are not fitting" (v. 4). Why? Because Christians are saints who inhabit a new world where "righteousness and peace and joy in the Holy Spirit" are the defining features (Rom. 14:17).

This is why the battle for the mind is so vital. The continuing presence of indwelling sin gives sin and Satan a welcoming landing strip in our lives. It is imperative that with the promised help of the Holy Spirit (Rom. 8:26) we daily "set [our] mind on things above, not on things on the earth" (Col. 3:2). This requires resolve and effort. But if we do not kill sin, sin will kill us!

This is a huge challenge to Christians living in cultures saturated with and obsessed by sex and crudeness. The challenge is heightened because the Lord Jesus Christ prayed to His Father not that He would take His disciples out of the world but that He would protect them from the evil one (John 17:15). Christians are never to retreat into cultural or spiritual ghettoes—as if that would be a protection from the world's excesses. No, the answer does not lie in retreating from the world but in thanking God.

Thanksgiving
Jesus called His disciples to live in the world as salt and light (Matt. 5:13–16). Amid the moral darkness and putrefying corruption of this fallen world, God's people are to live differently as gospel-light diffusers and moral preservatives. At the heart of this different lifestyle is thanksgiving. Christians have much for which to be thankful to God, "for of Him and through Him and to Him are all things, to whom be glory forever. Amen" (Rom. 11:36). What is to come out of our mouths is not crude joking or filthy, foolish talk but "giving of thanks" (v. 4). Christians should be noted not for possessing a complaining or critical spirit but for a thankful spirit. We are the recipients of sovereign, electing love and mercy. We are God's beloved children. We have been blessed in Christ with every spiritual blessing. God is personally working all things together for our good (Rom. 8:28). Nothing in all creation can separate us from God's love in Christ (Rom. 8:39). Thanksgiving should be the currency of our mouths at all times.

Solemn Incentives
The life of faith in Jesus Christ is to be marked by "true righteousness and holiness" (Eph. 4:24). Righteousness and holiness do not simply happen; they are the fruit of resolve and determined effort. Certainly it is the indwelling presence and power of the Holy Spirit that enables us to live righteous and holy lives (Rom. 8:13). But in the process of sanctification, believers are never passive. We are to work out our salvation knowing, however, that it is God who works in us to will and to work for His good pleasure (Phil. 2:12–13). From 4:1, Paul has consistently impressed on the Ephesians that the life that is worthy of their high calling in Christ requires their utmost effort and energy. Just as it cost Jesus to love us (v. 2), so it will cost us to love Him and live lives worthy of His costly love.

    The notion that the Christian life requires no effort, no determined resolve, flies in the face of the plain teaching of God's Word. When the grace of God invades our lives savingly, it trains us that "denying ungodliness and worldly lusts, we should live soberly, righteously, and godly in the present age" (Titus 2:12). Holiness is not a condition the believer simply drifts into. The Christian life, the life that pleases God, involves effort. In Colossians 1:29, Paul uses language that highlights the extreme effort he put into serving God and His church: "To this end I also labor, striving according to His working which works in me mightily."[2]

Paul is aware of the seductive presence and appeal of sin, what the writer to the Hebrews calls "the deceitfulness of sin" (3:13), so he reinforces his exhortations to holiness with three incentives.

First, "for this you know, that no fornicator, unclean person, nor covetous man, who is an idolater, has any inheritance in the kingdom of Christ and God" (v. 5). Paul is unequivocal: no holiness, no heaven. If there truly has been a birth from above (John 3:3), then that new birth will inevitably show itself in new life. That new life will be marked by new desires, new affections,[3] new hopes, new loves, and new hates. Where these are absent, the Holy Spirit cannot be present. And if the Holy Spirit is absent, we do not belong to Christ (Rom. 8:9). Paul will later tell the Ephesians that Christ loved His church and gave Himself up for her "that He might sanctify and cleanse her" and present the church "to Himself a glorious church, not having spot or wrinkle or any such thing, but that she should be holy and without blemish" (5:25–27). Holiness of life is not an optional extra for the Christian. Without holiness, "no one will see the Lord" (Heb. 12:14).

Second, not only will the sexually immoral, the impure, and the covetous have no heavenly inheritance, no matter how evangelical and passionate their Christian profession, but the "wrath of God"

---

2. The verb here, ἀγωνίζομαι, was used of wrestlers in the gymnastic games. It conveys the idea of hand-to-hand combat, of contending with strenuous zeal to win a prize.

3. Thomas Chalmers, perhaps the greatest of the nineteenth-century Scottish evangelical churchmen, wrote of the gospel producing "the expulsive power of a new affection." This was the title of a sermon he preached to his congregation of St. John's Church, Glasgow. *Sermons and Discourses of Thomas Chalmers* (New York: Robert Carter & Brothers, 1856), 2:271–78.

will come upon them (v. 6). It is possible that Paul has heard that false teaching was infecting the Ephesian church. He writes, "Let no one deceive you with empty words" (v. 6). Were some teachers suggesting that it did not really matter how you lived as long as you trusted Jesus? Paul calls this teaching "empty words" (v. 6), devoid of substance, because they are completely lacking in truth. This is not simply antinomian teaching; it is soul-imperiling teaching that will bring God's wrath down on us. People who live lives contrary to the will and commandments of God are not immature Christians; they are "sons of disobedience" (Eph. 2:2).

Authentic gospel ministers will therefore punctuate their preaching of God's glorious grace in Christ with warnings. Paul does this regularly. The letter to the Hebrews solemnly and dramatically, in the midst of wonderful Christ-exalting teaching, confronts the readers with a series of heart-searching warnings, culminating with the solemn words, "If we sin willfully after we have received the knowledge of the truth, there no longer remains a sacrifice for sins, but a certain fearful expectation of judgment" (10:26–27). It truly is "a fearful thing to fall into the hands of the living God" (10:31).

Third, Christians must not become "partakers" with "sons of disobedience" (5:7, 6, respectively), because of their new identity in Christ. Once they were "darkness," but now they are "light in the Lord" (v. 8). The gospel of grace had effected a glorious transformation in their lives. They were darkness. Spiritual and moral darkness had not only invaded their lives but had become their life. They were darkness—they had "walked according to the course of this world, according to the prince of the power of the air, the spirit who now works in the sons of disobedience" (Eph. 2:2). But through the gospel, they had become "light in the Lord." This was their new identity. Because Jesus is Himself "the light of the world" (John 8:12), all who are in Him are "the light of the world" (Matt. 5:14). As Jesus reminded His disciples, light is for shining, exposing spiritual and moral corruption, and illuminating a dark world with the light of God's transforming grace (Matt. 5:16). The Ephesians were "light in the Lord" and must live as such, showing in their lives that they truly belonged to the Lord, who is Himself light (1 John 1:5). This would mean that they "walk as children of light" (v. 8). As was noted before, walking suggests the idea of steady, resolved progress. Sanctification, growth in likeness to the Lord Jesus Christ, involves a lifetime of steady, purposeful walking in the light.

What Light Looks Like

The Christian's new identity as a child of the light will show itself in a lifestyle shaped by "all goodness, righteousness, and truth" (v. 9). The metaphor of light suggests the idea of transparency. The life of faith in Jesus Christ can he held up to the light without fear of being revealed as double-minded or motivated by selfish gain.

In recent years evangelical Christianity has been scarred by high-profile preachers living double lives. Their inevitable exposure has brought huge discredit on the gospel. These moral tragedies highlight the great need for ministerial accountability. Christian leaders must be held to the highest account. They must never be allowed to think that they are essential to the work of God's kingdom; no man is. These moral qualities, which were perfectly exemplified in Jesus, the light of the world, are to be the public face as well as the private pursuit of God's people.

Pleasing the Lord

Paul writes in verse 10, "finding [a present participle] out what is acceptable to the Lord." The form of the verb impresses on us that discovering what is acceptable to the Lord is not a one-time activity but the effort of a lifetime. There is a foundational principle here that helps Christians discern God's will. God's will is what pleases Him, and what pleases Him is "goodness, righteousness, and truth" (v. 9). This requires Christians to have Bible-saturated minds. We see this mind exemplified in the Lord Jesus Christ. When Satan tempted Jesus three times as He launched into His public ministry, Jesus responded by quoting three texts in Deuteronomy 6 and 8 (Matt. 4:1–11). Jesus knew what was pleasing to God and what

God's will was in His encounter with Satan, because He knew God's word.

Have you ever wondered how Jesus knew God's word so well that He effortlessly, in the midst of great hunger and thirst, could quote it accurately and appositely? Some words in the third Servant Song (Isa. 50:4–11) provide us with an unexpected answer:

> The Lord GOD has given Me
> The tongue of the learned,
> That I should know how to speak
> A word in season to him who is weary.
> He awakens Me morning by morning,
> He awakens My ear
> To hear as the learned.
> The Lord GOD has opened My ear;
> And I was not rebellious,
> Nor did I turn away. (vv. 4–5)

In other words, our Savior, in His true humanity, was not excused the daily discipline of applying Himself to hearing and taking to heart God's Word. He was among those with "the tongue of the learned."

There are no shortcuts to developing a Bible-saturated mind. Like our Lord Jesus Christ, we must apply ourselves every day to reading, hearing, and hiding God's word in our hearts and minds (Ps. 119:11).

When certain courses of action and practices are presented to a Christian, he or she must always seek to apply the standards of these three moral qualities: Is this good—is it consonant with God's character? Is this right—does it conform to the rule of God's Word? Is this true—will it help advance the cause of God's truth in the world?

What is "acceptable to the Lord [Jesus]" (v. 10) is that we seek as God's dear children to live according to the promises and precepts of God's word (Isa. 8:20). Just as Jesus perfectly pleased His Father by being obedient to death, even the death of the cross (Phil. 2:8), so Christians are similarly to please the Lord by their faithful obedience to His word.

Exposing Darkness

Positively, God's beloved children, "once darkness, but now... light in the Lord," are to "walk as children of light" (v. 8). But this positive command involves a necessary prohibition: "Have no fellowship with the unfruitful works of darkness" (v. 11). Paul is once again highlighting the double-sided character of the believing life: godliness is to be pursued and cultivated, and ungodliness is to be shunned and resisted. The "works of darkness" are detailed in Galatians 5:19–21, where they are called "the works of the flesh." These works spread like corrupting cancers in believers and churches, destroying all gospel credibility (Rom. 2:24).

Walking as children of light means, unavoidably, exposing "the unfruitful works of darkness," both their presence and their unholy, destructive nature. Sometimes this is done simply by being light in the Lord. Just as it is the natural quality of light to expose and dispel darkness, so Christians, who are light in the Lord, are to expose the unfruitful works of darkness, not first by verbal condemnation but by living, naturally, as children of light. By taking no part in the unfruitful works of darkness and simultaneously by doing what is good and right and true, Christians naturally, as God's new creations in Christ, shine the light of truth and righteousness into a world immersed in rebellion against God.

It is never enough, however, for Christians simply to expose the darkness by their godly living. We are called to speak God's truth, to bear verbal witness to Jesus, to give a reason for the hope that is in us (1 Peter 3:15). Jesus told His disciples that everyone who acknowledged Him before men, He would acknowledge before the angels of God; but those who denied Him before men He would deny before the angels of God (Luke 12:8–9). However daunting the prospect, Christians are to imitate their Savior in humbly but courageously bearing witness to the truth. This we can do only as we live out our union with Christ in His strength (Eph. 6:10).

Paul proceeds to highlight the double virtue of Christians being light diffusers in a dark world. First, "all things that are exposed are made manifest by the light" (v. 13). Sin's native environment is darkness. It flourishes when it can hide its vileness and ugliness. But when the light of truth and godliness shines into the darkness, sin is exposed for what it is. This is why many unbelievers feel uncomfortable around faithful Christians. My first encounter with biblical Christianity was meeting a young man whose life both intrigued and convicted me. His presence seemed to expose something of the emptiness in my own life. When we met some years later, I remarked to him that God used his life to speak powerfully into my life. I then said I had no recollection of him sharing the gospel with me. He was puzzled, he said, because he was always sharing the gospel with me. I have no doubt he had been, but what I remember was not his words but the impact of his life. It was his joyful, unaffected, Christlike life that hooked me and prepared me to hear the gospel.

Second, when the light shines into the darkness and sin becomes visible, sin becomes light (v. 13). It is not immediately clear what Paul means. Probably he means that the light of God's truth has the capacity not only to expose sin for what it is but also to transform sinners into new creations. The transformative power of a Christlike life and a Spirit-empowered testimony cannot be underestimated. Luke records in Acts the immense impact of Stephen's light-bearing witness to Christ on the life of Saul of Tarsus. When we read Acts 7:54–8:3 and then Acts 9, we are intended to see the connection between Stephen's courageous testimony and Saul's conversion. God used the gospel light and power of Stephen's life (Acts 7:55) to shine into Saul's sin-darkened heart and mind. Being a faithful light diffuser cost Stephen his life, but God used it to pierce Saul's internal darkness and eventually to make him the means of bringing multitudes into the kingdom of God.

Being a light diffuser in your family or place of work or college may prove costly. You may not, like Stephen, be publicly executed. You may, however, be ridiculed, shunned, passed over for promotion, or, even like the Lord Jesus Christ, be vilified and lied against. But it is your privilege to endure suffering like a good soldier of Christ (2 Tim. 2:3) and to fill up what is lacking in Christ's afflictions for the sake of His body, the church (Col. 1:24). No cross, no crown.

Verse 14 supports this understanding of verse 13. What verse from the Old Testament is Paul quoting? Not one verse, but probably a conflation of Isaiah 51:17; 52:1; and 60:1. He is gathering together from Scripture words that support his argument in verse 13. It has been suggested that Paul is quoting an early Christian hymn or the like. His introductory "He says," however, always precedes a quotation from God's written Word. Paul is showing us from God's Word that the great new covenant ministry of Christ is to shine the saving, transforming light of the gospel into the lives of men and women dead in trespasses and sins (Eph. 2:1). The gospel speaks into the spiritual deadness of men and women, summoning them to "awake" and "arise from the dead." Jesus's raising of Lazarus from the dead wonderfully illustrates the gospel message of God's Word (John 11:43–44).

It is fitting that Paul should tell us that Christ is the light that shines the transforming grace and power of God's truth into our lives. Jesus is the gospel. He is inseparable from the blessings that the gospel brings into our lives. All those blessings are only to be found "in Christ" (Eph. 1:3).

Walk Circumspectly

Paul concludes his exposition of the God-pleasing life by encouraging God's people to a measure of self-examination: "See then that you walk circumspectly" (v. 15). Paul is aware of the danger of Christians becoming complacent in their walk. The passing of time or a succession of pleasant circumstances can take the edge off the Christian's watchfulness. Jesus urged His disciples to "watch and pray, lest you enter into temptation. The spirit indeed is willing, but the flesh is weak" (Matt. 26:41). Watchfulness involves being alert to our own weaknesses and to the ensnaring schemes of the devil (Eph. 6:11). The wise take to heart the perfect wisdom of their Lord.

Paul proceeds to tell us how we can walk carefully, "redeeming the time, because the days are evil" (v. 16). Walking carefully in the ways of the Lord is best achieved by using our time wisely, not frittering it away indolently. It was when King David was idly walking around the roof of his palace, "at the time when kings go out to battle," that he saw Bathsheba, and the rest is history (2 Sam. 11:1–2).

The Christian life is lived out in "days [that] are evil" (5:16). The unholy trinity of the world, the flesh, and the devil is united in seeking the downfall and demise of every one of God's dear children. All Christians need to be aware that their adversary the devil is like a prowling lion, determined to devour them (1 Peter 5:8). Paul will develop this at greater length in 6:10–20.

20

Filled with the Spirit

EPHESIANS 5:17–21

Therefore do not be unwise, but understand what the will of the Lord is. And do not be drunk with wine, in which is dissipation; but be filled with the Spirit, speaking to one another in psalms and hymns and spiritual songs, singing and making melody in your heart to the Lord, giving thanks always for all things to God the Father in the name of our Lord Jesus Christ, submitting to one another in the fear of God.

From Ephesians 4:17, Paul has described the shape and the style of the life that is pleasing to God. This new life is the practical evidence of our new birth by the Spirit of Christ. Where this new life is absent, the Spirit of Christ cannot be present. New birth produces new life. This new life does not just happen but is the inevitable fruit of the indwelling presence of Christ to whom we have been united by faith, a union that is marked by our being "dead indeed to sin, but alive to God in Christ Jesus our Lord" (Rom. 6:11; see also Eph. 2:10). This wonderful truth, however, does not mean that growth in grace is automatic or that we somehow receive it by spiritual osmosis. Sanctification engages the Christian's determined resolve, as Paul has been impressing on us so insistently in the previous verses. Unless we "walk circumspectly," "redeeming the time, because the days are evil" (vv. 15–16), we will be sure to make no progress in sanctification, in living lives "acceptable to the Lord" (v. 10). The grace of God to us in Christ does not remove the need for resolved determination in the pursuit of holiness. We are to "[give] all diligence, [and] add to [our] faith virtue" (2 Peter 1:5), just as we are to be ever "endeavoring to keep the unity of the Spirit in the bond of peace" (Eph. 4:3).

More than anything, Paul wants these Christians in Ephesus to "walk as children of light" (5:8), which, as we have seen, will mean "finding out what is acceptable to the Lord" (5:10). It is remarkable how down-to-earth Paul is in his injunctions. He is writing to Christians who have been blessed in Christ "with every spiritual blessing in the heavenly places" (Eph. 1:3), and yet he continues to impress on them the responsibility they have to refuse sin and pursue righteousness. They may have been blessed in Christ with every spiritual blessing, but sin remains within them, the world around them is seductive, and the devil is a powerful, relentless, and conniving enemy (Eph. 6:10–20). So it is imperative that these Christians are not "unwise, but understand what the will of the Lord is" (v. 17).

This is the context in which we find Paul exhorting believers to "be filled with the Spirit" (v. 18). This is one of the most misunderstood exhortations in the New Testament. Throughout this section of his letter, Paul is highlighting the contours of the Spirit-filled life. Step-by-step, Paul is describing to us what the Spirit-filled life looks like, in church (5:19), in daily life (5:20), in fellowship (5:21), in the family (5:22–6:4), and finally in the workplace (6:5–9). It is striking that this section on relationships within the family is by far the longest section in Ephesians.

In verse 18, Paul contrasts a wine-filled life with a Holy Spirit–filled life, a contrast between two conditions and two lifestyles. One condition leads to "dissipation," to wild, dissolute, uncontrolled behavior, a lifestyle marked by self-indulgence. In contrast, the Holy Spirit–filled life leads to a lifestyle dominated by praise and thankfulness to God; humble, self-denying service to others within the fellowship of the church; and godliness in the workplace.

Living in Evil Days

The "therefore" that introduces verse 17 connects what Paul will say about the Spirit-filled life with what he has just been saying. He has told the Ephesians that "the days are evil" (v. 16). It is not that life in Ephesus was particularly more evil than life in Rome or Philippi or Thessalonica. The evilness of the days is a characteristic of life in every age of world history. The days are evil because we live in a world in active rebellion against God, the gospel of His Son, and people who have come to believe that gospel and have been transformed by its power and grace. "Therefore," Paul writes, "do not be unwise, but understand what the will of the Lord is" (v. 17).

Learning to Be Wise

Living as believers in evil days requires two things. First, we must not be "unwise" (5:17). In the context it seems clear that Paul is exhorting us not to live thoughtlessly but to be wisely conscious of the times in which we live. Jesus told His disciples to be "wise as serpents and harmless as doves" (Matt. 10:16). Peter told the elect exiles of the dispersion to "honor all people. Love the brotherhood. Fear God. Honor the king" (1 Peter 2:17). Living for Christ in a fallen world does not mean behaving foolishly or erratically. Christians are to live as responsible citizens and to respect authority—even the authority of a godless emperor!

Second, we must "understand what the will of the Lord is" (v. 17). Paul proceeds to spell out in surprising detail what God's will is for His children who are living in evil days. But before we consider the details, we should pause and note the principle. We are to understand what the Lord's will is. Throughout his letters Paul places great emphasis on the importance of the mind, of Christians being thinking people (Rom. 12:2). Instead of living foolishly—that is, unthinkingly and perhaps selfishly—we are to live with understanding. The life of faith is a thoughtful life; it seeks to make sense of what God has called His people to be and how He has called them to live. "In understanding be men," Paul told the Corinthians (1 Cor. 14:20 KJV).

The will of God that we are to understand is multifaceted, but at heart it is one. Paul tells the Thessalonians, "This is the will of God, your sanctification" (1 Thess. 4:3). He tells them, "In everything give thanks; for this is the will of God in Christ Jesus for you" (1 Thess. 5:18). God's ultimate will for every one of His children is that they be conformed to the image of His Son, "that He might be the firstborn among many brethren" (Rom. 8:29). God's will for us ultimately reaches its omega point in the exaltation of the Lord Jesus Christ among His adopted, blood-redeemed brothers. So the ultimate reason why we must understand the will of the Lord is not that we might live a blessed life but that our Lord Jesus will be highly exalted.

Drunk with Wine

Why does Paul begin his appeal for us to "not be drunk with wine, in which is dissipation," and "be filled with the Spirit" (v. 18)? Is it not surprising that as he exhorts us to understand the Lord's will he finds it necessary to tell us that this has nothing to do with getting drunk with wine? The apostle is not condemning the drinking of wine; he is condemning the drinking of wine to excess. Then as now, the church lived in a world dominated by self-indulgence. Many of the Ephesian Christians had probably at one time indulged the passions of their flesh (1 Cor. 6:9–11). They lived unto themselves. Their first thought was not how they could please the Lord today, as Paul instructs in 5:10, but what they could do to indulge their passions today, a picture he presents in 2:3. As Paul has already told them to put away lying (4:25) and stealing (4:28), he now tells them not to drink wine to excess. One of the fruits of the Spirit is self-control (Gal. 5:23). The life that is pleasing to God is not self-indulged but self-controlled; it is lived under the controlling, gracious constraint of God's Spirit. When self is indulged in excessive wine drinking, the result is dissipation. The Christian is to avoid anything that will lead to a loss of self-control. This principle is to mark the life of the church, particularly in its worship. Christian worship is never to be out of control but always controlled by Spirit and Truth (John 4:23–24).[1]

---

1. Most English Bible translations lowercase the words "spirit and truth." It

The Spirit-Filled Life

In contrast to wine-fueled self-indulgence, which leads to dissipation, the Christian is to "be filled with the Spirit" (v. 18) and thereby live a life that is pleasing to God. But what does it mean to be filled with the Spirit? Paul's principal concern is not to focus on the experience of the Spirit-filled life but on its evidences. There are a number of grammatical features in the phrase "be filled with the Spirit" that illuminate the shape and public profile of the Spirit-filled life.

A Command to Obey

Paul is issuing a command, not making a suggestion: "Be filled with the Spirit." Not to be filled with the Spirit is to live in disobedience to God. Christians have a divinely mandated command to be filled with the Spirit.

A Command to the Whole Church

The command is addressed to the whole church—that is, to Christians who already have the Spirit. Christians who are filled with the Spirit are not spiritual elites. The Spirit-filled life is the normal Christian life. Not to be filled with the Spirit is to live a deeply aberrant Christian life. Men and women, boys and girls—all are to be filled with the Spirit.

The Command Is in the Passive Voice

That is, "Let (or allow) the Holy Spirit fill you." What precisely is in Paul's mind? In what way are we to let the Spirit fill us? Paul noticeably makes no mention here of waiting for or seeking after special experiences. The filling of the Spirit is not an "experience" to undergo but a lifestyle to cultivate. In Colossians 3:16, a passage that parallels what Paul writes here, Paul urges the believers in Colossae, "Let the word of Christ dwell in you richly in all wisdom,

---

is highly possible, however, not least in the flow of John's gospel, that "spirit and truth" should be uppercase, as I have styled it here (see John 14:6).

teaching and admonishing one another in psalms and hymns and spiritual songs, singing with grace in your hearts to the Lord." The way in which we obey the command to be filled with the Spirit is by responding to the word of Christ, making room for its influence, giving our minds to its truth, our hearts to its teaching, and our wills to its obedience. The evidence that you are filled with the Spirit is that your whole life is shaped and directed by the Spirit-inspired word of God. The Spirit-filled life is richly indwelled by the word of God. Word and Spirit are spiritual Siamese twins. I heard a sermon many years ago that captured this concept in these memorable words: "With the word alone we dry up. With the Spirit alone we blow up. With word and Spirit together we grow up." As we allow God's word to take root in our lives and let the Spirit shape and style our lives according to God's precepts and promises, we live the Spirit-filled life. Jesus was the prototypical Spirit-filled man, and the hallmark of His life was His heart obedience to the word and will of His Father.

Does the word of Christ dwell in you richly? Is your life increasingly being conformed to the likeness of Christ, the Man of the Spirit, the Man who lived under the word? Or are there "no go" areas that you isolate from the searching, intrusive, humbling ministry of the word of God?

The Command Is in the Present Continuous Tense

The command to "be filled with the Spirit" is in the present continuous tense. Paul could not be clearer that the fullness of the Spirit is not a once-for-all, unrepeatable experience. The life of faith is a life of continuous fillings of the Spirit. There is never a moment when we arrive. There are always more fillings of the Spirit, more occasions when we will submit our lives to the wisdom, grace, instruction, truth, and power of God's word. This does not mean that the Lord will not punctuate your life with moments or even seasons of transforming, reviving power. But it does mean that we are not to live for these moments or seasons but seek every day to be filled with the Spirit by bringing every thought captive to Christ and our whole lives in happy submission to His word.

It is striking that Paul does not dwell on the state of the Spirit-filled life. Rather, he focuses on the marks of the Spirit-filled life. What follows is a description of the Spirit-filled life, which Christians today should take to heart.

Paul uses a series of present participles to highlight the dynamic character of the Spirit-filled life. He wants us to understand that any life filled with the Spirit will not be self-indulgent (cf. v. 18a) but will be marked by a serving spirit and a joyful, thankful, worshiping heart.

Life in Community

The Spirit-filled life is lived in community with other believers and is deeply relational, not lived in atomized isolation from other Christians: "speaking to one another in psalms and hymns and spiritual songs" (v. 19). It is remarkable that Paul begins his description of the Spirit-filled life here. We might have expected him to begin with the phrase "singing and making melody in your heart to the Lord" (v. 19). Why does he begin his description with the horizontal and not the vertical, with man and not with Christ? Paul is saying something significant to us: whatever else the Spirit-filled life is, it is a life that seeks to build up and bless fellow believers—that seeks to minister God's grace to God's people. Paul has learned well from the Lord Jesus Christ: "By this all will know that you are My disciples, if you have love for one another" (John 13:35). You might have expected Jesus to say, "If you have love for Me." The reality of our Christian profession is most tested by the way we treat and relate to other Christians. For the New Testament, this is a truth of the greatest importance. John writes in his first letter, "If someone says, 'I love God,' and hates his brother, he is a liar; for he who does not love his brother whom he has seen, how can he love God whom he has not seen?" (1 John 4:20).

Whenever God's Spirit fills a person with the truth and dynamic of God's word, He manifests His prevailing presence in love for the brothers. In particular, this love for the brothers will show itself in "speaking to one another in psalms and hymns and spiritual songs."

Christian worship has a deeply horizontal as well as a deeply vertical dimension: "speaking to one another." Christian worship that flows from a Spirit-filled life is never self-centered and certainly is not self-preoccupied. It is worship that is marked by the family spirit of mutual encouragement. We come before God not as a collection of disparate individuals, though we come with our unique individuality. We come to worship as the people of God, the body of Christ, the temple of the Holy Spirit.

This is one of the marked features of the Psalter. Again and again, the psalmists direct encouragement, challenge, and thankfulness to other worshipers and to themselves. In Psalm 103, David summons his own soul to "bless the LORD…and forget not all His benefits" (v. 2). In Psalm 105, the psalmist exhorts his fellow worshipers to "give thanks to the LORD," to "make known His deeds among the peoples," to "sing psalms to Him" and to "glory in His holy name" (vv. 1–3).

Psalms and Hymns and Spiritual Songs

There is debate among Christians as to what precisely Paul means by "psalms and hymns and spiritual songs" (5:19).[2] What we can all agree on is that the principal focus of these psalms and hymns and spiritual songs is "the Lord"—that is, Jesus (v. 19b). Those living the Spirit-filled life delight to encourage brothers and sisters in Christ by addressing them in songs that extol the glory and grace of the Lord Jesus Christ. Christian praise should therefore be richly theological and deeply devotional. The fundamental presupposition should never be the catchiness of the music but the scriptural character of the words. Just as Christian teaching and preaching should be scrutinized by the authority of God's Word, so Christian worship should be similarly scrutinized.

---

2. See Michael Bushell, *Songs of Zion: The Biblical Basis for Exclusive Psalmody* (Norfolk, Va.: Norfolk Press, 2011) for a robust defense of exclusive psalmody.

Making Melody to the Lord

The Spirit-filled life is further marked by "singing and making melody in your heart to the Lord [Jesus]" (v. 19). Those living the Spirit-filled life love to extol the grace, greatness, and glory of the Lord Jesus Christ to the Lord Jesus Christ. Jesus taught His disciples that the Spirit's new covenant ministry would be to bring glory to Him (John 16:14). They also delight to declare in song the praises of the Savior. As we sing to one another, we are also singing to the Lord. One of the new things God does to us when the gospel of His Son captures our hearts is to give us hearts that delight to sing His praise. David writes about this in Psalm 40:3: "He has put a new song in my mouth—praise to our God" (cf. Ps. 96:1; 149:1). The apostle John also wrote about the "new song" in Revelation 5:9. New songs of praise flow out of hearts that have tasted afresh the Lord's new works of grace.

The words of praise we sing with our lips are to be melodiously sounded in our hearts. Nothing is more offensive to God than praise that is mechanical, formal, and unengaging, even though it is formally orthodox. The prophet Isaiah wrote about God's response to the heartless worship and praise of His covenant people:

> When you come to appear before Me,
> Who has required this from your hand,
> To trample My courts?
> Bring no more futile sacrifices....
> I cannot endure [I hate] iniquity and the sacred meeting....
> When you spread out your hands,
> I will hide My eyes from you;
> Even though you make many prayers,
> I will not hear. (Isa. 1:12–15)

Jesus condemned the worship of the Pharisees for its heartlessness:

> Well did Isaiah prophesy of you hypocrites, as it is written:
> "This people honors Me with their lips,
> But their heart is far from Me." (Mark 7:6)

Paul is speaking here about heart praise that is directed to the Lord—that is, Jesus. The person and works of the Lord Jesus Christ are to be central to the praise of the church. We are not to praise a Jesus dislocated from the Holy Trinity. He is ever the Sent One of the Father, the One in whom the Spirit dwells without measure. But the heavenly Father's great delight and purpose is to see His Son exalted, and the great new covenant ministry of the Holy Spirit is to bring glory to the Savior (John 16:14). Adoring praise to Jesus Christ will be a distinguishing mark of a healthy Christian life and of a healthy church life. It is a wonderful thing that every Christian without exception has a song to sing.

Thankfulness

The Spirit-filled life will be marked by thankfulness, "giving thanks always for all things to God the Father in the name of our Lord Jesus Christ" (v. 20). The Spirit-filled life is thankful, not complaining. Paul's words are surely "faith stretching": "giving thanks always for *all things*" (emphasis added)! Is Paul being unrealistic? Life is so variable. Sooner or later troubles, difficulties, and even tragedies will touch our lives. Is the apostle saying that even then we are to give thanks? He is, absolutely. John Calvin makes this comment: "The innumerable benefits which we receive from God yield fresh cause of joy and thanksgiving."[3] Calvin is not suggesting that the life of faith is one of untroubled ease. His own life was literally engulfed with difficulties, illnesses, and disasters. But he always had cause for giving thanks because of the "innumerable benefits" he had received from God in Christ. Paul was too much of a realist to engage in flights of spiritual fancy. Remember, he is writing this letter from prison (Eph. 6:20). He is in chains, yet he can write "giving thanks always for all things." This is the conviction of a man who is persuaded that God is absolutely good. This goodness was seen in the

---

3. John Calvin, *Calvin's Commentaries: The Epistles of Paul the Apostle to the Galatians, Ephesians, Philippians and Colossians*, trans. T. H. L. Parker, David W. Torrance, and Thomas F. Torrance (Edinburgh: St. Andrew Press, 1965), 204.

giving of His Son to be the Savior of the world and in His blessing us in Christ with every spiritual blessing. We will never rise to giving thanks always and for everything until we are similarly persuaded that God is absolutely good. We can give thanks because in His Son God has given us His best and will therefore withhold no lesser blessing from us (Rom. 8:32). Our thanksgiving may be through tears and unrelieved perplexity, but it will be all the more real for that.

This is one of the remarkable features of the Spirit-filled life. If we are always for all things giving thanks, there will be no room for complaining. Some Christians, sadly, find it easier to moan and complain than to give thanks, always seemingly on the lookout for things to criticize. A complaining spirit is an anti-Christ spirit. It denies the goodness, wisdom, and love of God.

Submitting to One Another

The final mark of the Spirit-filled life that Paul highlights is mutual submission. The one living a Spirit-filled life has a servant's heart. This was supremely seen in the Man who had the Spirit without measure: "I am among you as the One who serves" (Luke 22:27). Jesus further impressed on His disciples the priority and preeminence of mutual love in their fellowship with one another: "By this all will know that you are My disciples, if you have love for one another" (John 13:35). In the family of God service, not status, is the mark of greatness.

This is a note that ought to be far more prominent among Bible-believing Christians than it presently is. The servant-hearted example of the Lord Jesus Christ is often sadly inconspicuous in church life. Nothing would do more to elevate the internal life of a church and enhance its gospel witness than an all-pervasive servant spirit among its members. Esteeming one another better than ourselves and going out of our way to seek the good of others in the church fellowship would add luster to church life and give an added credibility to our calling to shine like stars in the universe as we hold out the word of life (Phil. 2:15–16). Satan is always looking for opportunities to break asunder the unity of Christ's church. Yes, we need doctrinal unity, but we also need heart and soul unity (John 17:20–26; Eph. 4:1–6; Phil. 2:2–3). Purely formal doctrinal and confessional unity without love to Christ and love to His blood-redeemed people is a unity of form only. Such a unity is a charade, a disgrace to God, and a denial of the gospel.

Fear of God

What will this submitting to one another look like? The phrase "in the fear of God [Christ]" (v. 21) provides us with the most remarkable and wonderful illustration. Jesus was the Man of the Spirit par excellence. He modeled what the Spirit-filled life looks like, and not least in the way He served His dull-hearted disciples. John recounts in remarkable detail Jesus washing His disciples' feet (John 13:1–15). It was the responsibility of the servant of the house to wash the house guests' feet. Probably shaming His disciples, Jesus "laid aside His garments, took a towel and girded Himself. After that, He poured water into a basin and began to wash the disciples' feet" (John 13:4–5). Jesus's disciples were sinful men; they regularly failed their Lord. And yet He stooped down and washed their feet. Jesus had come not to be served, but to serve (Mark 10:45). He esteemed us as better than Himself when He put our interests above and before His own (Phil. 2:5–8). The gospel comes to unite us to the Servant-King and to make us partakers of His servant spirit. We are to "be kindly affectionate to one another with brotherly love, in honor giving preference to one another" (Rom. 12:10). We are to esteem one another as better than ourselves. We are to "love the brotherhood" (1 Peter 2:17).

Spirit-filled people have servant hearts. They look to serve. They love to serve and go out of their way to serve. Spirit-filled people reflect, however poorly, the life of the Lord Jesus Christ, the perfect Spirit-filled Man.

Is one reason—perhaps the reason—why the church's witness to Christ in the world is so weak and so often ineffective because we are so unlike our Servant King? "By this all will know that you are My disciples, if you have love for one another" (John 13:35). Is self-denying love for your fellow believers a hallmark of your life? Can the world see that you love your fellow Christians? The apostle John put the issue starkly and searchingly: "Beloved, if God so loved us, we also ought to love one another. No one has seen God at any time. If we love one another, God abides in us, and His love has been perfected in us" (1 John 4:11–12).

21

Christlike Submissiveness

EPHESIANS 5:22–24

*Wives, submit to your own husbands, as to the Lord. For the hus-
band is head of the wife, as also Christ is head of the church; and
He is the Savior of the body. Therefore, just as the church is subject
to Christ, so let the wives be to their own husbands in everything.*

It is deeply significant that having described the fundamental features of the Spirit-filled life, Paul proceeds to speak about wives and
husbands, husbands and wives, children and parents, and fathers
(and mothers) and children (5:22–6:4).[1] The Spirit-filled life is not
to be lived in a vacuum. It is to be lived out among the people of
God, within the family and in the workplace (6:5–9). Gospel credibility is established principally in the home. The gospel comes to
transform our relationship not only with God but also with one
another. In Christ, believers are new creations (2 Cor. 5:17).

God's Design
In Genesis 1 and 2 we learn that marriage was not a good idea
dreamed up by man but a relationship conceived and designed by
God. Marriage is one of the foundational building blocks in human
society. It is the union of one man and one woman for life (Gen.
2:24; Matt. 19:4–6). We live in an age when so-called same-sex

---

1. Ephesians 5:22–6:9 is helpfully, insightfully, and practically expounded in
David Martyn Lloyd-Jones's series of sermons *Life in the Spirit in Marriage, Home
and Work* (Edinburgh: Banner of Truth Trust, 1973).

marriage has been legitimized throughout the world. Even main-line churches, seduced by the mantra of modernity, have given their blessing to such unions. But no matter how hard men and women try, marriage is undeniably and incontrovertibly between one man and one woman. You can call a dog a pig, but if it barks, wags its tail, and is called Rover, it's a dog! More than ever Christians are called to live out the grace of Christ in their marriages, confounding our deeply selfish world with powerful pictures of love, harmony, selflessness, and deep joy.

In an increasingly amoral and anti-Christian world, Christians' convictions about the heterosexual, binding nature of marriage will inevitably bring them into collision with lifestyles that promote self-indulgent hedonism. This collision will be both dangerous and rich in gospel opportunity. Faithful, monogamous marriage is one of the essential, God-provided building blocks of societal cohesion. As social cohesion unravels, stable, faithful Christian marriages can function as salt and light, helping fulfill Jesus's command to His church: "Let your light so shine before men, that they may see your good works and glorify your Father in heaven" (Matt. 5:16).

Paul's teaching on marriage in Ephesians 5 is rooted in his wider teaching of the grace of God in the gospel. The force of Paul's repeated injunctions in chapters 4–6 can be rightly appreciated only when seen in the context of chapters 1–3. In those chapters Paul has set out the riches of the gospel of Christ. He has shown us how extravagantly the Lord has blessed us in Christ with all spiritual blessings. Without this context of grace, Paul's marriage injunctions could sound metallic. Throughout the Bible, as we have seen, there is a specific "grammar" to God's revelation. The commands of the gospel are rooted in and flow out of the blessings of the gospel. This is the difference between evangelical and legal obedience. Legal obedience operates out of a mere sense of duty to win favor; evangelical obedience operates out of a deep sense of love and gratitude to God, not to win His love but because we possess His love. This gospel grammar must shape and style how ministers of the gospel preach the Word. Preaching is essentially the overflow of a man's life. That overflow must impress on those who listen that God is full of grace and rich in mercy.

Love and the Family

Why does Paul devote so much of this letter to the subject of relationships within the family? John Stott explains the reason well: "The divine family ceases to be a credible concept if it is not itself sub-divided into human families which display God's love."[2] Similarly, Paul tells Timothy that a man is unfit to be an undershepherd in Christ's church unless he is "one who rules his own house well... with all reverence" (1 Tim. 3:4). The credibility of our Christian witness begins in our homes, among our families. There is an obvious connection with these verses and Ephesians 5:21. Paul has been highlighting the Spirit-filled grace of mutual submission. Now he picks up on the grace of submission and applies it to wives in their relationship with their "own husbands" (v. 22). Paul is not in any sense suggesting that wives are less than their husbands, that their relationship is one of inferior to superior. The Bible is adamant that men and women are equally made in the image and likeness of God and are "heirs together of the grace of life" (1 Peter 3:7). Rather, Paul is looking to show us what mutual submission looks like in the Christian family. If, as Calvin says, "where love reign, mutual services will be rendered,"[3] Paul's concern is to impress on God's people that love serves. In the New Testament, the idea of submission is voluntary yielding in love, pursuing the interests of others and not your own, no matter how noble. This was the mind-set of our Lord Jesus Christ (Phil. 2:5–8). This is why male chauvinism and female feminism are equally condemned in God's Word and why both of these react so violently to God's wisdom. In our world greatness is given to status, but in the Bible greatness is seen in service (Luke 22:24–27).

---

2. Stott, *God's New Society*, 213.

3. John Calvin, *Commentaries on the Epistles of Paul*, trans. William Pringle, Calvin's Commentaries, vol. 21 (Grand Rapids: Baker, 1993), 317.

This truth poses a huge challenge to gospel churches. Is it evident that those set apart to lead are men with a manifest servant heart? Evangelical Christianity has been scarred in its modern history both by the cult of personality and a spirit of overweening pride. If the Lord Jesus Christ, the Lord of glory, could say, "I am among you as the One who serves" (Luke 22:27), all Christian leaders should be marked by the same spirit and should be noted for leading by serving.

Wives and Husbands First

In focusing on family life, Paul begins with wives and husbands. Why not first with children? For this reason: the great issue in family life is not how parents relate to children or how children relate to parents. The great issue is how wives relate to their husbands and how husbands relate to their wives. It is the husband-wife relationship that sets the tone, direction, love, and obedience that are to shape family life, establish harmony within the home, and bring glory and honor to Christ. Some years ago I heard Elisabeth Elliot speak on marriage. One thing she said struck me powerfully and has remained with me: "The greatest good a father can do for his children is to love their mother. The greatest good a mother can do for her children is to love their father." Too often in the church we focus on the failures of children to grow into faith and discipleship, when the primary focus ought to be on the failures of their parents to provide them with the compelling power and grace of fathers and mothers who love one another and who live in glad submission to the wisdom and rule of Christ in His Word. I remember well visiting a couple whose teenage children were behaving badly and showing little interest in the gospel. As I listened to them, I knew what I needed to say. With some trepidation I said, "The reason why your children are the way they are is because you are the way you are." I knew the couple well, but wondered how they would respond. They simply replied, "We know." My point is not that if Christian parents truly love and serve one another their children will inevitably become sweet, faithful Christians. Rather, God is most often pleased to use the godly soil of parental love to provide the context for children to grow up in the Lord.

Godly Humility

Paul literally says, "Wives to your own husbands" ("submit" is not in the Greek text but is implied). Paul is applying the idea of submission that is to mark everyone within the Christian community (v. 21) successively to wives (vv. 22–24), children (6:1–3), and servants (6:5–9). Within the context of mutual submission in the church fellowship, Paul highlights the particular submission that is to be found first within the Christian family and second within the sphere of work.

Why does Paul not begin with husbands when he says that "the husband is head of the wife, as also Christ is head of the church" (v. 23)? Not because he is being polite! Rather, he is seeking to develop the Christian principle of godly, Christlike submission by giving it a practical and familial focus. Paul highlights three features of a wife's relationship to her husband: what she is to do, why she is to do it, and how she is to go about it.

First, wives are to submit to the divinely appointed headship of their own husbands. The wife-husband principle of submission is rooted in creation (Gen. 2:18;[4] 1 Tim. 2:11–15). Submission for a Christian is a voluntary yielding in love. It is not an acknowledgment that the person I submit to is superior to me and that I am inferior to him or her. When a wife submits to her husband, she is recognizing and embracing the fact that he is the God-appointed head and leader of their relationship and home. She is not to submit to her husband because he is more spiritual than she is or stronger, wiser, or more intelligent. He may be; he may not be. If God has appointed something, it must be right and wise and good.

---

4. עֵזֶר (ezer), meaning "helper," possibly "completer." Rather than demean the woman, God uses a word that is used of Him helping His people (Ex.18:4). Eve was to be Godlike in her relationship to her husband.

Second, she is to submit to him "as to the Lord" (v. 22); that is, as part of her obedience to Christ. The Lord who is all-wise commands it; she is to do it. The wife's calling is to model the relationship of the church to its Head and Savior, Jesus Christ. This is no demeaning calling. The Lord Jesus Christ lived under the headship of His Father (1 Cor. 11:3). He told his disciples, "I am among you as the One who serves" (Luke 22:27). The essence of true greatness is service, not status.

It should be said that a wife's submission to her husband will reflect, in part, her God-given personality and temperament. Some women are naturally of a quiet disposition while others are more outgoing. Wifely submission will not be monochrome, nor will it be devoid of discussion and debate—perhaps even animated discussion and debate. Husbands need the vital input and wisdom of their wives as they seek to lead them and their families in the ways of the Lord. In other words, there will be a necessary, inevitable, and desirable uniqueness to every Christian marriage. The Christian life is designedly idiosyncratic. God does not fit all his children into a preconceived spiritual shape. This is why it is only together, "with all the saints" (Eph. 3:18), that we come to a full knowledge and experience of God's love. The church is to reflect that glorious God-designed multiformity in its life, fellowship, and service.

In Everything

Wives are to submit to their own husbands "in everything" (v. 24). A wife's and every Christian's primary submission is to Christ: "We ought to obey God rather than men" (Acts 5:29). Husbands are delegated heads, no more. If any man asks of his wife what God forbids, his wife must refuse. The Christian's first allegiance is to God. When a husband asks anything of his wife that is contrary to the word and will of God, he asks too much, and his wife must refuse to obey. Indeed, as we will see, husbands are to love their wives as Christ loved the church and gave Himself up for her (v. 25). Christian husbands are to be the kind of Christlike men who make it easy for their wives to submit to their leadership. Love makes obedience sweet. The best of Christian husbands will not always get it right and will need to apologize humbly to their wives and even their children. They have the God-appointed responsibility to lead their wives and families, but only in the way that is pleasing and honoring to Christ. Paul's "in everything" is not an excuse for husbands to lord it over their wives (1 Peter 5:3). But just as the church is to submit to its sovereign King and Savior in everything, so wives have the high honor of modeling in their relationship with their husbands the privileged submission of the church to Christ.

What is a Christian wife to do if her husband acts unreasonably? Bethan Lloyd-Jones, the wife of Martyn Lloyd-Jones, was once asked that question. "But what if my husband wakes me up at 3 am demanding I fetch him ice cream? Am I to go and get it?"

Mrs. Lloyd-Jones replied, "Yes. And then phone for the doctor, because he is clearly not a well man."

Sadly, there are Christian men who behave unreasonably, who forget that their wives are to be cherished and served, not browbeaten and used. Love truly does make obedience sweet.

Why Submission?

The conflict between the church and the world is a root and branch conflict. Between the seed of the woman and the seed of the serpent is an elemental gulf (Gen. 3:15). This gulf in thinking and behavior is seen nowhere more than in the sphere of the family. The idea of wifely submission is laughable to the secular humanism that dominates the thinking of Western civilization in particular today. But the wisdom of the Creator will always trump the wisdom of man. To the world in general, the cross of Christ is foolishness and weakness, but it is the wisdom and power of God (1 Cor. 1:18, 21–25), and is so to those who are being saved (1 Cor. 1:18).

The reason wives are to submit to their own husbands is first and foremost because God commands it. A wife's godly submission to her husband belongs to her obedience to God. Submission is not a suggestion to consider; it is a command to obey. There is, however, a second reason for submission: "For the husband is head of the wife, as also Christ is head of the church; and He is the Savior of the body" (v. 23). Paul is taking us back to basics, back to God's creational order (Gen. 2:18, 21–24; 1 Tim. 2:11–14). Eve was created to be Adam's helper. She was God's gracious complement to Adam. Eve made Adam complete. She enabled him to fulfill his God-given calling on God's earth. Adam's headship was not that of a superior to an inferior. Both Adam and Eve were created in the image of God (Gen. 1:27). Paul is speaking here analogically, not absolutely—"as also Christ is head of the church" (v. 23). Man is a creature; Christ is the Creator. The point is that both the husband and Christ were appointed to their respective headships. When a husband is arbitrary or cold or self-pleasing in his headship, he is to be resisted, not submitted to. This is why an elder in the church is to be a man who "rules his own house well…with all reverence" (1 Tim. 3:4), so that he can first model godly, kindly, self-denying headship and, if needed, counsel, rebuke, and discipline husbands who fail to cherish their wives. Headship is never to be an excuse for being domineering.

Matthew Henry has a beautiful exposition of the relationship Adam was to have with his wife: "The woman was made of a rib out of the side of Adam; not made out of his head to rule over him, nor out of his feet to be trampled upon by him, but out of his side to be equal with him, under his arm to be protected, and near his heart to be beloved."[5]

Third, how are wives to submit to the God-ordained headship of their husbands? They are to do so "as the church is subject to Christ" (v. 24). Clearly Paul is speaking analogically, not absolutely, as we have seen. How is the church to submit to Christ? We can best answer that question by asking another question: How does the Lord expect His church to submit to Him? First, out of love to Him who first loved us. The first and greatest commandment, said Jesus, is that we love the Lord our God with all our heart and with all our

---

5. Matthew Henry, *Commentary on the Whole Bible* (Peabody, Mass.: Hendrickson, 1991), 10 (commenting on Gen. 2:21).

soul and with all our mind (Matt. 22:37). An unloving submission is deeply offensive to God. It is the posture of a body, not the love of a heart. Christians have every cause to love the Lord and to acquiesce humbly to His headship. In like manner, wives are to submit to their husbands in love, not out of a sense of mere duty. Second, wives should submit with confidence. The church knows that its Savior is worthy of unhesitating submission. He laid down His life for His church. Out of love for His church He "endured the cross, despising the shame" (Heb. 12:2) and became "obedient to the point of death, even the death of the cross" (Phil. 2:8). There is nothing the Lord Jesus Christ could ask of His church that would not be for its good, so its submission to Him is confident and unhesitating. Third, wives should submit with scriptural direction. The church's submission to Christ is never to be unthinking or mindless. The Lord never asks anything of His church that is not according to His revealed will. The Lord exercises His lordship over His church through the precepts and principles of His Word (Isa. 8:20; 2 Tim. 3:16–17). This truth protects the church from the fads and fashions that come and go with every succeeding generation. So the church's submission to Christ will never be mindless; it will always be shaped and informed by God's revelation in Holy Scripture.

The basic problem in the world today is that of authority. Until families are led and shaped by God's good and perfect will, society will continue its chaotic, anarchic ways. It is what the Bible calls the "deceitfulness of sin" (Heb. 3:13), which blinds political leaders of all persuasions to this truth.

The Bible's teaching on the relationship of wives to husbands is considered a relic of a bygone, patriarchal age. We are so sure we know better. And yet we live today, especially in the West, in a sea of marital breakdown that has produced increasingly dysfunctional societies. When people walk out on God and disregard the wisdom of His Word, chaos inevitably happens. Thus it ever has been (Judg. 21:25).

It would be appropriate at this point to ask some questions: Wives, do you submit to your husband's God-appointed leadership?

Do you submit gladly, out of love? Do you help him to live up to his calling? Do you pray for your husband to have the courage, grace, wisdom, and humility to be your head? Husbands, do you make it as easy as possible for your wives to submit to your headship? Do you treat your wife as your spiritual equal? Do you tell her, as the Lord so often tells His bride, that you love and cherish her? Do you treat her with gentleness and thoughtfulness? Do you listen to her and have the humility to lead her, when necessary, by following her?

22

Christlike Authority

EPHESIANS 5:25–33

Husbands, love your wives, just as Christ also loved the church and gave Himself for her, that He might sanctify and cleanse her with the washing of water by the word, that He might present her to Himself a glorious church, not having spot or wrinkle or any such thing, but that she should be holy and without blemish. So husbands ought to love their own wives as their own bodies; he who loves his wife loves himself. For no one ever hated his own flesh, but nourishes and cherishes it, just as the Lord does the church. For we are members of His body, of His flesh and of His bones. "For this reason a man shall leave his father and mother and be joined to his wife, and the two shall become one flesh." This is a great mystery, but I speak concerning Christ and the church. Nevertheless let each one of you in particular so love his own wife as himself, and let the wife see that she respects her husband.

Christian wives have the exalted privilege of mirroring in their relationships with their husbands the church's relationship to Christ. Christian husbands have the exalted, if daunting and humbling, privilege of mirroring in their relationships with their wives the Savior's relationship with His church.

It is striking that Paul does not write, "Husbands, rule your wives," but "Husbands, love your wives" (v. 25). Three times in these verses, husbands are commanded to love their wives (vv. 25, 28, 33). The most important characteristic marking a Christian husband's relationship with his wife is love. The counterbalance to submission is love. In the ancient world, a wife was expected to pander to her husband's every whim. Not so the followers of Jesus Christ. In the gospel, the God-given dignity of womanhood is restored. Husbands are to set their hearts and hands on ministering to the needs of their wives. As Paul reminded the church in Corinth, love "does not seek its own" (1 Cor. 13:5).

Paul highlights two models to reflect on and inform how husbands are to love their wives. First, husbands are to love their wives "as Christ also loved the church and gave Himself for her" (v. 25). The significant word here is "as"; just as—in the same way—Christ loved His church, so husbands are to love their wives. If wives think their calling to submit to their husbands is daunting, the husband's calling to love his wife as Christ loved His church is doubly so. If God did not assure us that there is always grace to help in time of need (Heb. 4:16), these callings would leave us overwhelmed. How did Christ love His church? He loved the church by giving "Himself for her" (v. 25). The heart of love, at least of the love of Christ, is selfless sacrifice. To secure the good of His church, the Lord Jesus Christ laid down His life (John 10:18). He did so not as a martyr but as a Savior. This was the destiny foretold of God's Messiah:

> He was wounded for our transgressions,
> He was bruised for our iniquities;
> The chastisement for our peace was upon Him,
> And by His stripes we are healed. (Isa. 53:5)

In His leadership role as the covenant Head of His people (Rom. 5:12–21), the Son of God gave His all to rescue His bride from a fate worse than death (Mark 10:45). There are three notes Paul strikes. First, Christ gave *Himself.* He "made *Himself* of no reputation.... And being found in appearance as a man, He humbled Himself and became obedient to the point of death, even the death of the cross" (Phil. 2:7–8, emphasis added).[1] It was not His time and energy that He gave to His church; it was Himself. Love gives of itself. Love seeks not its own. Love empties itself to secure the good

---

1. The text literally reads "Himself He emptied" (ἀλλὰ ἑαυτὸν ἐκένωσεν).

of its beloved. Husbands are to give themselves to their wives as Christ gave Himself for His church.

Second, Christ *gave* Himself. This is the language of sacrifice. The apostle John explains the nature of this love sacrifice: "In this is love, not that we loved God, but that He loved us and sent His Son to be the propitiation for our sins" (1 John 4:10). Just as the Lord Jesus Christ gave up all He cherished, even His life, to secure the good of His bride, so husbands are to love their wives. Selfless sacrifice marked Christ's love for His betrothed.

This is the life God calls husbands to. Husbands, do you lay aside what you want to do what your wife wants to do? Do you spend precious time with her? Do you go out of your way to antici-pate her needs and desires? Headship and rule and authority are principally about service. Husbands are to love their wives just as Christ loved the church. This is both an exalted and an overwhelm-ing calling. It is not a suggestion for husbands to consider; it is a command for husbands to obey.

Third, Christ gave Himself "for her" (v. 25). All Jesus did, He did for the benefit of His bride. The cross had a goal, and that goal was the perfecting and purifying of the church. The language Paul uses is richly evocative. The verb "to sanctify" contains the funda-mental idea of "to set apart." The purpose of Christ giving Himself was to set the church apart from the world to belong to God. The goal of Christ's saving work on the cross was to "deliver us from this present evil age" (Gal. 1:4) and "present her [us] to Himself a glorious church, not having spot or wrinkle or any such thing" (v. 27). But how is this to be done? There is a manifest progression in what Paul writes. First, Christ gave Himself up for His church. Second, He did this to sanctify the church "and cleanse her with the washing of water by the word" (v. 26). Third, He did this "that He might present her to Himself a glorious church…holy and without blemish" (v. 27).

Water and Word

Before the church could be "holy and without blemish," Christ first needed to "cleanse her with the washing of water by the word" (vv. 27, 26, respectively). Jesus told Nicodemus that "unless one is born of water and the Spirit, he cannot enter the kingdom of God" (John 3:5). In that verse Jesus is not referencing baptism; rather, He is alluding to Ezekiel 36:24–27, where the Lord promises to cleanse His people inwardly from their sins, put His Spirit within them, and cause them to walk before Him in obedience. It seems more likely that here Paul is thinking about the decisive place baptism played in the life of the church. John Stott says that the "'washing of water' is an unambiguous reference to baptism."[2] In the early church, baptism was intimately and inextricably associated with salvation (Acts 2:38, 41). Paul depicts the Christian life by using the imagery of baptism (Rom. 6:1–4). The point is not that baptism in any sense effects or secures salvation. Rather, baptism was the God-appointed public sign and seal of His wholly gracious salvation to the individual, the church, and the watching world. The added phrase "by the word" highlights the truth that without the word of the gospel of Christ, baptism is unintelligible, unfounded, and empty.

This close association of Word and sacrament is not something evangelical Christians have always been comfortable with. There has been a tendency to depreciate the sacramental signs, effectively separating the Word from the God-appointed signs and seals of God's covenant grace. Calvin has wise words to say about this in his commentary:

> Some try to weaken this eulogy of baptism, in case too much is attributed to the sign if it is called the washing of the soul. But they are wrong; for in the first place, the apostle does not say that it is the sign that cleanses, but declares that this is the work of God alone. It is God who cleanses, and the praise for this must not be transferred to the sign or even shared with the sign. But there is no absurdity in saying that God uses the

---

2. Stott, *God's New Society*, 227.

sign as an instrument. Not that the power of God is shut up in the sign, but He distributes it to us by this means on account of the weakness of our capacity.[3]

As the read and preached Word gives understanding and significance to the sealing sign, so the sealing sign visibly confirms the Word before our eyes. Without the Word, the sacraments are "dumb" signs—they communicate nothing. With the Word and received in faith, they are means of grace to the people of God.

The Ultimate Goal

The goal of God's salvation in Christ is not to rescue us from our sins but to make us "holy and without blemish" (v. 27). The past decisive act of sanctification and the present continuing process of sanctification (v. 26) reach their ordained goal in the purifying and perfecting of the church, a people completely blemish free (v. 27). The present state of Christ's church in the world is one of apparent weakness. It is increasingly despised, just like its Savior. It is marked by sin and failure and disunity. But the Lord of the church is ceaselessly at work by His Spirit to "present her to Himself a glorious church, not having spot or wrinkle or any such thing" (v. 27). What is in view here is the inevitable future glory of the church. When the Lord Jesus Christ promised to build His church (Matt. 16:18), He was not thinking only of the church's protection and preservation. What He is presently in the process of building is something to take our breath away! One coming day the church will be revealed in all its splendor—a splendor wholly accomplished by Christ through the transforming, sanctifying ministry of the Holy Spirit (Rev. 21:1–2).

The salvation accomplished by Christ is not a bare rescue from the coming wrath (Col. 3:6). Because faith takes a sinner into Christ, salvation in its fullest sense is all about being transformed into His likeness (Rom. 8:29; 2 Cor. 3:18). When Christ presents

---

3. John Calvin, *The Epistles of Paul the Apostle to the Galatians, Ephesians, Philippians and Colossians*, ed. D. W. Torrance and T. F. Torrance (Edinburgh: Oliver and Boyd, 1965), 206.

His bride to Himself, He will see a reflection of Himself, a blemish-free spouse, fitted to be the bride of Christ.

It belongs to the heart of a husband's love for his wife that he seeks her perfecting in grace. This will not be done easily or in one concentrated effort. This is the work of a lifetime. Some years ago a dear young friend of mine died, leaving behind a wife. During the months leading up to his death, he wrote a farewell letter of some 180 pages. The letter is full of the choicest passages from God's Word and quotations from eminent Christians throughout the ages. When I first read this farewell letter, the opening words gripped my attention: "The first responsibility of a husband is to see his wife safely to glory." Safely to glory! This is precisely what our Lord Jesus Christ did. He gave Himself, all He was, to save us from the coming wrath and make us fit for the glory of His presence as His chosen bride. "Husbands, love your wives, just as Christ also loved the church" (v. 25).

One Flesh

In verse 28, Paul restates God's charge for husbands to love their own wives. "So" or, "in the same way," husbands are to love their wives "as their own bodies." Just as the church is the body of Christ, united indissolubly to Him, in the same way husbands and wives are indissolubly united. They are "one flesh" (Gen. 2:24). Christian marriage is a union, not a partnership. To speak of your spouse as your "partner" would both demean his or her true significance and deny the God-created nature of the marriage bond. When a husband loves his wife, he loves himself. Paul uses two richly evocative words to describe how a husband is to love his wife as his own body that describe how caringly Christ Himself loves His own body, the church. The first word is "nourishes" (ἐκτρέφει). Paul uses this word later in Ephesians 6:4 where he encourages fathers to "fondly cherish" their children. The second word is "cherishes" (θάλπει). Paul uses this word on only one other occasion (1 Thess. 2:7). The root meaning is "to keep warm," "to give kind and generous comfort." Tenderness flows out of Paul's language. Christian husbands should be noted for the kind, thoughtful, tender, and supportive way they lead their wives. Anything less dishonors Christ and brings public disgrace to the cause of the gospel.

It is no surprise, therefore, that in verse 31 Paul grounds his exposition in the creational ordinance of marriage (citing Gen. 2:24). The Bible's teaching on marriage is not shaped by cultural expectations but by God's creational ordinance and wisdom. It is imperative that when we speak of the Bible's authority we always do so in the context of the Creator's perfect wisdom. God is not a prisoner of the ever-changing expectations and explorations of this fallen world. He has spoken. His word reflects His unchanging will and perfect wisdom.

The Profound Mystery

As Paul concludes his exposition of the elemental husband-wife relationship, he acknowledges that their union as one flesh is "a great mystery" (v. 32). The true nature of the mystery, however, does not lie in the union of a man with a woman, but in the union of Christ and His bride, the church. As noted earlier, Paul uses "mystery" not to highlight the esoteric and unknowable (see comments on Eph. 3:4–6) but to speak about truths God has revealed that we could never fathom. One such truth is that the marriage of one man to one woman emblematizes and points to a greater marriage, that of Jesus Christ to His church.

God's ultimate purpose does not terminate on men and women. It terminates on His Son (Rom. 8:29). Many Christians have understood the Song of Songs ("the Superlative Song") as typifying this profound mystery of Christ's relationship with His bride, the church. Whether the Song is to be understood this way may be a matter for serious discussion. What is not in doubt is that the extravagant love Solomon lavishes on the bride and the bride lavishes on Solomon pictures Christ's love for His bride—His body, the church—and His church's love for Him. Isaiah's words to God's exiled people capture the intimacy of the relationship: "As the bridegroom rejoices over the bride, so shall your God rejoice over you" (Isa. 62:5).

This is why a husband and wife who love Christ first will love one another best. A Christian's best interests are always served when God's priorities are his or her priorities. It is when we seek first God's kingdom and His righteousness that all things will be added to us (Matt. 6:33). That fundamental kingdom principle runs like a golden thread throughout the Bible. The first answer of the Westminster Shorter Catechism succinctly and beautifully expresses the truth: "Man's chief end is to glorify God and enjoy him forever." When the gospel of God's grace comes into our lives, it centers our lives in God and orders our priorities. Where these are absent, the transforming power of the gospel can hardly be present. It cannot be said often enough: by our fruits we will be known (Matt. 7:20; John 15:8).

Verse 33, the final verse in the section, finds Paul reasserting the respective relationships of wives and husbands. Husbands must love their wives, and wives must respect their husbands. Christian marriages are to be display models that exhibit to a fallen, morally twisted world the wisdom of the Creator. The thought is both deeply humbling and deeply exciting.

23

Obedient Children

EPHESIANS 6:1–3

Children, obey your parents in the Lord, for this is right. "Honor your father and mother," which is the first commandment with promise: "that it may be well with you and you may live long on the earth."

Paul now particularly addresses the children in the church who belong to those addressed in 1:1 as "the saints who are in Ephesus, and faithful in Christ Jesus." The visible, professing church of Christ (and we have access to no other church) "consists of all... throughout the world that profess the true religion, together with their children."[1] By virtue of their covenant baptism, children are members of Christ's church. As such, Paul addresses them concerning their relationship to their parents.

Covenantal Presumption

The specter of covenant presumption lurks over the history of God's church in the world. The new covenant church was no less a stranger to covenant presumption than the old covenant church (Heb. 10:26–31). The repeated calls in the New Testament for God's people to work out their own salvation with fear and trembling (Phil. 2:12), to "go on to perfection" (Heb. 6:1), and to bear fruit and so prove to be true disciples of Christ (John 15:8) highlight God's concern that church members not rest on their profession of

---

1. Westminster Confession of Faith, 25.2.

Christ but evidence in their lives the Savior's transforming grace. A bare profession of faith that is not married to a gospel lifestyle of obedience and love is "faith without works" and is dead (James 2:14–26). Covenant privileges do not unite anyone to Christ—only self-abandoning faith does.

There is a manifest concern in Paul's teaching about the Christian family. His concern is not simply that Christian families live harmonious, happy, and God-honoring lives. He understands that the Christian family is a "store window" for the gospel (Matt. 5:16). He knows that the church's gospel credibility relies on the credibility of families and individuals whose lives have been transformed by the gospel of God's grace in Christ.

Children and Parents

Thus far Paul has appealed to wives to submit to their husbands as the church submits to Christ and to husbands to love their wives as Christ loves His church. Now he urges—commands—children to obey their parents. There is an obvious progression in Paul's thinking. Before Paul speaks to the children in the church, he first speaks to their parents. Children are planted in the soil of their parents' relationship. What children see in their parents will deeply influence how they respond to God's command to them to obey and honor their parents. Often when children in the church are rebellious, their rebellion is the fruit of the spiritual dysfunction of their parents' relationship. Where husbands are not selflessly loving their wives and where wives do not submissively love their husbands, the spiritual fallout can be deadly.

Fundamental Principle

Basic to what Paul writes in these verses is the biblical truth that individual and societal happiness depends on listening to God and obeying His word. This conviction stands in dramatic contrast to the thinking that generally prevails throughout society. Happiness is generally thought to be the product of pursuing your own thing, of trusting your own instincts, of listening to your inner voice. The

Bible, however, tells us that our best interests and present as well as future happiness depend on us following the wisdom of our Creator, the God who "so loved the world that He gave His only begotten Son" (John 3:16).

Paul's teaching in 5:20–6:4 lies at the heart of the philosophy of Christian parenting. There are many secular books on parenting based on anti-Christian principles. This is not to say that such books are uniformly unhelpful. The goodness of God's general revelation means that men and women sometimes "by nature do the things in [God's] law" (Rom. 2:14). The Christian will therefore approach secular books on parenting with discrimination and not outright rejection. What Christian parents must be absolutely clear about is that the fundamental wisdom they need for raising their children is to be found in the pages of God's wise and good Word. Children of believers are "a heritage from the LORD" (Ps. 127:3). They are the Lord's before they are ours and are to be raised as the precious gifts from God that they are.

Obey Your Parents

Wives are to submit to their husbands, husbands are to love their wives, and children are to obey their parents. Paul expands on what he means in verse 2: "Honor your father and mother." He is not speaking about a bare, grudging, enforced obedience. Rather, he is encouraging obedience that is the fruit of a heart that honors parents. Again, we need to understand that this command is relative. Where parents ask or demand of their children what God forbids, obedience to them would be sin. This is why the church, through its pastors and elders, should have a consistent shepherd-like care of the flock. Pastoral visitation is often sadly neglected in the church today. Godly, kindly, and nonintrusive visitation should be woven into the life of every Christian congregation. Pastors and elders must never lord it over the flock, but they must not neglect the flock. The Directory for the Publick Worship of God says, "It is the duty of the minister not only to teach the people committed to his charge in publick, but privately; and particularly to admonish, exhort, reprove, and comfort them, upon all seasonable occasions, so far as his time, strength, and personal safety will permit."[2] Such consistent pastoral visitation will greatly encourage parents and their children and assist the church's elders in better appreciating the different familial dynamics that make up a congregation of the Lord Jesus Christ.

Legal Obedience and Evangelical Obedience

There is a world of distance between a grudging obedience and an obedience that is the response of a thankful heart. The spirit in which children obey their parents is all important. Christian theologians have distinguished two kinds of obedience: legal obedience and evangelical obedience. Legal obedience is done out of mere duty or in order to secure some kind of advantage. Evangelical obedience is done out of love, not to secure an advantage but to express gratitude for kindness received. In Jesus's parable of the prodigal son (Luke 15:11–32), when the older son hears of his father's openhearted welcome to his younger brother, he says, "Lo, these many years I have slaved for you" (v. 29, author's translation).[3] He did not serve his father with delight but with a grudging, slave-like spirit. He was the father's son, but he did not honor his father. The only obedience that is acceptable to God is willing, gladly given heart obedience. Bare obedience can be given reluctantly and disrespectfully. The disrespect may not be heard, but it will be felt and seen.

Fathers and mothers are God's appointed representatives to exercise His authority in the home. Refusal to obey and honor parents is rebellion against God. Parents are not perfect and will make mistakes. But children can cope with their parents' failures when they see how much their parents love them. Parents need to often

---

2. "The Directory for the Publick Worship of God," in *The Subordinate Standards and Other Authoritative Documents of the Free Church of Scotland* (Edinburgh: Offices of the Free Church of Scotland, 1955), 159.

3. In the context, "to slave" is a more appropriate translation than "to serve" (δουλεύω, "to be a slave").

ask themselves, "Am I making it easy for my children to honor and obey me?"

Reasons for Obedience

It is a repeatedly striking feature of God's Word that reasons for and encouragements to obedience are attached to exhortations to obedience. Here Paul gives the church children four reasons why they should obey and honor their parents.

First, they should obey and honor their parents, "for this is right" (v. 1). Paul probably is not thinking about God's specific command as such, but of the created order. There is an inherent, created rightness in children obeying and honoring their parents. God's revelation in creation shouts out that without order and authority and respect there will be chaos because of unbridled self-interest (Rom. 1:18–20). In every human society in every age of history, there has been the recognition and acknowledgment of the necessity of authority. Sadly, authority can be and often has been abusively enforced. The authority, however, that is to mark the life of Christ's church is always to be a gracious and merciful authority. Elders are never to domineer over those in their charge (1 Peter 5:3). Husbands are always to love their wives self-denyingly (Eph. 5:25). Fathers, as we will soon see, are never to provoke their children to wrath (Eph. 6:4). Masters were to oversee their slaves knowing that with the Lord "there is no partiality" (Eph. 6:9).

Second, children should obey and honor their parents because God specifically commands it (v. 2). The gospel does not excuse us from keeping God's commandments; rather, it enforces the church's commitment to those commandments. It is not only natural to obey parents but it is scriptural to do so. Paul is quoting from the fifth commandment (Ex. 20:12; Deut. 5:16). When children refuse to obey and honor their parents, their controversy is not first with their parents; it is ultimately with God. This is highlighted in Leviticus 19:1–3. God commanded Moses to tell the people of Israel, "You shall be holy, for I the LORD your God am holy. Every one of you shall revere his mother and his father." How children relate to their parents is to reflect their reverence for God.

This is one reason why it is the responsibility of parents to impress on their children that God is natively and perfectly good. His commands are an expression of His goodness and of His desire to bless us and do us good. Who God is, is the greatest of all encouragements to doing all He says. The preface to the Ten Words (Ex. 20:1–2) roots the commandments in the soil of God's love and mercy.

Third, children should obey and honor their parents because their relationship to Jesus Christ requires it. Children's obedience to their parents is "in the Lord" (v. 1). It is certainly true that an adult or child Christian owes their primary obedience and allegiance to Christ. A child's obedience to his or her parents is to be "in all things" (Col. 3:20). But "in all things" is qualified (Acts 5:29). Christian parents must therefore be careful that they do not ask of their children anything that is contrary to God's revealed will or to the grace of the gospel. It is probable, however, that Paul's main concern is to tell the church children that obedience to their parents is their appropriate response to their Savior and Lord: "You are Christian children. You belong to the Lord Jesus Christ by creation, covenant, and redemption. So obey your parents." Obedience to parents is one of the principal ways in which children in the church evidence their love for Christ. The Gospels tell us almost nothing about Jesus's life from the events of His birth to His baptism by John. Luke, however, tells us that in those years he was "subject" to his parents (2:51). Jesus was the prototypical godly child. He is "our childhood's pattern," as the hymn puts it.[4]

Fourth, children should obey and honor their parents because God will bless them if they do: "that it may be well with you and you may live long on the earth" (v. 3). Paul, as we have seen, is quoting from the fifth commandment, conflating Exodus 20:12 and

---

4. Cecil Frances Humphreys Alexander, "Once in Royal David's City," in the public domain.

Deuteronomy 5:16. This, Paul says, "is the first commandment with promise," the promise being prosperity and long life (v. 2). The first thing we need to say is that this is a general, not an invariable, promise. Paul is making the general point that God's promised blessings will not rest on the disobedient. It is not going well for many young people (and older people too) because they disregard the fifth commandment. The happiness our hearts yearn for will never be experienced as long as we live without serious regard for God's commandments. Under the old covenant, God's covenant blessings were closely linked to the land. But the land was never to be an end in itself. It pointed forward to the eternal rest that God had prepared for His people (Heb. 4:1–11). Abraham was "the heir of the world" and not simply of the land (Rom. 4:13). This is why Paul alters the original—or a better way to understand it is that he explains the inherent trajectory of the original "upon the land" to "on the earth."[5]

In Western culture, children are boys and girls who live at home and depend on their parents for sustenance. Once they attain their "majority," they are no longer children but adults and are free from the constraints of submitting to parental discipline. In Eastern cultures (and the Bible belongs to the East), children are considered to have a lifelong responsibility to respect and care for their parents and are never considered free from their obligation to honor and even obey their parents. The escalating disintegration of family life in the West, due in large measure to societies turning away from the truth and wisdom of God's Word, has led to the increasing disappearance of family loyalty and commitment. The care of the elderly is often thought to be the responsibility of the state and not of the family. It may be that an "old folks' home" is the best environment for an elderly parent, but it should be a last, not a first, option.

Life in the twenty-first century is different from life in the first century. It still remains, however, the clear teaching of God's Word

5. ἐπὶ τῆς γῆς more accurately reads "on the earth." The focus is not the land of Israel but the whole earth.

that children of all ages are commanded by God to honor their parents. Paul is surely not just thinking of Christian parents, though there is a special appropriateness in Christian children honoring the parents who raised them "in the training and admonition of the Lord" (Eph. 6:4).

The gospel of Christ has come to transform not only our relationship with God but our relationships with one another. This is so much the case that the apostle John could write, "If someone says, 'I love God,' and hates his brother, he is a liar; for he who does not love his brother whom he has seen, how can he love God whom he has not seen?" (1 John 4:20). Obedience to parents is something that "is well pleasing to the Lord" (Col. 3:20). The Christian family truly is a store window for the gospel, for good or for ill.

A Challenge to Children

These verses are a challenge to church children. It is one thing to profess faith in Christ and another to show by your life that your profession of faith is genuine. Israel's great sin under the old covenant was the sin of covenantal presumption. They were proud of their status as God's covenant people. He had richly blessed them (Rom. 9:4–5). But, nonetheless, Paul wrote, "My heart's desire and prayer to God for Israel is that they may be saved" (Rom. 10:1). It is easy for children and their parents to become content with covenant privileges and not to trust in the Lord Jesus Christ alone for salvation. Jesus said that if we want to show that we truly are His disciples then we need to "bear much fruit" (John 15:8). He also said that only as we keep His commandments will we abide in His love (John 15:10). The gospel of God's grace is a life-transforming dynamic. Where transformation is absent, grace cannot be present. Children obeying and honoring their parents, not grudgingly but gladly "in the Lord," is fruit that pleases God and shows that they truly are Christ's disciples.

24

Wise Parenting

EPHESIANS 6:4

And you, fathers, do not provoke your children to wrath, but bring them up in the training and admonition of the Lord.

It is important we understand that Paul is not setting before the church unattainable ideals regarding God-honoring family life. What we read here is God's revealed will for Christian families. We will, no doubt, be overwhelmed by the responsibility God has laid upon us. But the Holy Spirit has been given, and He "helps in our weaknesses" (Rom. 8:26).[1]

Fathers

Fathers are mentioned not because mothers are redundant and play no part in the spiritual rearing of their children, but because they are the God-ordained covenant heads of their families. Fathers have the chief responsibility to shepherd their wives and children in the way of the Lord. The biblical pattern for child-rearing is not that the father works to provide sustenance for his family while the mother stays at home and cares for the children. Rather, the father has the chief responsibility to raise their children in the "training and admonition of the Lord" (v. 4). If fathers are too busy to do this, then they are too busy! Life in our modern world can be frenetic.

---

1. The double compound συναντιλαμβ *compo* (help, come to the aid of) contains the idea of "together with." The Spirit helps us as we work, not as we remain passive.

Husbands and fathers can be stretched simply to provide for their families. To be biblically faithful and God-honoring fathers, men will need to give much thought as to how they can best fulfill their calling to nurture their children in the faith and ways of the Lord. The greatest good a father can do for his children is to make time for the welfare of their souls. Good parents care for the physical, mental, social, and emotional well-being of their children. The best parents will give time and energy to cultivating the spiritual well-being of their children. It was Eli's neglect of the spiritual care of his sons that led to their tragic death (1 Sam. 3:13).

Fathers, do you take seriously your privileged calling to take the lead in cultivating the spiritual nurture of your children? You may feel deeply ill-equipped for this task, but God gives "grace to help in time of need" (Heb. 4:16). The Holy Spirit is your promised helper.

Watch the Way You Raise Your Children

It is striking that Paul begins his instruction to fathers with a negative: "Do not provoke your children to wrath" (v. 4). Paul was aware that in Roman society the *paterfamilias* (the head of Roman family life, the oldest living male) often was imperious, even arbitrary. He had absolute power over his children. He could sell them into slavery or even kill them. Christian fathers are called to model the grace of the heavenly Father in caring for their children. It is easy for fathers (and mothers) to "provoke" or "exasperate" their children. This can be done by imposing thoughtlessly your convictions on them; by showing unthinking or even deliberate favoritism (for example, Isaac favored Esau over Jacob); by not making quality time for them; by not taking the time to understand how they "tick"; by living an inconsistent spiritual life before them; by not treating them as individuals with their own idiosyncratic personalities and temperaments. Martyn Lloyd-Jones made the comment, "If parents gave as much thought to the rearing of their children as they do to the rearing of animals and flowers, the situation would be very different."[2] Our children are precious, God-given lives. They are vulnerable, susceptible to all kinds of unhelpful influences. Fathers and mothers greatly need to do all within their power to ensure that nothing they say or do hinders their children from sweetly receiving "the training and admonition of the Lord" (v. 4).

Fondly Cherish Them

Rather than provoke or exasperate their children, fathers are to "bring them up in the training and admonition of the Lord" (v. 4). Paul has already used this verb in Ephesians 5:29, where the NKJV translates it "nourish."[3] John Calvin helpfully brings out Paul's meaning when he paraphrases "fondly cherish" them.[4] Paul is further impressing on fathers that the attitude that marks their spiritual care of their children is all important. It is possible to do all the required things, Bible reading and prayer especially, but to do them mechanically, clinically, with little evident joy and enthusiasm. In horticulture you can give plants the required nutrients, but if the temperature is not right they will die notwithstanding. The spiritual atmosphere in which we raise our children is paramount. The Lord Jesus Christ is our perfect example. In Isaiah's first Servant Song (Isa. 42:1–4), we are told that the Lord's Servant, His Messiah, would not break a bruised reed or quench a smoking flax. His mission and ministry would be marked by undeviating faithfulness (Isa. 42:4), but no less would it be marked by gentleness and generosity. Just as we are called to speak "the truth in love" (Eph. 4:15), so we are called to raise our children with Christlike tenderness. Parents must exercise their God-given authority over their children, but in a manner that draws their children to them, not in a way that repels them.

---

2. Lloyd-Jones, *Life in the Spirit*, 290.

3. ἐκτρέφω (to feed, nourish).

4. Calvin, *Commentary on Ephesians*, 329.

Training and Admonition

The spiritual care and nourishment of children is to be shaped and styled by "the training and admonition of the Lord" (v. 4). Children are not to be left to make their own way in life. They are the Lord's heritage (Ps. 127:3), and His desire is to have "godly offspring" (Mal. 2:15).[5] Fathers are commanded to give themselves to the spiritual nurture of their children. It is not a suggestion they are invited to consider; it is a command they are enjoined to obey. Jesus's words to those who cause one of His little ones "to sin" (Matt. 18:6) should never be far from the minds and hearts of Christian fathers. It is, of course, the Lord Himself who nourishes and matures our children in the faith. If our dependence is not wholly in Him, all we do will accomplish nothing. But it pleases the Lord to use means to accomplish His ordained ends, and the faithful, consistent, loving ministry of fathers to their children is one of His principal means for advancing and maturing godly offspring.

Training

"Training" is, literally, "child training."[6] There are possibly two emphases in this child training. Paul is highlighting the necessity of training—of diligent, determined, regular application of the Lord's ways to children. This emphasis is seen in Deuteronomy 6:4–9. Through Moses, God tells parents to teach His holy commandments to their children diligently and in every sphere of life out of hearts that love Him and His commands. Child training is not to be spasmodic, irregular, or occasional; it is to take place "when you walk by the way, when you lie down, and when you rise up" and is to be done "diligently" (Deut. 6:7). Such child training is not to be relegated only to times of family worship, important though those times surely are. The whole of life is to be the context of God-honoring child

---

5. Malachi 2:15 relates "godly offspring" to a husband's committed faithfulness to his wife. This is the pattern that dominates Paul's teaching throughout this section of his letter.

6. παιδεία.

training, as parents fondly cherish their children and seek to mold them, by the grace of God, into people who please the Lord.

There is a second emphasis contained in the idea of training. This note is seen in Hebrews 12:5–6, where the Lord's chastening (παιδεία) is connected with His reproving His children. He rebukes them because He loves them "and scourges every son whom He receives" (Heb. 12:6). Child training without correction and chastisement soon dissolves into indulgence (Heb. 12:7–8). There is always the danger of zealous fathers becoming overly harsh toward their children. This is why Paul has established the context of fondly cherishing before he instructs fathers to be training their children. Parental correction and chastisement should always be measured and thoughtful and should never be done in anger. It will vary from child to child, because what will work for one child may not work for another. This will take careful and considered thought as fathers consult with mothers how best to bring up their children in the discipline of the Lord.

Admonition

Parental discipline is to be united with parental "admonition." "Admonition" means literally "to place in the mind."[7] It may also convey a note of warning or instruction. In the Bible, instruction is always directed first to the mind—not just to the mind, but first to the mind. God's truth is to impact and take control of the mind. The Christian life is to be transformed by the renewing of the mind (Rom. 12:2). There is a constant, unceasing battle for the mind, and Christian parents are to give themselves to placing the Lord's instruction in the minds of their children. The principal and principial content of the Lord's instruction is His Word, Holy Scripture. God's Word is our "only rule of faith and obedience."[8] The precepts, promises, and principles of God's Word will form the essential content of our instruction. Paul tells us that "all Scripture is given

---

7. νουθεσία (admonition, instruction, warning).
8. Westminster Larger Catechism, answer 3.

by inspiration of God, and is profitable for doctrine, for reproof, for correction, for instruction in righteousness, that the man of God may be complete, thoroughly equipped for every good work" (2 Tim. 3:16–17). The Lord's instruction is everything we need to live godly, faithful, and Christ-honoring lives in a fallen world. Fathers and mothers together have been given the vast privilege of teaching their children. No doubt reading God's Word with our children and teaching it to them requires wisdom, thought, and proportion. It should never be done mindlessly, coldly, or formally. The New Testament reminds us that teaching children, physically and spiritually, begins with giving them the milk of the Word (1 Cor. 3:2; Heb. 5:12–13). But we are to move on from the milk of the Word to "solid food" (Heb. 5:12, 14). This requires great wisdom and much patience. We must guard against the danger of force-feeding and overfeeding our children, as well as barely or occasionally feeding them. While there are many helpful books on how to read and pray with our children, the fundamental need is that we teach them out of the overflow of hearts that love God and His commandments (Deut. 6:5–6).

Creeds and Catechisms

Throughout history, many churches have found creeds and cate-chisms richly useful in placing God's instruction in the minds of children. The Westminster Shorter Catechism magnificently and memorably covers the breadth, length, height, and depth of the teaching of God's Word. In catechetical form it introduces us to and instructs us in the "admonition of the Lord" (v. 4).

Christian parents cannot begin to teach their children too early. Paul reminds Timothy that from his childhood he had been acquainted with the sacred writings which are able to make us wise for salvation through faith in Christ Jesus (2 Tim. 3:15).

Teaching children the training and admonition of the Lord is demanding work. Each child has his or her own unique, God-given personality. The image of God that the gospel comes to re-create in us is indeed likeness to Christ, who is the image of the invisible

God (Col. 1:15; see also 2 Cor. 3:18). But that image is deeply idiosyncratic and must be treasured and valued as such. While deeply daunting, the training and admonition of children is God-honoring and Christ-pleasing work and is vital for their saving and sanctifying. More than that, the Holy Spirit is our constant helper and encourager. Parents are called to be faithful and prayerful: faithful, because God blesses those who honor Him; prayerful, because without Him we can do nothing. He alone gives the increase and causes our training and admonition to bear fruit to His glory (1 Cor. 3:5–8).

25

God Pleasers

EPHESIANS 6:5–9

---

*Bondservants, be obedient to those who are your masters accord-
ing to the flesh, with fear and trembling, in sincerity of heart, as to
Christ; not with eyeservice, as men-pleasers, but as bondservants
of Christ, doing the will of God from the heart, with goodwill doing
service, as to the Lord, and not to men, knowing that whatever good
anyone does, he will receive the same from the Lord, whether he is
a slave or free.*

*And you, masters, do the same things to them, giving up
threatening, knowing that your own Master also is in heaven, and
there is no partiality with Him.*

In the ancient world, slavery was commonplace. It has been calculated that in the Roman Empire there were perhaps sixty million
slaves.[1] In the New Testament we never read about any attempt
to abolish the institution of slavery. Does this mean that the Bible
is indifferent to slavery? Far from being indifferent to slavery, the
teaching of the New Testament opposes slavery and promotes
values that effectively challenged and undermined this vile social
institution. In 1 Timothy 1:9–10, Paul lumps "kidnappers"—those
who stole, captured, bought, and sold fellow human beings—
together with the fornicators, liars, murderers, and the unholy and

---

1. Quoted in Stott, *God's New Society*, 250. Slavery was a multifaceted evil in
the Roman Empire. Some slaves were subject to the most degrading treatment.
Others, especially those in the cities, could hold positions of some responsibility,
especially in well-to-do families.

profane. Such people, he said, practice vices that are "contrary to sound doctrine, according to the glorious gospel of the blessed God" (vv. 10–11; see also Ex. 21:16).

Paul also wrote a letter to a certain Philemon regarding one of his slaves, Onesimus, who had stolen away from Philemon and run off to another city. There Onesimus met Paul and became a Christian. Paul loved him like a son but sent him back to his master. In the Roman Empire, a runaway slave could be punished with death. But that would not happen to Onesimus. Paul wrote and urged Philemon to accept his former slave back "no longer as a slave but more than a slave—a beloved brother" (Philemon 16).

What Paul wrote to Philemon highlights both the priority and the transforming power of the gospel. For Paul to advocate the immediate abolition of slavery would have been a recipe for social anarchy and the intense persecution of the church throughout the Roman Empire. But even more, Paul's first concern was not the abolition of slavery but the reconciliation of sinners, free and slave, to God. This priority of values was not novel to Paul. Jesus said, "What will it profit a man if he gains the whole world, and loses his own soul?" (Mark 8:36). For a slave to gain his freedom and then die unreconciled to God, lost, without hope and without God, would for Jesus and Paul have been an unmitigated tragedy.

Slavery is an indefensible evil. Men and women, whatever their color, culture, or economic status, are equally made in God's image and likeness (Gen. 1:26–27). The New Testament is clear that when men and women come to faith in Christ, "there is neither Jew nor Greek, there is neither slave nor free, there is neither male nor female; for [they] are all one in Christ Jesus" (Gal. 3:28). It is no surprise that Christians were at the forefront of the movement to abolish slavery in the late eighteenth century. Chief among them was William Wilberforce, Earl of Shaftesbury.[2] To treat men and women as if they were commodities to be bought and sold for personal

---

2. See the most recent biography by William Hague, *William Wilberforce: The Life of the Great Anti-Slave Trade Campaigner* (London: Harper Perennial, 2008).

profit and convenience is not only a crime against humanity but blasphemy against God and deserving of the severest punishment.

Through the preaching of the gospel in Ephesus, some slaves, "bondservants," had been converted and added to the church (v. 5). They belonged not as second-class citizens, but as "fellow citizens with the saints and members of the household of God" (Eph. 2:19). Starting in verse 5, Paul specifically addresses them and their earthly masters.

Bondservants of Christ

In the context of the middle years of the first century, it is remarkable that Paul should have specifically addressed slaves, along with wives, husbands, parents, children, and masters. No less than these other groups, slaves belonged to the church, "the saints who are in Ephesus" (1:1). Foundational to how the bondservants in the church are to behave toward their masters is their identity as "bondservants of Christ" (v. 6). Paul's summons to these bondservants to obey their earthly masters is addressed to men and women whose fundamental identity was found in their relationship to Jesus Christ, not in their relationship to any earthly master. They were to obey their "masters according to the flesh, with fear and trembling, in sincerity of heart, as to Christ" (v. 5).

In the Roman world, three words dominated: *Caesar ipse dixit* (Caesar has spoken). Caesar was undisputed lord and master. But for Christians, there was but one Lord and Master, Jesus Christ. Every Christian owed their first and fundamental allegiance to Him and to no other.

Obeying Men to Please God

Paul tells the church members who are bondservants that their freedom in Christ does not mean they are no longer to obey their earthly masters. Paul is speaking into the way things were in society. He is neither condoning nor condemning the way things were. He is telling the Christian bondservants to behave in a way that will commend the gospel.

They are to obey their earthly masters with "fear and trembling" (v. 5). Paul uses the identical phrase in Philippians 2:12. There he applies it to all Christians regarding their relationship with the God who had saved them. In both contexts the words mean "with respect and reverence." Christian slaves were to treat their masters with respect due to their status. They were also to do this "in sincerity of heart," not feigning respect but actually giving respect (v. 5). The heart nature of their relationship with their earthly masters is highlighted by the words "not with eyeservice, as men-pleasers, but as bondservants of Christ, doing the will of God from the heart, with goodwill doing service, as to the Lord, and not to man" (vv. 6–7). Just as wives are to submit to their husbands "as to the Lord" (5:22) and husbands are to love their wives as Christ loved the church, so Christian slaves are to give due respect to their masters, "as bondservants of Christ, doing the will of God from the heart, with goodwill doing service, as to the Lord, and not to men."

A New Identity

The key words, as already noted, are "as bondservants of Christ" (v. 6). Paul is reminding them of their new identity in Christ: "Remember who you are. Remember to whom you owe your first allegiance. Live not to please mere men but to please the Lord who freed you and made you His bondservants."

What Paul writes here has a transgenerational application. Perhaps no one reading this today is a slave, at least in the social sense that the slaves in the church in Ephesus were. But the same principle that was to shape their relationship with their earthly masters is to shape and style the relationships Christians are to have with those whom we serve in our daily employments. Christians are always to be noted for being respectful and diligent workers—and not only when they are being watched! Every Christian is to live *coram Deo*, before the face of God. Our first concern in work, as in all of life, is not to please the boss but to please and honor the Master.

The gospel comes not only to transform our relationship with God but also, at the same time, to transform our relationships with other people. There is a social dimension to the gospel. Jesus made this point powerfully when He answered the question,

"Teacher, which is the greatest commandment in the law?"

Jesus said to him, "'You shall love the LORD your God with all your heart, with all your soul, and with all your mind.' This is the first and great commandment. And the second is like it: 'You shall love your neighbor as yourself.'" (Matt. 22:36–39)

Where the second is absent, the first cannot be present.

Paul is not seeking to dismantle the social distinctions that were embedded in Roman society. He is, however, seeking to show a watching world the transforming power of the gospel. Behind all that Paul writes here is the conviction that people need not only to hear but also to see the gospel.

Receiving Good from the Lord

In verse 8, Paul directs the minds and hearts of the whole congregation, and not of the slaves only, to the day when God will "render to each one according to his deeds" (Rom. 2:6). God is no man's debtor (Heb. 6:10). When we live first to please God and do so by keeping His commandments, the good we do will not be forgotten: "Whatever good anyone does, he will receive the same from the Lord, whether he is a slave or free" (v. 8). There is not a law for the slave and another for the free. God acts impartially in the bestowal of His gracious blessings (v. 9). The "cash value" of heart obedience may not be evident in this life. But whatever good any Christian does will, sooner or later, be acknowledged by the Lord.

The Christian is to live in the light of eternity. One day we will all "appear before the judgment seat of Christ, that each one may receive the things done in the body, according to what he has done, whether good or bad" (2 Cor. 5:10). It is not always easy for Christian slaves to behave toward their earthly masters as God has commanded. But God is no man's debtor.

Masters, God Shows No Partiality

How were masters to treat their slaves? Paul does not command or even ask them to free their slaves. Why? Paul's primary concern, and it is the primary concern of the Bible as a whole, is not social transformation but the cause and credibility of the gospel of Christ. This does not mean that the Bible is unconcerned about social transformation. The gospel and its manifold implications confront the selfishness, racism, sexism, and greed that so disfigure every human society. But first things first. In His ministry, Jesus did not initiate a crusade for societal transformation. His primary concern was to impress on His hearers the vital necessity of being "rich toward God" (Luke 12:21). In His parable of the rich fool (Luke 12:13–21), Jesus highlights the folly of having everything this world counts important and actually having nothing of lasting value.

Paul urges Christian masters to treat their slaves with respect and dignity. He tells them to "do the same things to them" (v. 9); that is, if the masters want respect, they should give respect. This is a nonnegotiable Christian principle: treat other people as you would have them treat you. Paul specifically tells them not to threaten their slaves (v. 9). Just as fathers are not to provoke their children (Eph. 6:4), so masters are not to threaten their slaves—that is, abuse their authority selfishly. The abuse of authority in any relationship is wicked. For Christians it should be unthinkable. Earlier Paul characterized a husband's authority as servant-hearted love (Eph. 5:25). For the Christian masters in the congregation, the use of threats, verbal or physical, is completely out of place. God is the master of both the slaves and the masters. They are both ultimately answerable to Him, and He shows "no partiality" (v. 9). God will not give masters special treatment because of their social standing. He is no respecter of persons (Acts 10:34).

This section of the letter highlights the countercultural character of the Christian faith. The fundamental concern of the gospel of Jesus Christ is not to give men and women blessings that will die with them at death. What will it profit a man if he does gain the whole world and then loses his soul (Matt. 16:26; Mark 8:36)? But this in no sense means that the gospel has nothing to say about the sins that scar the societies of this world. The gospel comes to make us new creations (2 Cor. 5:17). It comes to center our lives in God and to redirect us from self and toward God and others. It comes to show us the vanity of passing things and the attractiveness of eternal things and to persuade us that our greatest need in life is to be right with God through faith in Jesus Christ.

These convictions compelled Christians not only to oppose the slave trade but also to promote a whole range of social reforms in the later years of the eighteenth century. According to the New Testament, true religion involves caring for widows and orphans in their affliction (James 1:26–27). To profess the gospel of Christ and at the same time ignore the physical needs of fellow Christians places a huge question mark over our Christian profession (James 2:14–17; 1 John 3:16–18).

26

The Enemy

EPHESIANS 6:10–12

Finally, my brethren, be strong in the Lord and in the power of His might. Put on the whole armor of God, that you may be able to stand against the wiles of the devil. For we do not wrestle against flesh and blood, but against principalities, against powers, against the rulers of the darkness of this age, against spiritual hosts of wickedness in the heavenly places.

From Ephesians 5:15 through 6:9, Paul has been unpacking what it means to "be filled with the Spirit" (5:18). He has especially highlighted what the Spirit-filled life will look like within the Christian family. The credibility of the church's mission to the world rests on how the gospel impacts and transforms relationships within the family. One of the foundational characteristics of an elder is that he "[rule] his own house well, having his children in submission with all reverence" (1 Tim. 3:4). The Christian family is to be a showcase for the transforming grace of the gospel, especially its reconciling grace.

Know Your Enemy

It should be no wonder, then, that the devil will do all he can to destroy that showcase. Too often we link these verses about the devil and his schemes to times of persecution and pressing temptation and fail to grasp the immediate context. The devil has plans and "devices" (2 Cor. 2:11) to attack the Christian family. Spiritual warfare is as present in the home—perhaps even more so—as anywhere else. Many Christians will testify that the home is the place of our greatest spiritual failures and inconsistencies. It is often in the midst of the ordinariness of family life that the devil sets his most subtle ambushes. Watch and pray.

One of the marked features of our Lord Jesus Christ's earthly ministry was His awareness that His mission and person were opposed every step of the way by Satan. The beginning of His public ministry was marked by His baptism by John in the Jordan and then immediately by His temptations in the wilderness by the devil (Matt. 4:1–11). The whole course of our Savior's life was marked by the unceasing opposition of the devil. This was Jesus's self-conscious assessment of His public ministry (see Luke 22:28). But the devil's antagonism to Jesus was also seen in his desire to overwhelm and destroy Jesus's disciples (Luke 22:31—the "you" is plural). It is little wonder that among Jesus's last words to His disciples were, "Watch and pray, lest you enter into temptation" (Matt. 26:41).

This spiritual warfare has its origins in God's announcement to the serpent in the garden of Eden:

> And I will put enmity
> Between you and the woman,
> And between your seed and her Seed;
> He shall bruise your head,
> And you shall bruise His heel. (Gen. 3:15)

The entire Bible is an exposition of that divinely instituted antagonism. And yet many Christians have little awareness of the spiritual warfare that they are engaged in. It is wonderfully true that our Lord Jesus, "having disarmed principalities and powers…made a public spectacle of them, triumphing over them in it" (Col. 2:15). Satan is a defeated foe; but he is still a troublesome, vindictive foe, full of "wiles" (v. 11), and we need to know our enemy and how to stand against him. The first rule in warfare is know your enemy.

The Devil Is Real, Not a Figment
Benjamin B. Warfield, the great Princeton biblical theologian, described Christianity as "unembarrassed supernaturalism." And

it is. The New Testament is adamant that our "adversary the devil walks about like a roaring lion, seeking whom he may devour" (1 Peter 5:8). It is imperative for our own spiritual good and for the good of Christ's church and its mission to the world that we know our enemy and know that we can, in Christ, overcome him. This is precisely what Paul is concerned to say in these verses: "You Christians in Ephesus need to know the fact, nature, and methods of the enemy you face and God's glorious provision for you if you are to stand firm in the faith of our Lord Jesus Christ."

Power to Prevail

So as Paul draws his letter to a close, he has one final, deeply significant thing to say to the Ephesians: "Finally, my brethren, be strong in the Lord and in the power of His might" (v. 10). He wants the Ephesians to know that the resources they need to enable them to stand "against the wiles of the devil" will be found "in the Lord" alone (vv. 11, 10, respectively). Even as redeemed men and women, we need nothing less than the "power of His might" if we are to keep standing in the "evil day" (6:10, 13). Paul is highlighting the spirit of utter dependence on the Lord that must characterize our engagement in spiritual warfare. He makes the same point to the believers in Corinth: "For though we walk in the flesh, we do not war according to the flesh. For the weapons of our warfare are not carnal but mighty in God for pulling down strongholds" (2 Cor. 10:3–4).

This dependence on the Lord and His might was what characterized the life and ministry of our Lord Jesus Christ. Throughout His earthly ministry, Jesus lived in faithful, obedient dependence on the upholding support of His Father and the anointing enabling of the Holy Spirit (Isa. 42:1; Matt. 12:18). As Jesus faced the temptations and assaults of the evil one, He did so drawing by faith on the promised support of His Father and the Spirit. In everything, Jesus is the prototypical Man of faith. It is the new covenant ministry of the Holy Spirit to replicate in believers what He first formed and forged in Jesus. The Gospels give us a dramatic example of Jesus's repelling the devil as He lived in His trustful, servant-obedience to

His Father. As Jesus began His public ministry, He was "led up by the Spirit into the wilderness to be tempted by the devil" (Matt. 4:1). On three occasions, the devil tempted Jesus to step outside His Father's will and abandon the way of the cross. On each occasion Jesus replied, "It is written.... For it is written.... It is written again..." (Matt. 4:4, 6, 7). As He found Himself in a barren wilderness, hungry after forty days of fasting, confronted by the devil, Jesus drew upon the authority, wisdom, grace, and truth of the Word of God. He had complete trust in the Holy Scriptures. He armored Himself against the insidious, pressing temptations of the evil one with God's written Word. This Word was not a lucky charm to ward off evil. It was the living Word of the living God, embedded with God's own infallible wisdom. Jesus was exercising trust and confidence in the goodness, wisdom, and power of His Father.

No matter how powerful and pressing the devil's opposition and temptations are, in the Lord there is strength to prevail. Christians are "more than conquerors through Him who loved us" (Rom. 8:37).

Paul will unpack just what the armor of God is in verses 13–18. For now he is impressing on us that we need "the whole" armor of God if we are to stand against "the wiles of the devil" (v. 11).

Purposeful Responsibility

Notice that we are to "put on" the whole armor of God (v. 11). This emphasis on Christians' responsibility to avail themselves of the armor God has provided is highlighted throughout these verses: "Therefore take up the whole armor of God...having girded your waist with truth, having put on the breastplate of righteousness...having shod your feet with the preparation of the gospel of peace...taking the shield of faith...and tak[ing] the helmet of salvation, and the sword of the Spirit, which is the word of God" (vv. 13–17). Putting on a suit of armor takes determined effort. Paul is accenting the responsibility believers have in their warfare with the devil and his schemes. God has made a great provision for His people in our spiritual warfare, but we are responsible for taking hold of this great provision. It is by faith that we take up and put on the whole armor of God. Faith is self-abandoning trust in God and in His rich gospel promises in Christ. Faith is the spiritual dynamic that animates and shapes the life of a Christian. Paul has told us in Ephesians 1:3 that the Father has blessed us in Christ with every spiritual blessing. Among those spiritual blessings is the whole armor of God. Faith believes God's word and personally appropriates the rich blessings that faith alone draws out of Christ.

The Fact of the Devil

Most people today, inside and outside the church, will happily speak about the fact of evil. Few will speak about the fact of the devil. The reality and activity of the devil punctuate the entire Bible, from Genesis through Revelation. We first encounter him in Genesis 3 when he seduces Adam and Eve into rebellious disobedience against God. The book of Job begins with Satan appearing among the sons of God (angels) and being given permission by God to assault His faithful servant Job (Job 1:6–12). Satan is a fallen creature. He can do nothing beyond what the sovereign Lord gives him permission to do. Evil is a dark mystery. How could this creature rebel against a holy, sovereign, omnipotent God? When did he do so? How was he able to seduce Adam and Eve into sin? Why does God give this evil one sovereign permission to do anything at all? These and other questions no doubt rise in our minds. But God's ways are higher than our ways, as Isaiah reminds us (Isa. 55:8). His ways are past finding out, as Paul tells us (Rom. 11:33).

The solemn fact is that God's people collectively and individually have a powerful, malignant, organized, deceitful enemy. The devil has wiles, well-planned and thought-out strategies, all aimed at harming, and if possible destroying, Christian believers. Paul wants us to be absolutely clear about the reality of the devil. He is no comic-book figure. He is out to get you, and he will do all he can to accomplish this. So it is vital for you to know your enemy.

Often Christians think that their great enemy is "flesh and blood" (v. 12), godless authorities, troublesome neighbors, belligerent fellow workers, and indwelling sin in their own lives. These are indeed enemies that must be recognized and resisted. But behind flesh and blood, the devil is invisibly but unceasingly devising his stratagems, provoking godless authorities and stirring up indwelling sin. Paul is counseling us to understand that the warfare we are in has an enemy headquarters that is out of sight! Paul tells us that the Christian warfare is "against principalities, against powers, against the rulers of the darkness of this age, against spiritual hosts of wickedness in the heavenly places" (v. 12). He is not thinking about unjust, ungodly political regimes. Rather, he is highlighting the organized, structured, powerful, and malignant opposition that is provoked by the devil against God's church. Is this how you think as a Christian? It is surely sobering to read Paul's description of the world we live in, this present darkness. This world is not neutral toward the Lord Jesus Christ and His gospel. It is under "the sway of the wicked one" (1 John 5:19), "the god of this age" who blinds the minds of unbelievers (2 Cor. 4:4). Behind all the opposition and persecution that the church corporately and believers individually face, there are the schemes of the devil.

Do you live your Christian life seriously in the light of this elemental conflict? The whole Bible is simply an unfolding exposition of the conflict God Himself initiated in Genesis 3:15. Christians have been drafted into this conflict to "fight the good fight of faith" (1 Tim. 6:12). Sometimes the conflict can be overwhelming. Jesus recognized when Peter urged Him to avoid the cross that the opposition He was facing was satanic: "Get behind Me, Satan!" (Matt. 16:23). When Paul reflected on the disunities that were disturbing the peace of the church in Corinth, he said, "We are not ignorant of his [Satan's] devices" (2 Cor. 2:11). The worst kind of enemy is an unseen enemy. This is why we need "the whole armor of God" (v. 11). Nothing less will do.

27

The Whole Armor of God

EPHESIANS 6:13–17

Therefore take up the whole armor of God, that you may be able to withstand in the evil day, and having done all, to stand.

Stand therefore, having girded your waist with truth, having put on the breastplate of righteousness, and having shod your feet with the preparation of the gospel of peace; above all, taking the shield of faith with which you will be able to quench all the fiery darts of the wicked one. And take the helmet of salvation, and the sword of the Spirit, which is the word of God.

Having introduced us to the great enemy who is malignantly determined to bring unceasing harm to God's people and cause, Paul now introduces us to the various elements that make up the whole armor of God. For Paul it is a matter of great urgency that God's people put on the whole armor of God.

Standing Firm

Warfare with the devil is so serious that we need the whole armor of God "to withstand in the evil day, and having done all, to stand" (v. 13). In the life of faith we are called to "go on" (Heb. 6:1), to "grow in the grace and knowledge of our Lord and Savior Jesus Christ" (2 Peter 3:18), and to be transformed "from glory to glory" (2 Cor. 3:18). But there are days when it takes all the faith we have and all the resources God has given us in Christ simply to stand and not be overwhelmed. It is a great thing to stand for Christ, bloodied, battered, and broken, but still standing, unmoved, unyielding, unbowed. This is especially so when the evil day comes.

The Evil Day

Paul does not specify as such just what the "evil day" is (v. 13). He could simply mean that we live in an evil day when Christ and His gospel are assailed on every side (cf. Gal. 1:4—"this present evil age"). It is more likely, however, that Paul is thinking about a time of particular, concerted pressure, a time when the devil is "roaring" (1 Peter 5:8) and uses all his energy and powers to destroy the church (Acts 8:3). John Owen, the English Puritan, describes what the evil day looks like: "[Temptations] will have a season wherein their solicitations will be more urgent, their reasonings more plausible, pretences more glorious, hopes of recovery more appealing, opportunities more broad and open, the doers of evil made more beautiful than ever they have been."[1]

At such a time believers are particularly vulnerable. The evil day may come when you are low in spirit, suffering poor health, or experiencing some difficulty. Or it may come when you are in the spiritual heights and have let down your defenses, much like David in 2 Samuel 11. Or the evil day may come and attack you when you least expected an attack. Who would have thought that bold, courageous Peter would collapse spiritually before the questioning of a servant girl? Your imagined strong point may be your spiritual Achilles', heel. Do you imagine that Abraham thought for one moment that he would risk his wife's moral purity to save his own skin? He did (Gen. 12:13). Did King David think for one moment that he would steal another man's wife, plot his murder, disgrace his family, and publicly dishonor the Lord and His church? He did (2 Samuel 11–12). Did it cross Peter's mind that he would deny his Savior with curses? He was so sure of himself (Mark 14:29). But he did. Paul's solemn warning to the church in Corinth is one every

---

1. Owen, *Works*, 6:99.

Christian needs to take to heart: "Therefore let him who thinks he stands take heed lest he fall" (1 Cor. 10:12).

A deep sense of your weakness and vulnerability is vital to standing firm in the evil day and every other day. If the devil was bold enough to tempt the Lord Jesus Christ (Matt. 4:1–11), you can be sure he will not hesitate in any way to attack you.

But we need more than a deep sense of our weakness and vulnerability when faced with the trial of the evil day. More vitally, we need a deep sense of dependence on the Lord and His promised grace to help us in our times of need (Heb. 4:15–16).

God's Gracious Provision

Paul now details the comprehensive provision the Lord has made to help His people face the assaults of the enemy. Our gracious God knows our frame and remembers we are dust (Ps. 103:14). He knows how weak and vulnerable every one of His blood-bought children is and has made magnificent provision for each one. In his massive and exhaustive commentary on the Christian's armor, William Gurnall makes this comment: "In heaven we shall appear not in armour but in robes of glory; but here they are to be worn night and day; we must walk, work, and sleep in them, or else we are not true soldiers of Jesus Christ."[2] The Christian's warfare with the devil is not episodic; it is perpetual. Certainly there will be evil days of intense warfare. But warfare with the devil is no less present when our times are pleasant and God's blessings are inundating us. The warfare is unceasing. It was for Christ, and it will be for His people. It was for this reason that our Savior counseled His disciples to "watch and pray, lest you enter into temptation" (Matt. 26:41).

---

2. William Gurnall, *The Christian in Complete Armour* (1662; repr., London: Thomas Tegg, 1845), 40. Gurnall's full title is *The saints' war against the Devil, wherein a discovery is made of that grand enemy of God and his people, in his policies, power, seat of his empire, wickedness, and chief design he hath against the saints; a magazine opened from whence the Christian is furnished with spiritual arms for the battle, helped on with his armour, and taught the use of his weapon; together with the happy issue of the whole war.*

The most important thing to grasp about this armor is that it is "of God" (v. 11). It is not armor that we manufacture out of the threadbare resources at our disposal. Rather, it is armor that is not only from God but is of God. This truth will help us rightly to interpret the meaning of the individual pieces of armor that Paul highlights in this passage.

Christ Our Armor

Before we consider each of the various elements that comprise the armor of God, it will be helpful to see this armor as being uniquely and perfectly found in Christ. In Romans 13:14, Paul urges the believers in Rome to "put on the Lord Jesus Christ, and make no provision for the flesh, to fulfill its lusts."[3] Paul is telling them that the Lord Jesus Himself is God's provision for the needs of His people. As we will see, the armor, in different ways, represents the Savior.

The Secure Belt of Truth

Paul most likely has in his mind's eye a fully equipped, battle-ready Roman soldier. Every Roman soldier had a belt around his waist to secure his clothing and keep it from flapping in the wind. If this is so, the Roman soldier's belt had a foundational significance. His belt was there to secure any loose garments. Without the belt to keep everything in place, the soldier could be hindered in battle. The belt enabled the soldier to fight unencumbered. With his belt in place, he was prepared and ready for action. The belt of truth was foundational. But what spiritual truth did Paul have in mind? Some commentators have thought that Paul is speaking about the foundational truth and authority of God's Word (Martyn Lloyd-Jones). Others are sure that what is in Paul's mind is truth in the sense of personal integrity, sincerity of heart, and truthful and genuine motives (John Calvin, Matthew Henry, and William Hendriksen). While Paul may deliberately be using a double meaning, if the

---

3. It was reading this text that finally brought Augustine to give his life to Christ. His account of his conversion is found in his *Confessions*, 88–89.

armor is of God, it is more likely that what Paul has in mind is the foundational truth of the Christian revelation. If Christ's church and individual members of it are to stand firm in the evil day, it is vital that their lives be anchored in and securely tied to God's revealed truth concerning His Son. The escalating tragedy of the Christian church in the past one hundred years has been associated with its abandoning the truth and authority of God's revelation in the face of unbelief. The present spiritual and moral debility of the church is due preeminently to one thing: it has let slip, often willfully, the belt of truth. If God's saving truth in Christ is not what binds the life and mission of the church, it becomes prey to "every wind of doctrine" (Eph. 4:14) and ends up a spiritual and societal irrelevance, a parody of its divine identity and calling.

Foundational to Jesus's life and ministry was His absolute commitment to God's infallible word (John 10:35). His whole ministry was given to fulfill the "Law or the Prophets" (Matt. 5:17). God's word defined His life and shaped His ministry and mission. Jesus was preeminently the Man of the word. He lived under its authority and unambiguously taught its truth. For Jesus, "It is written," was enough. The authority and infallibility of God's revealed truth is the church's foundational bulwark against the devil's schemes (Isa. 8:20). When the devil sought to tempt Jesus into abandoning His saving mission, Jesus repulsed him three times, each time hurling the truth and authority of God's word in his face (Matt. 4:1–11). The God who cannot lie and who does not change has spoken. His word is truth (John 17:17). His word is "given by inspiration of God" (2 Tim. 3:16). It is the "sound doctrine" of our Lord Jesus Christ that is to be taught in the church (2 Tim. 4:3). God's revealed truth is the unshakable rock on which we stand against the schemes and designs of the devil.

When the church has drifted from the infallible truth and authority of God's word, it becomes prey to the devil and his schemes. Conversely, when the church affirms its absolute confidence in God's truth, it sees through the devil's wiles, exposes them for what they are, and confirms itself afresh in the truth of the gospel.

Christian sincerity of heart is informed and shaped by the truth and authority of God's written Word. Under the ministry of the Holy Spirit, the power and authority of God's truth is transformative. It produces the family likeness in our lives as we are conformed to our Lord Jesus Christ (Rom. 8:29), which is seen in heart integrity. What so marked the life and ministry of the Lord Jesus and what distanced Him from the religious leaders of His day was His unimpeachable inward integrity. His life was entirely consistent. What He was in public, He was in private. What He was "in the pulpit," He was in the daily routines of life. It was this inward integrity of heart that gave such authority to His teaching; He taught "as one having authority" (Matt. 7:29). In Jesus there was no guile, no deceit, no mixed motives, and no hidden agenda. King David came to understand, amid the wreckage of his sin with Bathsheba, that God desires and delights in "truth in the inward parts" (Ps. 51:6). Without inward integrity of heart, our lives are a sham. There is to be nothing "double-minded" about the man and woman of faith (James 1:8; see also 2 Tim. 1:5). If there is unreality and hypocrisy in any form in our hearts, we have no protection from the devil and his schemes. The armor of God will not hang upon lives where there is an absence of heart integrity. William Gurnall perhaps best captures what is in Paul's mind: "Some by truth mean a truth of doctrine; others will have it truth of heart, sincerity; they I think best that comprise both.... One will not do without the other."[4]

Paul has just been expounding what God-honoring marriages and family life look like. If men are not loving their wives as Christ loved His church (Eph. 5:25), how can they expect to be protected from the wiles of the devil, no matter how loudly they proclaim their Reformed credentials? If wives are not humbly and lovingly submitting to their husbands, "as to the Lord" (Eph. 5:22), how can they expect to be protected from the wiles of the devil? If professing Christian parents are not fondly cherishing their children "in

---

4. Gurnall, *Christian in Complete Armour*, 207.

the training and admonition of the Lord" (Eph. 6:4), how can they expect to be protected from the wiles of the devil?

I recently heard a staggering statistic: over two thousand pastors are "forced" to leave the gospel ministry every year in the United States. How many of those men leave because they lack deep-seated inner heart integrity? God knows. It is sadly possible in these days for a politician to be a cheat, a womanizer, a liar, and much worse and still, remarkably, be a valued politician. People imagine that a person's inner life need not affect his or her public service. But in the service of God, the inner life is everything. Sooner or later God will bring these people's inner lives into the light to be exposed for what they are. This is why earlier Paul urged the Ephesians to "walk as children of light" (5:8). It is only as "we walk in the light as [God] is in the light, [that] we have fellowship with one another, and the blood of Jesus Christ His Son cleanses us from all sin" (1 John 1:7).

Gird Your Waist

Paul writes, "Having girded your waist with truth" (6:14). We must resolve to be men and women who deliberately and self-consciously take up God's truth and bind it around our lives. There will be times when you will be tempted to trim the truth, to hide the truth, or to manipulate the truth to place yourself in a better light or to save you from the cost of being a faithful disciple of Christ. The devil will use his schemes to try to persuade you that a little compromise is neither here nor there. The moment you allow your heart to be infected with hypocrisy in whatever form, who knows what havoc the devil will wreak in you and in your church? Gird your waist with the belt of truth. Resist the temptation to take lower ground. But if you have allowed hypocrisy to find its way into your heart, confess it to the Lord now. Be assured that the Lord is rich in mercy, slow to anger, and abounds in covenant love. He is the God of new beginnings: "Thou knowest the way to bring me back, my fallen spirit to repair."[5]

---

5. Charles Wesley, "Weary of Wandering from My God," in the public domain.

A compromising spirit too easily slips into our lives—and what good is a suit of armor if the enemy has already found a way behind it and pressed a poisoned dagger into your heart? The hymn writer captures the thrust of Paul's teaching:

> How can we fight for truth and God,
> Enthralled by lies and sin?
> He who would wage such war on earth
> Must first be true within.[6]

The Savior Christians are united to is pure; He is the perfect ἀνυπόκριτος (genuine, sincere) Man. His inner life was a life of truth. Is yours? Has God's truth made you a man or woman of truth?

The Breastplate of Righteousness

Paul proceeds to what is possibly the most vital piece of a soldier's armor: "the breastplate of righteousness" (v. 14). For a soldier to go into battle without the protection of a breastplate would be virtual suicide. He would be leaving unguarded his most vulnerable area against the assaults of his enemy. What does Paul have in mind when he urges the Ephesians to "put on the breastplate of righteousness"? Remember, not only is the armor from God, it is "of God" (v. 11). Like the belt of truth, the breastplate of righteousness may have a deliberate double meaning, but there is little doubt that Paul is thinking principally about the righteousness of Christ.

Imputed righteousness. Calvin is quite clear that what Paul has in mind is a "devout and holy life."[7] Just as we need truth in the inward parts in order to fight "the good fight of faith" (1 Tim. 6:12), no less do we need righteousness of life, a life shaped and styled by the word and will of God. Without such a life, the devil will easily overwhelm us and crush us. But because Paul writes here of the breastplate of righteousness, a breastplate that is of God, it seems

---

6. Thomas Hughes, "O God of Truth Whose Living Word," in the public domain.

7. Calvin, *Commentary on Ephesians*, 338.

more likely that what he principally, if not exclusively, has in mind is Christ, the Lord our righteousness (Rom. 5:18; 1 Cor. 1:30). Our own righteousness would be no ultimate deterrent—or indeed any deterrent—to the devil and his schemes. Our righteousness, even at its redeemed and sanctified purest and best, is deeply flawed. Indeed, "all our righteousnesses are like filthy rags" (Isa. 64:6).

There is in the church today a deeply flawed teaching that is causing much harm to God's people which asserts that our acceptance with God rests both on Christ's and the believer's righteousness. This teaching makes something in a person of acceptable worth to God. Those who hold to this teaching do not think in terms of the famous hymn: "Jesus, Thy blood and righteousness my beauty are, my glorious dress."[8] Rather they must adapt the hymn to make it reflect their thought: "Jesus, Thy blood and righteousness *and my righteousness* my beauty are, my glorious dress." How remote this teaching is from what we read in the Word of God. The New Testament is categorical that Christ alone is the believer's righteousness (2 Cor. 5:21; Phil. 3:8–9). It is Christ Himself we are to "put on" (Rom. 13:14). Christ cannot be separated from His benefits. He is the great benefit of the gospel. Why can the devil not bring any charge against God's elect? Because "it is God who justifies" (Rom. 8:33). Why can no one condemn God's elect? Because "it is Christ who died, and furthermore is also risen, who is even at the right hand of God, who also makes intercession for us" (Rom. 8:34). Against Christ the Righteous One, in whom believers are, the devil's schemes must fail. Christ is our defense against the enemy of our souls. The life of faith, the Christian life, is lived out in Christ (Gal. 2:20). Because I am in Christ, the devil has no more hold over me than he had over my Savior. At first, this may seem an overstatement of the highest magnitude. But if we truly are "in Christ" (Eph. 1:3) and His righteousness has been imputed to us by the God of grace, then we are completely secure.

---

8. Nicolaus Ludwig von Zinzendorf, "Jesus, Thy Blood and Righteousness," trans. John Wesley, in the public domain.

But this "breastplate of righteousness" is to be "put on" (v. 14). We are to believe that it is ours because it is ours by God's gracious gift (Phil. 3:9).

Experience and feelings. The breastplate of Christ's righteousness is our sure defense against all the attacks of the enemy. This is especially so in one area of daily experience. The devil will do his utmost to tempt Christians to base their lives on their feelings. But our feelings rise and fall; they ebb and flow. Feelings are never a true barometer of our standing in Christ. Our best and highest feelings can be treacherous, which is why Edward Mote wrote, "I dare not trust the sweetest frame, but wholly lean on Jesus' name."[9] The same is true of spiritual experiences. The Christian faith is deeply and pervasively experiential. You cannot truly know the presence of God and not be moved by it. But it would be the height of folly for Christians to face the assaults of the devil on the basis of their feelings and experiences. Nothing but the perfect righteousness of Christ will answer whatever charge the devil lays against you.

The same is true, perhaps even truer, for Christians who are blighted by gloom and despondency. There are times when our feelings and experiences can blot out the sunshine of our heavenly Father's love. What then are we to do when the devil comes with his accusations? We find hope not by looking into ourselves but by looking out to Christ, the Lord our righteousness. As Paul reminded the church in Rome, "There is therefore now no condemnation to those who are in Christ Jesus" (Rom. 8:1).

Imparted righteousness. The New Testament, however, never separates imputed righteousness from imparted righteousness. The two must always be distinguished, but they must never be separated. The perfect righteousness of Christ which is imputed, or placed in the account of believers, is also imparted to them. Through the gospel, believers are being transformed "from glory to glory" (2 Cor. 3:18). Union with Christ unites us to a holy and righteous Savior and

---

9. Edward Mote, "My Hope Is Built on Nothing Less," in the public domain.

makes us partakers of His life (John 15:1–11). An unholy Christian is a theological oxymoron, a moral monstrosity (1 John 2:3–6). Christians sin—and sometimes very badly! But Jesus was absolutely clear that by our fruits we would be known. An unrighteous life that is not being shaped by God's truth in union with Christ is an un-Christian life. Christ is our righteousness. He is our sure defense against the wiles of the devil. But if He truly is the life in which and out of which we live (Gal. 2:20), then His life will manifest itself in and through our lives: "If you know that He is righteous, you know that everyone who practices righteousness is born of Him" (1 John 2:29). The devil's schemes thrive in unrighteous lives, even if they confess Christ with evangelical passion.

Gospel Shoes
The next piece of gospel armor turns attention to God's provision for our feet: "having shod your feet with the preparation of the gospel of peace" (v. 15). The devil is a master at knowing our weakest points and will attack us there. Paul clearly has in mind Isaiah 52:7:

> How beautiful upon the mountains
> Are the feet of him who brings good news,
> Who proclaims peace,
> Who brings glad tidings of good things,
> Who proclaims salvation,
> Who says to Zion,
> "Your God reigns!"

Paul is not addressing the church's pastors and preachers; he is addressing the whole church. Every Christian is called to wear gospel shoes, to be ready to give a reason for the hope that is in them (1 Peter 3:15).

A Roman soldier's footwear was important for two reasons. First, the studs on the soles provided protection against slipping and sliding. Christians are always in danger of slipping and sliding! Second, the studded soles gave the soldier mobility. Because he had good shoes, the soldier could move freely and quickly in the roughest terrain. Christians are always to be going on, never settling to stand still. If this is the picture in Paul's mind, he is thinking of God's provision to keep His people from slipping and falling and to continue on. This provision is described as "the preparation of the gospel of peace" (v. 15).

There are two ways to understand Paul. He could mean that the gospel of peace gives the believer security against the devil's assaults (Rom. 5:1). It is from the sure foundation of the gospel of peace that we wage warfare against the kingdom of darkness and its evil prince. When the enemy presses hard against God's people, when we find ourselves cast down, what defense do we have? The sure defense of the gospel of peace. Because God has justified us in Christ, we are at peace with Him, and nothing and no one can take that blood-secured peace away. Peace with God is the first and foundational blessing of the gospel. Because Christ Himself is our peace (Eph. 2:14), the gospel makes us impregnable and unimpeachable.

It is possible, however, that the genitive may well be objective, in which case the shoes are the believer's readiness to announce the gospel of peace, which is the precise point of Isaiah 52:7. "Missionary work," says Johannes Blauw, "is like a pair of sandals that have been given to the church in order that it shall set out on the road and keep going on to make known the mystery of the gospel."[10] If this is what Paul has in mind, he is telling us that the gospel of peace is for spreading. The gospel is not only a treasure to glory in; it is also good news we are to share with the world. As we bring good news of happiness, Satan's dark kingdom is invaded and sinners are plucked as brands from the burning. It is a maxim in military warfare that the best form of defense is attack.

Too often the church has become prey to the schemes of the devil because it has lost sight of its calling or has even abandoned its calling to announce good news. One of the devil's most potent wiles is to absorb the church with itself. We end up spending precious

---

10. Johannes Blauw, *The Missionary Nature of the Church: A Survey of the Biblical Theology of Mission* (New York: McGraw-Hill, 1962), 125, quoted in Stott, *God's New Society*, 280.

time debating theological niceties while people are perishing. In no sense am I advocating a cavalier disregard of doctrine. Rather, I am saying that we must take to heart the gospel passion of men like Richard Baxter:

> The work of conversions is the first and great thing we must drive at; after this we must labour with all our might. Alas! the misery of the unconverted is so great, that it calleth loudest to us for compassion.... I confess I am frequently forced to neglect that which should tend to the further increase of knowledge in the godly, because of the lamentable necessity of the unconverted. Who is able to talk of controversies, or of nice unnecessary points, or even truths of a lower degree of necessity, how excellent soever, while he seeth a company of ignorant, carnal, miserable sinners before his eyes, who must be changed or be damned? Methinks I see them entering upon their final woe.[11]

Baxter's passion can be used as an excuse for doctrinal indifferentism. But if evangelism—holding out the gospel of God's grace in Christ to a dying, perishing world—is not at the heart of our church's life, the devil has gained access and corrupted the church's life! If the soldiers in the Lord's army are fighting one another, what hope do they have of fighting and defeating the enemy? Earlier, in 4:3, Paul urged the Ephesians to "[endeavor] to keep the unity of the Spirit in the bond of peace." It is the gospel of God's justifying peace in Christ that binds the church together and gives no opportunity to "give place to the devil" (Eph. 4:27).

Shield of Faith

Paul next urges the Ephesians to "[take] the shield of faith" (v. 16). It has often been said that the Christian life is fought on a battlefield and not on a playground. Paul tells Timothy that he has "fought the good fight" (2 Tim. 4:7). But if we are to fight this good fight of the faith (1 Tim. 6:12), we must fight it not in our own strength, but

---

11. Baxter, *Reformed Pastor*, 95.

out of our union with Jesus Christ. This armor is of God. All the resources a Christian needs for fighting the good fight of the faith are found in Christ.

The shield Paul has in mind measured 4 feet by 3 feet, and a soldier could hide behind it. For the Christian, the shield that defends us from "all the fiery darts of the wicked one" is faith (v. 16). Often Christians have been guilty of focusing too much on the quality of their faith rather than on the object of their faith, Jesus Christ. Faith is essentially "extraspective."[12] It is not faith that justifies us; it is faith in Jesus Christ. And, strictly speaking, it is not faith in Jesus Christ that saves us but Jesus Christ received by faith. We have seen all along that Jesus Christ is our armor. Justifying faith anchors itself in the virtues and victories of Another. The faith that will enable you to "quench all the fiery darts of the wicked one" (v. 16) is faith in Jesus Christ—His finished priestly work (John 19:30), His continuing priestly work (Heb. 4:15–16; 7:25), and His great and precious promises.

It is imperative that we understand that when the Bible speaks about faith, it is not speaking about mere intellectual assent to certain propositions. Saving faith includes intellectual assent to God's truth, but it is more than that. Faith essentially is trust, self-abandoning trust in Jesus Christ. Faith involves submitting all you are to the lordship of Christ. This is the faith that is the believer's shield against all the fiery darts of the wicked one.

What are these fiery darts of the evil one? In essence, they are the well-aimed, powerful, often sudden and unexpected temptations and accusations of the devil. The aim of these fiery darts is to confuse and, if possible, disable the child of God.

For many Christians, these fiery darts are the devil's persistent accusations that they are not saved, that God has not really fully and freely forgiven all their sins. Such fiery darts can be deeply

---

12. John Murray, *The Epistle to the Romans* (London: Marshall, Morgan and Scott, 1960), 123: "The specific quality of faith is trust and commitment to another; it is essentially extraspective and in that respect is the diametric opposite of works."

disturbing and distressing for the Christian. We know too well our sins and inconsistencies and are troubled and humbled by them. But, explains Paul, by taking the shield of faith, you will extinguish these distressing darts. Faith takes hold of Christ and lifts Him against all the devil's darts. Faith says, "I am persuaded that neither death nor life, nor angels nor principalities nor powers, nor things present nor things to come, nor height nor depth, nor any other created thing, shall be able to separate us [God's elect] from the love of God which is in Christ Jesus our Lord" (Rom. 8:38–39). Faith in Christ repulses all the devil's fiery darts as it cries out, "Having been justified by faith, we have peace with God through our Lord Jesus Christ" (Rom. 5:1). Peter tells the "pilgrims of the Dispersion," "Resist [the devil, remaining] steadfast in the faith" (1 Peter 1:1; 5:9).

For other Christians, the devil's fiery darts are those thoughts and suggestions that appear suddenly, without any warning, and paralyze them with fear and failure. Perhaps you have said to yourself, "How could I, child of God that I am, think such a thought?" John Bunyan clearly knew something of this. In *Grace Abounding*, Bunyan's spiritual autobiography, he recounts how "a very great storm came down upon me, which handled me twenty times worse than all I had met with before. It came stealing upon me, now by one piece and then by another. First, all my comfort was taken from me; then darkness seized me; after which whole floods of blasphemies, both against God, Christ, and the Scriptures, were poured upon my spirit, to my great confusion and astonishment."[13] The choicest of God's children have experienced the devil's powerful and sudden fiery darts. Our Lord Jesus was confronted with the temptation to think and act upon blasphemous thoughts when the devil came upon Him in the wilderness and sought to assail His mind with the vilest of temptations. But the Lord has provided for us what He provided for our Savior: the shield of faith. Yes, Jesus hurled the

---

13. John Bunyan, *Grace Abounding to the Chief of Sinners* (London: George Larkin, 1666), 22, http://www.chapellibrary.org/files/4813/7642/2821/bun-abounding.pdf.

truth of God's word against the devil's temptations, but He did so in faith. The apostle John speaks about faith as "the victory that has overcome the world" (1 John 5:4). The devil's fiery darts can come from any and every direction, so you must always be on your guard (1 Peter 5:8).

Helmet of Salvation

The next piece of armor that Paul urges the Ephesians to "take" is "the helmet of salvation" (v. 17; see also Isa. 59:17). The helmet offered the Roman soldier protection for his head. Paul is obviously concerned that the minds of God's people be protected from the assaults of the evil one. In the Christian life, as in all of life, your mind matters. How you think shapes how you live. This is why the advertising industry so alluringly and suggestively targets our minds. Win the battle for the mind, and you win the person—and their money. The Bible gives tremendous prominence to the importance of our minds. Paul appeals to the Christians in Rome not to be "conformed to this world," but to "be transformed by the renewing of your mind" (Rom. 12:2). He tells the Christians in Philippi, "Whatever things are true, whatever things are noble, whatever things are just, whatever things are pure, whatever things are lovely, whatever things are of good report, if there is any virtue and if there is anything praiseworthy—meditate on these things" (Phil. 4:8).

It is not surprising therefore that Paul now turns to the importance of the helmet of salvation for protection against the schemes of the devil. Again, Paul accents the responsibility believers have to take this helmet of salvation. God has provided it, but we have to take it.

What is the helmet of salvation? There are perhaps two ways (not mutually exclusive) to understand what Paul means by the helmet of salvation. He could mean, "Take up the knowledge that by God's grace, the Lord Jesus Christ has saved you by His perfect atoning sacrifice. Repulse the assaults of the devil with the finished, perfect work of your Savior." Satan is malignantly adept at plying our minds with plausible reasons why our hope before God is built on the shakiest of foundations. Our lives are so full of contradictions and inconsistencies. We experience lapses of faith and failures of trust, and we even fall into grievous sin. Our minds can be besieged with a host of reasons that may rob us of any assurance. What then are we to do? Take the helmet of salvation. Don't look into yourself to find crumbs of comfort. Look out to your Savior and His perfect salvation. What guards our minds is the salvation perfectly accomplished for us by our Lord Jesus. He has made a once-for-all, perfect, complete, and unimpeachable atonement for sin. This is Paul's argument in Romans 8:31–34. The hymn writer perfectly captures this truth:

> When Satan tempts me to despair
> And tells me of the guilt within;
> Upward I look, and see him there
> Who made an end of all my sin.[14]

If only the devil can get us to focus on ourselves, our minds will easily become befuddled and distracted. The knowledge of God's so great salvation in Christ is an impregnable defense against Satan's assaults, no matter how violent or vile.

Do you see how practical doctrine is? Doctrine is not merely for believing; it is for living, for applying to our lives that they may be shaped and styled by its truth.[15] Armor your mind with the truth of God's salvation in Christ.

It is possible, however, that Paul means something a little different by the helmet of salvation. In his magnificent sermons on the Christian armor, Martyn Lloyd-Jones understands the helmet of salvation to refer more to the Christian's hope of salvation.[16] The

---

14. Charitie Lees Bancroft, "Before the Throne of God Above," in the public domain.

15. "True theology is not theoretical, but practical. The end of it is living, that is, to live a God-like life." Martin Bucer, as quoted in *Martin Bucer's Doctrine of Justification*, by Brian Lugioyo (Oxford: Oxford University Press, 2010), 54.

16. David Martyn Lloyd-Jones, *The Christian Soldier* (Edinburgh: Banner of Truth Trust, 1977), 315.

hope of salvation is the ultimate consummation of our salvation (Rom. 8:23–25). It is one of the devil's strategies to suggest to us that the gospel has brought us nothing but difficulties, problems, and hardships. The letter to the Hebrews was written in part to expose and explode that particular temptation of the devil, to show God's hard-pressed children that they had in Christ "an anchor of the soul, both sure and steadfast, and which enters the Presence behind the veil, where the forerunner has entered for us, even Jesus" (Heb. 6:19–20; see also Rom. 8:18–25).

Every Christian knows the "sufferings of this present time" (Rom. 8:18). How are we then to keep ourselves from sinking under the weight of those sufferings? By taking the helmet of salvation and reminding ourselves that our hope of salvation is a living hope, a sure and certain hope. One day all the distresses and sufferings of this present life will be swallowed up in glory (2 Cor. 4:16–18). Again, the hymn writer puts the matter well:

> Th' eternal glories gleam afar
> To nerve my faint endeavor;
> So now to watch, to work, to war,
> And then to rest forever.[17]

It has been suggested that the Roman soldier's helmet had a decorative as well as a protective purpose. If so, then it is not overstating the text to suggest that nothing more adorns our Christian profession and commends it to a watching world than a humble, settled confidence in what God has done for us in Christ. Christ's salvation should never make us proud or arrogant but rather humble and thankful.

For many Christians, the great danger is to be more taken up with our own spiritual state than with God's great salvation in Christ. We must daily do what the writer to the Hebrews urged his readers to do: "Consider...Jesus" (3:1). What do you feed your

---

17. James G. Small, "I've Found a Friend, O Such a Friend," in the public domain.

mind on? Do you see just how practical doctrine is? Your salvation is impregnable because your Savior is impregnable. Augustus Toplady understood this truth well: "More happy, but not more secure, the glorified spirits in heav'n."[18] Your mind is the devil's main access into your life and into the life of Christ's church. So "seek those things which are above, where Christ is" (Col. 3:1).

The Sword of the Spirit

It is often remarked that the "sword of the Spirit, which is the word of God" (v. 17) is the first piece of offensive equipment in the Christian's and church's armor. But is this so? Surely the belt of truth, the breastplate of righteousness, the gospel shoes, the shield of faith, and the helmet of salvation have offensive power. The belt of truth exposes and dispels the lies of the devil. The breastplate of Christ's righteousness sends the devil scurrying away. The gospel of peace plunders the devil's kingdom. It is our faith in Christ that "overcomes the world" (1 John 5:4). The helmet of salvation is not purely defensive. Even when the helmet is serving a defensive purpose, it testifies to the grace and power of Christ and drives the enemy of our souls away at the same time.

Nonetheless, "the sword of the Spirit, which is the word of God," is the church's mighty, God-given weapon to defeat the schemes of the devil (2 Cor. 10:4–5; Heb. 4:12).

There are probably two reasons Paul calls the Word of God the "sword of the Spirit." He uses this name first because God's Word was brought into being preeminently by the special ministry of God's Spirit (2 Peter 1:21). God's Word is the word of man in the sense that it did not come through mindless robots. Scripture bears the unmistakable and undeniable imprint of man. Each book of the Bible betrays the stylistic and even grammatical peculiarities of its author. But God's Word did not originate with man: "Prophecy never came by the will of man." God's Word originated in God: "But holy men of God spoke as they were moved by the Holy Spirit"

---

18. Augustus Toplady, "A Debtor to Mercy Alone," in the public domain.

(2 Peter 1:21). Foundationally and fundamentally, the Holy Spirit is the primary author of Holy Scripture. Paul tells Timothy that "all Scripture is given by inspiration of God" (2 Tim. 3:16).[19] The confidence Christians can have in Scripture rests in the fact that because it is God's breathed-out Word, it is flawless and abidingly true (Isa. 40:8). God's Word is His revelation to us of His mind and heart (1 Cor. 2:12–13). This is why John Calvin wrote, "We owe to the Scripture the same reverence which we owe to God, because it has proceeded from him alone, and has nothing belonging to man mixed with it."[20]

This does not mean that we have answers to all the critical questions that seek to mock the self-attested inerrancy of God's Word any more than we have all the answers to those questions that mock the hypostatic union in Christ of deity and humanity. Great indeed "is the mystery of godliness" (1 Tim. 3:16). The Word of God truly is the sword of the Spirit.

Second, the Word of God is the sword of the Spirit because it is the great weapon the Spirit uses to advance God's kingdom in this world and plunder and despoil the kingdom of Satan. God's Word—read, preached, and lived—is the principal ordinary means God uses to convince, convict, and persuade sinners of the truth of the gospel. The proclamation of God's Word was the heart and substance of Jesus's earthly ministry (Mark 1:14). Jesus used God's Word to defend himself against the powerful and plausible temptations of the devil (Matt. 4:1–11).

There is a striking picture of the exalted Savior in the opening chapter of Revelation that highlights the absolute centrality of God's Word: "He [Jesus] had in His right hand seven stars, out of His mouth went a sharp two-edged sword, and His countenance was like the sun shining in its strength" (Rev. 1:16). John is giving us

---

19. Paul uses the Greek compound θεόπνευστος, which literally is "God breathed."

20. John Calvin, *Commentaries on the Epistle of Paul to Timothy, Titus and Philemon* (Grand Rapids: Baker, 1993), 249.

a picture of how Jesus rules His church and confronts His enemies (Rev. 19:15).

It was the early church's unswerving conviction that it must devote itself "to prayer and to the ministry of the word" (Acts 6:4). When Peter addressed the great crowd at Pentecost, he preached God's Word (Acts 2:14–41), and thousands were added to the church. When Paul came to Corinth, he taught the people "not in words which man's wisdom teaches but which the Holy Spirit teaches" (1 Cor. 2:13). As he faced the prospect of imminent death, Paul gave solemn farewell counsel to Timothy, his younger fellow minister of the gospel: "I charge you therefore before God and the Lord Jesus Christ, who will judge the living and the dead at His appearing and His kingdom: Preach the word! Be ready in season and out of season" (2 Tim. 4:1–2).[21]

If the Word of God truly is the sword of the Spirit, why do we see so little of the power of this sword of the Spirit in our day? The question first must be qualified. In many parts of the world today, the sword of the Spirit is evident in great power. Throughout Asia, Africa, and South America, God is mightily at work gathering countless thousands into His kingdom through the faithful preaching of His Word in dependence on the Holy Spirit. But it can hardly be denied that in the past two hundred years, particularly in the West, there has been a massive loss of confidence in the truth, sufficiency, and Spirit-wrought effectiveness of the Word of God. Three reasons in particular account for this seismic loss of confidence.

First, the church has been infected by what are called mistakenly the assured results of modern scholarship. This scholarship denies the credibility of the Bible's supernatural revelation. It debunks the supernatural person of Jesus Christ. It reduces the "gospel of God" (Rom. 1:1), which claims to be "the power of God to salvation for everyone who believes" (Rom. 1:16), to a fanciful tale with, at best, an attractive moral ethic. Should it surprise us if God's blessing

---

21. "In season and out of season" (εὐκαίρως ἀκαίρως) might be better translated, "When times are good and when times are bad."

is absent from the preaching of His Word when that preaching is often little more than moral injunctions dressed up with a veneer of piety?

Second, the church has become obsessed with cultural relevance. The church is called in every age to be culturally relevant, to bring the gospel of Christ to the world as it is, not as it was. However, the emphasis on the visual in this age, allied to the Internet revolution, has often seduced the church into thinking that preaching God's Word is now passé. Drama is in; preaching is out. Endless singing is in; expository sermons are out. Although the early church lived in an age fascinated with drama, it had unbounded confidence in the truth, power, and authority of God's Word. It was persuaded that "faith comes by hearing, and hearing by the [preached] word of God" (Rom. 10:17). Paul wrote to the church in Corinth, reminding them that when he first came to Corinth his message was not "with persuasive words of human wisdom, but in demonstration of the Spirit and of power," so that their faith would not rest "in the wisdom of men but in the power of God" (1 Cor. 2:4–5). Even more pointedly, he told the Corinthians in his second letter that he refused to "[walk] in craftiness nor [handle] the word of God deceitfully, but by manifestation of the truth," he sought to commend himself and his fellow missionaries to every man's conscience in the sight of God (2 Cor. 4:2).

God's principal means for confronting the pretensions and lies of this age and every age is the dynamic of His Spirit-inspired Word.

Third, the church has often drifted into a spirit of self-confident pride. That pride can take many ugly forms. We can have pride in our doctrine, and yet right doctrine is vital. We can have pride in our history and heritage, and yet there is much in a church's history and heritage to prize. We can have pride in our denominational distinctives, though those distinctives may honor God. The church and its ministers too often are not marked by a sense of absolute dependence on the Lord, His Word, and His Spirit. God's word to His desperately weak and dispirited people at a critical time in their history should be the unshakable conviction of the church in every age: "'Not by might nor by power, but by My Spirit,' says the LORD of hosts" (Zech. 4:6). If the Bible truly is the sword of the Spirit, let us have unbounded confidence in the truth of its message, and let us pray that the Holy Spirit will take that Word and use it mightily in the lives of many.

28

Praying in the Spirit

EPHESIANS 6:18–24

*…praying always with all prayer and supplication in the Spirit,
being watchful to this end with all perseverance and supplication
for all the saints—and for me, that utterance may be given to me,
that I may open my mouth boldly to make known the mystery of the
gospel, for which I am an ambassador in chains; that in it I may
speak boldly, as I ought to speak.*

*But that you also may know my affairs and how I am doing,
Tychicus, a beloved brother and faithful minister in the Lord, will
make all things known to you; whom I have sent to you for this
very purpose, that you may know our affairs, and that he may comfort your hearts.*

*Peace to the brethren, and love with faith, from God the
Father and the Lord Jesus Christ. Grace be with all those who love
our Lord Jesus Christ in sincerity. Amen.*

These verses are filled with instruction on prayer. Paul is writing to
a congregation and is particularly addressing the fellowship of the
saints, not the individuals within it. What he says about prayer has
direct relevance to the families and individuals within the church.
But it is the church as the people of God—the body of Christ—
that he exhorts to pray always. What is the connection between
Paul's injunction that the church should be "praying always with all
prayer and supplication in the Spirit" (v. 18) and the various pieces
of the armor of God that he has just been urging the Ephesians
to take up in their warfare against the evil one? Some suggest that
"praying always with all prayer and supplication in the Spirit" is the

culminating piece of armor that Christians are to take up and put on. But it is better to understand that Paul is telling us prayer is what makes the other pieces of the armor of God effective in our lives. The hymn writer captures well Paul's thinking: "Put on the gospel armor, each piece put on with prayer."[1]

There is nothing robotic or mechanical about the Christian life. In prayer we confess our helplessness and our confidence in the love and power of God. John Bunyan expressed this belief: "Pray often, for prayer is a shield to the soul, a sacrifice to God, and a scourge for Satan."[2] Without prayer all we are and do for Christ and His church has the smell of death about it. Prayerlessness is practical atheism. The first picture we are given of the early church in the New Testament is of a people at prayer (Acts 1:14; 2:42; 6:4). John Owen once said that he would rather judge a man's theology from his prayers than from his books. Owen was not decrying knowledge and understanding. He was, however, recognizing something of the profoundest importance, a truth that Robert Murray M'Cheyne expressed well: "A man is what he is on his knees before God, and nothing more."

Is prayer fundamental or supplemental in your life and in the life of your church fellowship? Do you take up and put on the armor of God in conscious, prayerful dependence on the Holy Spirit? Is the absence of prayer, which should be the spiritual heartbeat of a church's life, the reason why the church languishes in weakness throughout the Western world?

Praying Always

Prayer is not to be an occasional, episodic, and sporadic feature of the Christian's life. Paul exhorts the Ephesians to be "praying always" (v. 18). He could mean that prayer is to be the basic disposition of the life of faith; we are to live before God in an attitude of

---

1. George Duffield, "Stand Up, Stand Up for Jesus," in the public domain.
2. John Bunyan, "Mr. John Bunyan's Dying Sayings," in *The Complete Works of John Bunyan* (Galesburg, Ill.: Bradley, Garretson, 1872), 4:80.

prayer. Prayer is not merely something we do when times are hard. We are to pray always. Prayer comforts and assures us in our darkest trials and sanctifies our brightest joys. It is also possible that he means that in every circumstance in life, when faced with the assaults of the evil one, we are to pray. Nothing is more vital in the life of faith than a self-conscious sense of our own need and of God's provision in Christ to meet our need. John Calvin understood the significance of prayer in the life of faith: "It is, therefore, by the benefit of prayer that we reach those riches which are laid up for us with the Heavenly Father.... So true it is that we dig up by prayer the treasures that were pointed out by the Lord's gospel, and which faith has gazed upon."[3]

The True Spirit of Prayer

What does it mean to pray "in the Spirit" (v. 18)? Is Paul suggesting that there can be prayer that is not in the Spirit? It is possible. Jesus warned His hearers about the danger of honoring the Lord with their lips while their hearts were far from Him (Mark 7:6, quoting Isa. 29:13). He especially warned His own disciples against praying like hypocrites, heaping up "vain repetitions as the heathen do. For they think that they will be heard for their many words. Therefore do not be like them" (Matt. 6:7–8). Like worship as a whole, prayer is to be "in spirit and truth" (John 4:23)—or, in Spirit and Truth. To pray in the Spirit is to pray in dependence on the Spirit and in conformity to what the Spirit desires, and these desires are set forth in God's Word and culminate in His desire to glorify Jesus (John 16:14). Prayer in the Spirit is never mindless but always sincere and from the heart. It may be fluent, or halting and stumbling. It will always, however, be in heart dependence on God, in humble conformity to His revealed will, laying hold of His inexhaustible grace and kindness and His unfettered omnipotence.

---

3. Calvin, *Institutes*, 3.20.2.

All Prayer and Supplication

Paul could have said "with all prayer," but he adds "and supplication" (v. 18). Prayer has many elements: thanksgiving and adoration, confession of sin, petition, and intercession. In adding "and supplication," Paul is encouraging the Ephesians to pray earnestly.[4] Christian prayer is never to be formal or mechanical. It is always to be earnest and from the heart. We are to pray with the earnestness of Jacob, "I will not let You go unless You bless me!" (Gen. 32:26). The Lord's appointed watchmen were to give Him no rest until He established Jerusalem and made it a praise in the earth (Isa. 62:7). Our Lord Jesus told His disciples that "men always ought to pray and not lose heart" (Luke 18:1). Cold, listless prayers are a contradiction of faith. Faith believes God and will call out to Him, cry out to Him, and plead with Him to fulfill His great and precious promises to His children in their times of need.

Being Watchful with All Perseverance

Whether Paul is self-consciously doing so, he is echoing the teaching of the Lord Jesus Christ who told His disciples to "watch and pray" (Matt. 26:41). This spiritual alertness is all the more vital because our "adversary the devil walks about like a roaring lion, seeking whom he may devour" (1 Peter 5:8). Paul knows well the myriad of distractions and hindrances that the devil will put in the way of prayer. He knows also that while our spirit may be willing, our flesh is weak (Matt. 26:41). We are never to imagine that our God needs persuading to help His children. Rather, in persevering through difficulties and personal sluggishness to make supplication to God for His people, we evidence our high commitment to the priority of prayer, which testifies to our conviction that God is "able to do exceedingly abundantly above all that we ask or think" (Eph. 3:20), that without Him we can do nothing (John 15:5).

---

4. δέησις, which contains the idea of plea or entreaty.

Supplication for All the Saints

Paul has earlier told the Ephesians that it is only together with "all the saints" that we can know the surpassing love of Christ (3:18). Now he urges them to make supplication for "all the saints" (v. 18). The new covenant church of Christ is God's multinational, multicultural people. The church comprises men and women and boys and girls from every nation, tribe, people, and language under heaven (Rev. 7:9), and we are to pray for them all. Jew and Gentile, rich and poor, black and white, educated and uneducated, powerful and weak, high and low—all are to be prayed for earnestly. The battle Christians are in is not a private war. In prayer we pray *with* all the church to *our* Father and *for* all the church (the saints). The devil fiercely and unceasingly opposes all God's children. We are all in the same battle, fighting under the colors of our captain, Jesus Christ. Paul told the church in Corinth that when one member of the body suffers, all suffer together (1 Cor. 12:26). So make supplication for all the saints. When Benjamin B. Warfield was asked what Calvinism is, he replied, "Christianity on its knees." He could hardly have spoken a truer word.

And for Me

Paul was never slow to ask God's people to pray for him (Col. 4:3; 1 Thess. 5:25; 2 Thess. 3:1). He is in prison. Humanly speaking, his ministry as Christ's ambassador has been cut short. But Paul knows the power of prayer, or, even better, the power of the God to whom prayer is made (Eph. 3:20–21). He is an "ambassador in chains" (v. 20), but an ambassador of the Savior who first commissioned him (Acts 26:16–18). Paul specifically asks prayer for two things. First, "that utterance may be given to me" (v. 19). Paul was not naturally word deficient and clearly knew how to make utterance. What he is asking prayer for is that he may utter incisive, heart-convicting, soul-penetrating, and, above all, Christ-exalting words. Every preacher, indeed every Christian, needs to know that mere utterance, however eloquent and earnest, is never sufficient. We need Spirit-given utterance that has its origin in heaven, not on earth.

Second, Paul asks prayer for boldness in proclaiming "the mystery of the gospel" (v. 19; see comments on Eph. 3:1–6). He does not ask that his chains be removed. He does not ask for physical comforts, though in his farewell letter to Timothy he asks for his cloak and his books in 2 Timothy 4:13. His burning concern is that the glorious gospel of God be proclaimed boldly.[5] He is an ambassador with a divinely given message of God's glorious salvation in Jesus Christ. Paul was a "one thing I do" man (Phil. 3:13). He was gospel obsessive. His ministry was his life. He sought to live out the injunction he gave to Timothy: "Preach the word! Be ready in season and out of season"—when times are good and when times are bad (2 Tim. 4:2). There were no doubt times when Paul was tempted to be less than bold in his preaching the gospel. He knew what it was to be fearful (Acts 18:9) and even to fear of life itself (2 Cor. 1:8). Paul was no spiritual superman. He needed the Lord to support him and embolden him in his preaching ministry, and he was not slow to expose his need of God's empowering Spirit. He knew well that such boldness belonged to his calling as an ambassador of Christ—"as I ought to speak" (v. 20). When churches pray for their ministers, these two things should be in the forefront of their praying: their minister's need for words to speak, and boldness with which to speak them. Such Spirit-anointed preaching is the great need of every age.

Concluding Greetings and Grace

We noted in the introduction that one reason, and perhaps even the reason, Paul wrote this letter was to let the Ephesian church and perhaps others know how he was faring in prison. For this reason he had sent "Tychicus, a beloved brother and faithful minister in the Lord" to give them information (v. 21). He would tell them everything.

---

5. παρρησία, an attitude of openness that stems from freedom and lack of fear. In speech it conveys the idea of boldness, plainness, and perhaps even outspokenness.

There is little information in the New Testament about Tychicus. He is first mentioned in Acts 20:4 and is described as "of Asia." He was clearly a man highly regarded by Paul, as he entrusted him to carry this letter to the Ephesians and the letter to the Colossians (Col. 4:7, 16). He also accompanied Onesimus (see Paul's letter to Philemon) back to Colossae (Col. 4:7–9). Paul calls him "a beloved brother" and "faithful minister…in the Lord" (Col. 4:7). It seems likely that the church in Ephesus knew Tychicus. He was a proven servant of the Lord. The two qualities Paul mentions, beloved and faithful, should mark the lives and ministries of every Christian, and especially every Christian man called into the gospel ministry. Few Christian graces more commend a man's service to God and His people than these.

But characteristically, Paul's greater concern in sending Tychicus was that he might encourage the Ephesians' hearts. Not even being chained in a Roman prison could make Paul forget he was a pastor, commissioned by Christ to serve His church.[6]

Peace, Love, and Grace

Paul began his letter with a greeting and a soaring doxology (1:1–14). The letter concludes with Paul richly blessing this church "from God the Father and the Lord Jesus Christ" (v. 23). Paul uses perhaps the four most distinctive words in his gospel vocabulary: peace, love, faith, and grace.

"Peace" (v. 23) is the wholeness and richness of life that belongs to God's children. Paul is not seeking a trouble-free life for them, but a life overflowing with the rich sense of God's presence, a life of well-being that the darkest of life's circumstances cannot annul.

"Love" (v. 23) is God the Father's and the Lord Jesus Christ's wholly gracious and undying commitment to be our God. It was this love that was the fountainhead of the gospel and rescued us

---

6. Sinclair Ferguson makes this insightful comment: "Paul was prepared to send out the best men he knew to help others, and did not keep them jealously for himself. There is a lesson here for the whole church." *Let's Study Ephesians* (Edinburgh: Banner of Truth Trust, 2005), 192.

from the darkness and death of Satan's kingdom and brought us into the light and life and liberty of the children of God. Paul joins "faith" with "love." He does so perhaps to remind the Ephesians that it is only by self-renouncing trust in Jesus, which is faith, that we enter into the saving blessings of God's love.

"Grace" (v. 24) is the word that most characterizes the Christian religion. Grace is God's undeserved kindness and mercy to judgment-deserving sinners. The gospel of Christ is the gospel of amazing grace. It was God's grace that elected us, found us, saved us, keeps us, and will bring us safely to glory.

But while God's grace is glorious and free, it is not cheap. So Paul writes his final words, "who love our Lord Jesus Christ in sincerity" (v. 24). Where the grace of God has been savingly planted in our lives, it will show itself in love to the Savior, a love of unceasing gratitude for blessing us with every spiritual blessing. Once we were dead in trespasses and sins, but Christ redeemed us by His own blood. Once we were in darkness, but in Christ we are "light in the Lord" (Eph. 5:8) and God's own "dear children" (Eph. 5:1). It would be good for us to ask ourselves whether we love our Lord Jesus Christ with love that is incorruptible. Nothing can substitute for a heart that loves Him who first loved us.

This was the great truth the Lord Jesus Christ impressed on Peter when He publicly rehabilitated him after His resurrection. Three times Jesus asked Peter if he loved Him (John 21:15–17). Jesus was telling Peter that his cowardly failure was at heart not a failure of nerve but a failure of love. This is why the heart of authentic Christian ministry will always be the exposition of the person and work of Christ. When Christians struggle with obedience or find their hearts becoming lukewarm or even cold, their great need is to rediscover the glory of their Savior and the grace of His love to them. No one understood this better than the English Puritan, John Owen:

> Let us live in the constant contemplation of the glory of Christ, and virtue will proceed from him to repair all our decays, to renew a right spirit within us, and to cause us to abound in all duties of obedience…when the mind is filled with thoughts

of Christ and his glory, when the soul thereon cleaves unto him with intense affections, they will cast out, or not give admittance unto, those causes of spiritual weakness and indisposition.... And nothing will so much excite and encourage our souls hereunto as a constant view of Christ and his glory.[7]

This is why Paul wrote, "We preach Christ crucified" (1 Cor. 1:23). And this is why he spends three chapters expounding the glory and grace of Christ before he begins to urge the church in Ephesus to "walk worthy of the calling with which [they] were called" (Eph. 4:1).

Paul's letter to the Ephesians scales the heights of the Christian faith and life. He wrote to a church living in the midst of the mighty Roman Empire. For another two and one-half centuries, the church would exist as a *religio illicita*, an illegal religion. It would have great hardships and periodic waves of persecution. In God's kindness and mercy, the letter to the Ephesians would help provide the encouragement and hope that would enable the church to stand and, having done all, to remain standing.

Soli Deo gloria.

---

7. Owen, *Works*, 1:460–61.